THE FAMILY AS CONSUMERS

THE FAMILY
AS
CONSUMERS

Irene Oppenheim, Ph.D.

NEW YORK UNIVERSITY

THE MACMILLAN COMPANY
New York

COLLIER-MACMILLAN LIMITED
London

PREFACE

THIS book is intended as a text for college students in consumer economics and family finance. The purpose of this book is to provide a source of comprehensive and concise information for the men and women in college so that they may become better acquainted with the problems and potentials of family spending and consumption in the modern world. Courses in consumer economics and longer sequences of courses in areas related to the family's use of money are increasing as awareness of the need for information and education in this area grows.

It was planned that this book would be unique in several ways. There is an overview of the choices available to families in an affluent society, discussion of the relationship of these choices to home and family living, and consideration of the potentiality for strengthening family and community life through the effective use of time and money. Individuals and families make decisions involving the use of money every day; almost every type of activity, from buying a car to selecting a place to bowl, involves choices in the use of money. Personal and family happiness and satisfaction are related to the manner in which choices are made and money used. Since much of the responsibility for the decisions of family expenditures, whether major purchases or day-to-day buying is in the hands of women, this book focuses on the important role of women in planning and managing family consumptions. Until quite recently very little attention has been given to educating women for their role in the management of family spending. However, it has long been recognized that women exert a considerable influence on the national consumption trends.

IRENE OPPENHEIM

ACKNOWLEDGMENTS

I HAVE received considerable help from many people in writing this book. I would like to thank with great appreciation all the people who assisted me with various portions of the job. Although I cannot mention everyone by name, I am particularly indebted to Dr. Henrietta Fleck, Chairman of the Home Economics Department at New York University for advice and suggestions at all stages of this endeavor.

Mr. John Marcus of the Prudential Life Insurance Company and Dr. Harlan Miller of the Institute of Life Insurance made many fine suggestions for Chapter 13, "Life Insurance." Mr. Jerry Miller of the Institute of Health Insurance was very helpful in revising Chapter 14, "Protecting Family Health." Mr. Robert Howard of the American Bankers Association made suggestions for Chapter 10, "Savings and Family Funds." Mr. Michael Strunak of the Social Security Administration read Chapter 12, "The Social Security System." Miss Vocille Pratt of the Welfare Administration, Department of Health, Education and Welfare also read portions of this same chapter. Mr. Wallace Janssen of the Food and Drug Administration gave me some suggestions on the discussion, in Chapter 17, of the activities of the Food and Drug Administration.

Many people assisted me in securing illustrations and references. I am indebted to Dr. George McKinney, Vice-President of the Irving Trust Company, who assisted me in locating graphic and reference material. Mr. Robert Baker and Mr. Howard Linder of the National Industrial Conference Board gave me many useful suggestions and made some charts available. Mrs. Leone Ann Heuer, Director of the Money Management Institute of Household Finance Corporation, had pictures made from some of their filmstrips. Mr. Frank Zumbro of Du Pont made available a number of pictures from Du Pont publications, Mr. Irving Gottsegen of Montefiore Hospital had pictures made for me from some of their publications. Mr. Wray Smith, Director of Consumers Union, made illustrations from their files available. Mrs. Erma Hinek of Consumers Research helped me secure some illustrations from their publications. Mrs. Phyllis Barnett of the American Bankers Association was very kind in making pictures available and helping me locate additional ones. Dr. George Fersh of the Council on Economic Education made available a number of pictures from their films. Mr. Brooke Alexander of *Fortune* magazine was very helpful in securing several illustrations. Miss Frederica Bienert, formerly of *What's New in Home Economics* kindly assisted me in locating illustrations of food products.

viii]

My friends, colleagues, teachers, and students contributed a great deal to my understanding of consumer problems through discussion, questions, and comments. I am particularly indebted to Dean John C. Payne of New York University who, with great kindness and rare tact, taught me how to organize and outline a manuscript.

Last, I would like to express my appreciation to my family for encouragement and help at every stage. My father, Dr. Samuel Gartner, read the entire manuscript and made many useful suggestions. My mother, Mrs. Bessie Gartner, did considerable editing. My husband, Don, made many helpful suggestions throughout the job, and our daughter Ellen showed a grand sense of humor in living with me through the process.

IRENE OPPENHEIM

CONTENTS

THE FAMILY AS CONSUMERS

1

THE AMERICAN FAMILY: AN ECONOMIC FORCE

The acceleration of change in 20th-century society is affecting the home in many ways. . . . Technological advances and socioeconomic changes
have made an enormous difference in activities
that go into maintaining a household.[1]

SINCE the advent of the twentieth century, American society has experienced a wide variety of rapid changes in its
composition and its manner of living. Many of these are
due to the ever-increasing complexity of our technological establishment.
This development, which had its beginnings in the late nineteenth century,
shows no sign of slowing down. It has affected our national life in every
possible way, from our role in the arena of world politics to the outlook,
status, and prospects of each individual residing in this, the richest, most
prosperous nation ever known to mankind.

As a nation, we occupy 5 per cent of the world's area and have about 5 per
cent of the world's population, but we produce about half of the factory-made
goods and have 40 per cent of the monetary income of the world. Modern
America has succeeded in providing most of its citizens with a standard of
living that even rich men could not obtain a century ago, one that is still
luxurious and unobtainable by much of the world. Almost everyone has at
least a bare minimum of the basic requisites for survival: food, shelter, clothing, and medical care. Public and private welfare agencies try to assure that
even people unable to obtain these necessities are provided with them. More
than this, improvements in education, communication, and technology have
resulted in many Americans being better read and better informed than ever
before. Specifically, such items as good books, radios, television sets, tele-
phones, automobiles, and a host of labor-saving appliances have become
commonplace in this "affluent society."

[1] U.S. Dept. of Health, Education and Welfare, Office of Education, *Management Problems
of Homemakers Employed Outside the Home* (Washington, D.C.: Government Printing Office,
1961), p. xi.

Today, the average American works about ⅓ the hours that his grandfather did, in order to earn the price of a suit.

FIGURE 1. *(Courtesy of Money Management Institute of Household Finance Corporation.)*

Not surprisingly, family life has also changed to meet these new conditions. For one thing, the family has changed from a productive and, in many cases, self-sustaining unit to a consuming group that is dependent upon national conditions for its economic well-being. Thus, while in the past such factors as weather and local events were of primary concern, now the family is affected directly by such formerly distant considerations as national productivity, inflations, depressions, and trends in unemployment.

The increase in productivity per worker has led to a decrease in the average work week (see Figure 1) and a consequent increase in the amount of leisure time available. This coupled with the development of more tools and appliances that have greatly reduced the housewife's chores, has resulted in more time for such pleasures as play, hobbies, vacations, and further education. A growing proportion of the nation's effort is being directed toward satisfying people's desires in this regard.

This continual increase in material goods has brought Americans no nearer to utopia. What seems to have happened is that new problems have arisen to take the place of those that have been solved. The most obvious one is that in the midst of a society of plenty there still exist many large pockets of poverty, places where people live in slum housing and have inadequate diet. We have yet to solve the questions of adequate and sensible production and equitable distribution of our great resources. More disturbing, perhaps, are the problems that have arisen as a result of recent conditions. Juvenile delinquency and mental illness seem to be increasing; many young people are insecure and uncertain of their roles and obligations in this new society; the fate of the older members of the community is growing more and more ambiguous; and family disintegration is on the rise. These are only a sample of the difficulties faced by the American family today; how they are solved determines to a large extent the happiness of family members, both as individuals and as components of a functioning social organism.

The Modern American Family

We are the most married nation in the world: approximately 94 per cent of the 181 million people in this country were members of families in 1961. (A family is defined as "two persons or more related by blood, marriage or adoption and residing together.")[2] This is caused primarily by the increasingly early age at which young people marry; the average age at marriage has been declining steadily since the depression of the 1930's.

Family size is also on the increase. Average family size in 1961 was 3.36 members. The usual family contained parents and their children.

> Since 1950 there has been an increase in the average number of children per household but a decrease in the average number of adults per household. . . . The decline in number of adults . . . resulted from a variety of influences: . . . fewer married couples found it necessary to share housing with others . . . [and] adults, other than married couples, are now far more likely to be living in their home alone or with nonrelatives. . . . An additional factor was the decline in the proportion of adults who live as lodgers or resident employees.[3]

Not only are women having more children, but they are having them at an earlier age. The proportion of young children in our total population is increasing.

New Trends in Family Life

We have already mentioned some of the ways in which modern technology has taken much of the drudgery out of our lives. Out of this highly mechanized way of life, several new characteristics in family life have emerged:

1. *Modern families are urban.* We are becoming a nation of city dwellers and suburban home owners. (See Figure 2.) Few families live on farms; most

[2] U.S. Dept. of Commerce, Bureau of the Census, "Household and Family Characteristics: March 1961," *Current Population Reports,* Series P-20, No. 122 (March 22, 1963), p. 5.

[3] U.S. Dept. of Commerce, Bureau of the Census, "Household and Family Characteristics: March 1961," *Current Population Reports,* Series P-20, No. 116 (May 1, 1962), pp. 1-2.

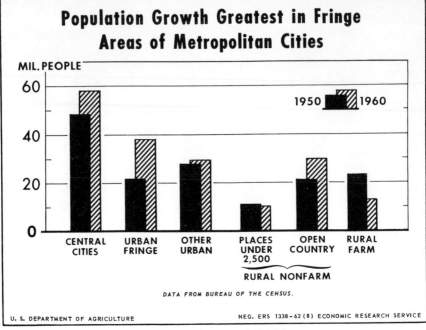

FIGURE 2. *(Courtesy of USDA.)*

of our people live in cities. Only 3.5 million families resided on rural farms in 1961, rural farm residence being defined as including people on "places of 10 acres or more yielding agricultural products which sold for $50 or more in the previous year . . . and persons living . . . on places of less than 10 acres yielding agricultural products which sold for $250 or more."[4] This development is an inevitable consequence of the shifting of more and more of the nation's productive capacity away from the farms to the more populous urban and suburban areas.

2. *Modern families are mobile.* One out of every five families moves each year. Many types of industrial employment take families from one community to another. Military service requires people to relocate in new places. Even school children travel farther to consolidated school districts.

Paid vacations and credit plans encourage holiday travel. Financing of automobiles enables more people to purchase cars. Advertising stimulates interest in seeing far-off places or in just going out for an evening.

3. *Activities centered around the family are decreasing.* As families moved from the farms to the cities and from a family business of raising food to an industrial life of specialized employment, family life patterns changed. Jobs, schools, and social activities now tend to separate family members. Both

[4]U.S. Dept. of Commerce, Bureau of the Census, *Current Population Reports,* Series P-20, No. 116 (May 1, 1962), p. 4.

parents and children are away from home much of the day. Smaller homes with limited space encourage recreation outside the home. Today many of the more densely populated urban areas are better equipped to satisfy the specialized social, athletic, and cultural interests of the individual family members than whole family groups.

4. *Family members are better educated than ever before.* Partly because educational achievement is a requisite for success in our society, partly because, in a sense, there is nothing else to do, and partly because of compulsory attendance laws, more children are staying in school longer than ever before. The Bureau of the Census reports that the average person age 25 and over had completed 11.4 years of school.[5]

Furthermore, a study done in 1959 indicated that "47 per cent of the high school seniors planned to go to college, 33 per cent planned not to go, and 20 per cent were undecided or did not report. More girls than boys planned to attend college—49 per cent vs. 45 per cent. Fifty-one per cent of the urban youth, 47 per cent of the rural nonfarm youth and 32 per cent of the rural farm youth planned to attend college."[6] In 1960, 3.6 million students were enrolled in college.[7]

Some Groups of Special Interest

The increasing fragmentation of the family into its component parts, as noted above, has led to the peculiar situation that, in some important respects, family members are considered not so much as members of a particular family or type of family but rather as members of some particular undifferentiated peer group. This is true especially of women, teen-agers, and the elderly, each of whom we shall consider in turn.

THE CHANGING ROLE OF WOMEN. The women of this nation have probably experienced the greatest role changes in our modern society. The prevalence of mechanization has partially displaced women from their traditional role in the home. Except where there are young children, women need no longer spend long hours in activities concerned with the physical maintenance of the family. Smaller families, mechanical equipment and a host of service industries have greatly reduced household labor.

While studies have shown that the majority of women still look upon marriage and childbearing as their principal responsibility, more and more women are assuming the dual role of homemaker and wage earner. The most dramatic increase has been in part-time employment. As John and Mavis

[5] U.S. Dept. of Commerce, Bureau of the Census, "Educational Attainment: 1962," *Current Population Reports,* Series P-20, No. 121 (February 7, 1963), p. 1.

[6] National Education Association, *NEA Research Bulletin,* Vol. 40, No. 1 (February 1962), p. 20.

[7] National Education Association, *ibid.,* p. 40.

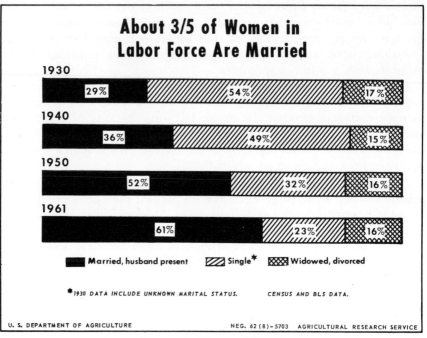

FIGURE 3. *(Courtesy of USDA.)*

Biesanz state, "No longer does a girl grow up expecting to be a homebody, a wife and mother. She always considers that probability, in fact usually wishes for it, but she also dreams of a career."[8] (See Figure 3.)

The very evident changes in the situation of women have led many people to question the nature and purpose of their education. Most of these people are concerned with the problem of helping women function more effectively in their new roles, as well as enabling them to make their maximum contribution to American life. Some of the specific issues which have been raised are:

1. What do present trends suggest about the future roles of women in the home, in the community, and in the labor force?

2. What type of education would help to prepare them for these various roles? Should their education be the same as that of men, equal to that of men, designed for a particular type of paid occupation, or a combination of preparation for wage earning and homemaking?

3. How can the nation utilize the abilities and skills of women to the most constructive ends?

4. What facilities might be made available for the retraining and re-education of women after their children no longer need their full attention?

[8] John Biesanz and Mavis Biesanz, *Modern Society* (Englewood Cliffs, N.J.: Prentice-Hall, 1955), p. 232.

5. What are the implications of restricted opportunities for women in the future flexibility of our society?

6. How can we help to meet the problems of increasing family disintegration and juvenile delinquency?

7. Is there any way by which we can help families develop a greater sense of responsibility for the problems in their own communities?

The problem of education for women is a challenging one. New types of educational programs are needed: a high school program organized by school and community leaders might help young people recognize their responsibility for family and community life, to become acquainted with the wide variety of attitudes and value systems which exist in American communities, and to develop skill in meeting people and changing situations. Such a program would take youngsters into constructive community activities and help them to work with family and community groups other than their own.

Another educational problem involving women today is the education of their children. Most people seem to accept the idea that the education and rearing of young children are still largely family tasks, and more particularly, that of the women. Among many modern families, women have had to assume an even greater share of the responsibility for the upbringing of children, since the fathers may see little of their children. Complicating this situation is the fact which was already mentioned that women are becoming mothers at an increasingly early age. Many young mothers are not well prepared to rear their children.

THE TEEN-AGE EXPLOSION. Much has been written about teen-agers. The increase in the birth rate started at the end of World War II and has produced an ever-growing number of teen-agers in the past decade. These young people are finding themselves in a world where their status is uncertain. They are treated neither as children nor as adults, their employment opportunities are limited, and inadequate provisions have been made for the utilization of their leisure time. Many have responded to this situation by venting their insecurity and dissatisfaction through irresponsible and antisocial behavior. The channeling of this force into constructive pathways is a problem yet to be solved.

Furthermore, through the power of sheer numbers, teen-agers have become an important factor in the national economy, both as producers and as consumers. We shall have more to say about this in Chapter 15, "The Teen-Age Consumer."

THE PROBLEM OF THE AGING. Senior citizens, those persons over 65 years of age, are also growing in numbers, thanks to the tremendous strides taken by medical science in the past few decades. About 9 per cent of our nation now are senior citizens.[9]

---

[9] U.S. Dept. of Commerce, *Statistical Abstract of the United States 1964* (Washington, D.C.: Government Printing Office), p. 22.

Economically, too, our senior citizens are gaining in importance. Retirement incomes are increasing: better retirement plans, more social security benefits, and higher salaries in the years preceding retirement enable people to save more for the years in which they are unable or desire not to work. These older people are thinking young; they want to live their own lives and do not want to be considered "old folks."

The Family as a Business

The modern American family is a small business enterprise. It receives money as a wage or salary or profit for goods or services rendered; in turn, it uses this money to provide for itself and perhaps to increase its earning power. The family must use this income to meet the legal obligations of taxes and social security, provide the necessities of living—food, clothing, shelter, and medical care—pay for hobbies, amusements, and vacations, and purchase desired luxuries. In short, the family income must provide for the spending of the family group.

The average American family occupies an enviable position in that it is much richer than the average family in most other parts of the world. This can be explained by the high productive output per worker that prevails in this country because of the high degree of industrialization; mechanized tools enable workers to produce more per hour than by hand production methods. "The productive output per worker in the United States has increased 5.6 times from 1850 to 1950."[10] As a result, American workers need to work fewer hours than do workers in other countries to buy an equal amount of food, clothing, and other commodities.

Family Income

The average family income in the United States in 1962 was $6,000. This represented a considerable rise over the previous twelve years; in 1947 it was $3,000. (Since consumer prices also have risen, about one half of this rise indicated an increase in purchasing power.) However, this relative affluence was not evenly distributed; for example, in families where the head was 65 years or older the average income was under $2,000.[11]

Personal income varies widely because of a large number of factors, two of the more important being age and occupation. Generally, income is found to rise to about age 35, remain fairly constant to 55, taper off to 65 and drop sharply thereafter. The correlation between required educational preparation and financial reward is quite high, those occupations requiring the most training are usually the highest paying.

[10] Thomas R. Carskadon and George Soule, *USA in New Dimension* (New York: Macmillan, 1957), p. 3.
[11] U.S. Dept. of Commerce, Bureau of the Census, "Consumer Income," *Current Population Reports*, Series P-60, No. 40 (July 26, 1963), pp. 1-3.

TABLE 1
Mother's Employment by Income of Father and Age of Children*

Whether Mother Employed, and Income in 1958 of Father	Total Single Children	DISTRIBUTION OF CHILDREN BY INCOME OF FATHER AND WHETHER MOTHER EMPLOYED (NUMBER IN THOUSANDS)					
		Under 3 Years	3-5 Years	6-11 Years	12-17 Years	18-24 Years	25 Years and Over
Total single children	59,958	10,587	10,635	18,505	13,643	4,952	1,636
Per Cent Distribution All income classes combined	100.0	100.0	100.0	100.0	100.0	100.0	100.0
Mother employed	23.5	13.2	17.2	24.5	32.9	32.4	18.3
$0 to $1,999	14.1	13.1	11.4	11.5	16.1	18.8	41.7
Mother employed	3.8	2.5	2.3	3.2	5.6	6.5	7.2
$2,000 to $3,999	24.1	28.5	23.1	23.2	22.6	23.5	25.0
Mother employed	7.0	4.8	5.3	7.3	8.9	9.5	4.0
$4,000 to $5,999	33.8	34.8	37.8	35.0	31.6	29.4	18.9
Mother employed	8.0	4.1	6.5	8.4	11.3	10.1	5.5
$6,000 to $9,999	21.9	19.8	22.5	24.2	21.8	19.5	11.0
Mother employed	4.1	1.5	2.7	4.9	5.8	5.4	1.2
$10,000 and over	6.1	3.8	5.1	6.2	7.9	8.7	3.4
Mother employed	0.7	0.3	0.3	0.7	1.4	0.8	0.4

* U.S. Dept. of Commerce, Bureau of the Census, *Current Population Reports*, Series P-20, No. 112 (December 29, 1961), p. 25.

Some interesting correlations have been found between the number of working mothers and the income of the father and the ages of the children. (See Table 1.) A much higher percentage of women work when the father earns $6,000 or less. At all income levels, the highest percentage of employed women occurs when the children are between the ages of 6 and 24; these are the years when the care of the children requires less of the mother's time and more of the family income. (See Figure 4.)

From the figures cited above, it can be seen that an enormous amount of money is available to families over a period of years and, consequently, a wide range of choices is possible. For instance, if a family replaces its automobile every three years over a forty-year period, the difference between buying a new car at $2,000 and a used car at $900 amounts to about $15,000, enough to send several children to college at current costs. If we consider the relative costs of a new car purchased on the installment plan versus the used car bought for cash, the difference might be as great as $40,000.

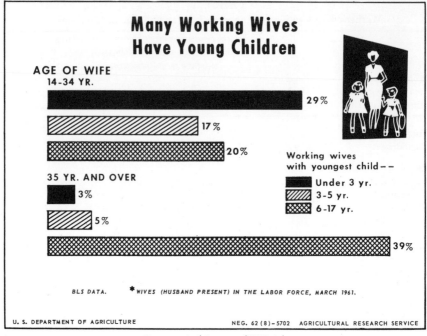

FIGURE 4. *(Courtesy of USDA.)*

Thus, the handling and use of family income is a matter of making the income and expenditures harmonize with family needs and desires. In the process, even families of moderate income have the opportunity to make many choices in the disposition of this income.

Family Spending

The total personal income of Americans in 1960 was over $400 billion, an average of $2,226 per man, woman, and child. Taxes averaged 12½ per cent, about $279. Thus the disposable income, or income after taxes, was $1,947 per person. As a group, we spent $1,820 each for goods and services; we saved $127."[12]

This high ratio of spending to saving is unquestionably the outstanding feature of American spending habits, one directly related to the style of living enjoyed by this nation of consumers. Almost all the goods and services used in the typical American home are provided by industries and agencies especially created to fill these needs. A hypothetical example will show some of the ways in which the system operates.

When Mr. Jones gets up in the morning, he is awakened by an alarm clock.

[12] New York State Cooperative Extension Service, "Who Gets the Consumer's Dollar," *Focus on the Food Markets* (March 19, 1962), p. 1.

The clock was purchased in a department store, shipped to his home by a delivery service, and furnished with electricity from hydroelectric plants hundreds of miles away. He washes with water brought by ducts and waterways from mountain streams at a considerable distance. The pipes and conduits were paid for by his taxes and built and maintained by the municipal government of his local community. The bacon he eats for breakfast probably came from hogs in the Midwest and was processed in a plant several hundred miles from his home. Perhaps the eggs came from a local farmer; most likely the bread came from nearby. When he leaves for work, Mr. Jones will drive his car, which was made in Detroit and assembled about a hundred miles from his home, over roads built and financed by the local, state, and federal governments.

This example shows very clearly that it is virtually impossible for anyone in this country to exist in an economic vacuum, that no one can remain uninfluenced by the prevailing economic conditions of the nation. Every economic action is predicated upon several others in this most complex and intertwined of systems. Conversely, no action can be taken which will have no effect upon the system; specifically for our purpose here, each decision to buy or not to buy affects a multiplicity of agencies.

The consumer demand created by family buying is an important influence on the American economy. For example, the production of automobiles is

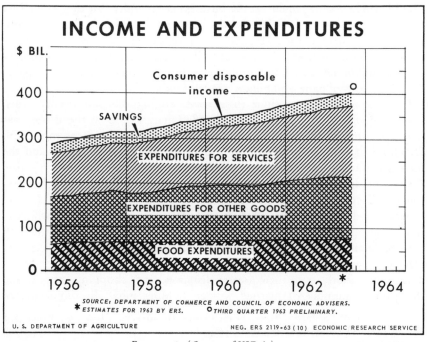

FIGURE 5. *(Courtesy of USDA.)*

based on anticipated consumer demand. Predictions of future trends of family purchases will have an effect on the total economy. If the forecast is that many people will want to purchase cars in the following year, then more cars will be produced. Many workers will be employed to produce the steel, to manufacture the necessary parts, and to assemble the completed automobiles. Employed workers buy food, clothing, household appliances, and some luxuries. If they are unemployed, however, their family spending is of course sharply reduced. The spending of millions of families, which is called "aggregate spending," results in a trend which influences the entire nation.

Obviously, it is impossible to say with certainty exactly what will happen in the future, but some definite trends in family consumption seem to be evident at the present time. The most prominent of these is that the population will continue to grow at a rapid rate. Our population has seen an increase during every census period since the first census was taken in 1790. While in the past the increase could be accounted for by immigration, by the excess of births over deaths, and by territorial expansion, recent developments indicate that the important factor in the future will be the increasing birth rate, coupled with the ever-lengthening life span of our citizens. According to estimates prepared by the Bureau of the Census, the population of the United States will be 215 million by 1970 and 261 million by 1980.[13]

More people mean a greater need for all the goods and services we presently use. "Some 4 million babies will be born in 1962 and their appearance should bring encouragement to the business community, for they constitute an important new market. Here's what economists estimate they will consume during their lifetime: 1 billion pairs of shoes; 25 billion pounds of beef; 63 million suits and dresses; 11 million new cars; 91 billion gallons of gas; 6.5 million refrigerators; 1 million new homes; 200 million tons of steel; 65 million tons of paper; 50 billion quarts of milk."[14]

Family income will continue to increase. During the past twenty years, family income, even allowing for the inflationary action of the dollar, has risen consistently. Increased productivity (each worker produces more with each hour of work by using newer and better tools and methods) and the increased number of wage earners per family are responsible for this rise. Predictions are for both improved methods of production and a higher percentage of employed married women.

Service industries and the production of labor-saving equipment will continue to expand. In the last fifteen years many factors, in addition to the high level of family income, have influenced the increased use of services and mechanical appliances. The busy life of the suburban housewives, the development of suburbs with their greater distances from shopping centers, and the growing number of married women holding jobs, all stimulated the

[13] U.S. Dept. of Commerce, Bureau of the Census, *Our Growing Population* (Washington, D.C.: Government Printing Office, 1961), pp. 1, 12.

[14] National Consumer Finance Association, *Finance Facts* (December 1961), p. 1.

utilization of agencies and devices to decrease the amount of housework required. Items that save time and energy have become popular: frozen foods,
drip-dry clothing, power lawn mowers, diaper service, home freezer service,
and cleaning service, to name but a few. With the expected upward trend
in family income, the demand for such services and appliances is likely to
grow proportionately.

THE USE OF CONSUMER CREDIT. The widespread use of credit buying, especially for hard goods, automobiles, and homes, is a relatively recent
phenomenon, but it is now accepted as a regular method of purchase. Some
economists have expressed considerable concern over what they consider to
be the unwise application and the overuse of installment buying, but it seems
clear that this form of purchasing is gaining in popularity. Young married
couples and families with incomes from $4,000 to $8,000 are the heaviest
users of consumer credit. The use and abuse of this method will be discussed
at length in Chapter 4, "Financing Family Spending."

THE ROLE OF WOMEN IN FAMILY CONSUMPTION. Families make
decisions about consumer activities every day, and much of the responsibility
for these decisions is in the hands of women. In addition to sharing in major
family purchasing, they do most of the daily buying which consumes so
large a share of the family income. Women's buying even exerts an influence
on national consumption trends. Much of the household equipment produced in such abundance since World War II has been designed to help
women care for their homes and families. Designers of automobiles are interested in women's tastes in color and style; so too are home builders, dress
designers, and store managers.

The increase in the number of working women means that women will
be doing even more buying, since working women add to family income
and help to stimulate family buying. In 1940 only 28 per cent of the women
over age 14 were part of the nation's labor force, but by 1957 some 36 per
cent were working outside the home and by October 1960, the figure was
almost 37 per cent. Projective data indicate that by 1970 over 38 per cent
will be employed, about four million more than in 1960.

Among the women in paid employment are many married women. Most
of these wives work because they need a second income in the family to pay
for household commodities they could not otherwise afford. Some of these
goods, such as washing machines and dishwashers, may replace the work
formerly done by the housewife; others, such as a second car, a color television set, or a hi-fi or stereo phonograph, serve to raise the family's standard of living. Among the well-educated married women, many work because
they find more satisfaction and fulfillment in work away from their homes.

In general, employed homemakers have a lighter work load at home than
full-time homemakers. Frequently they have smaller families or adult children. Also, labor-saving appliances and convenience foods free them of much
work formerly required in the household.

Studies have shown that when a wife is employed outside the home, many costs are higher than when the wife does not work.[15] For example, in urban households in the northeastern part of the United States, 75 cents more was spent for food each week when the homemaker was employed. Among the factors that contribute to increased food costs when the wife works is that the family tends to eat more prepared or partially prepared foods. Food costs are only one example; clothing consumption, dry cleaning, laundry services, the second car, and many other aspects of family consumption are often increased when women enter paid employment.

Women are assuming a new role in the management of family money. Formerly, their job was to manage the household expenditures with funds provided by the husband. Today many women both earn money and have a greater voice in its disposition, for large purchases as well as for household needs.

Family Spending and the National Economy

As we have already indicated, family spending and the health of the national economy are interrelated. If the economy is doing well, most people are working and receiving wages and salaries. They are therefore in a position to buy the goods and services their work has helped to produce.

However, the relationship is not quite as simple as this. High employment does not always mean that people will buy. If production is high and people do not buy, goods that have been produced remain unsold. When this happens, producers stop making more goods and begin to lay off employees. Then many workers and their families will have curtailed incomes and will be unable to buy freely.

A period when production is low and many people are unemployed is referred to as a depression. It is a vicious cycle: as production is decreased and unemployment increased, there is a downward spiraling effect; people do not have money to buy, and unless they buy there is no reason to produce. National governments have tried to control this downward trend with massive programs of government spending, sometimes known as "pump priming."

Understanding why people stop buying when production is high is difficult. Efforts are made to forecast large-scale buying intentions as a predictor of the economic health of the nation. Several factors are thought to influence buying intentions. The most important among these are optimism or pessimism about the future and the amount of consumer debt outstanding.

When people are optimistic in their expectations, or if they think a shortage of an item will occur, they tend to buy freely. On the other hand, if they do not expect to have a job next month, they buy less. Ups and downs in the stock market and in the cold war affect this outlook greatly.

Considerable controversy exists as to what level of consumer debt is the

[15] Cf. U.S. Dept. of Labor, Bureau of Labor Statistics, *Employment and Earnings,* Vol. VII, No. 5 (November 1960), and Women's Bureau, *Part-Time Employment for Women,* Bulletin 273, 1960.

point at which people stop buying. For a long time it was thought to be between 12 and 13 per cent of disposable income. Those people who feel that
this level is not necessarily a stopping point cite the fact that the proportion
of outstanding consumer debt to disposable income has risen over the last
fifteen years and that the productivity of workers aided by modern machinery
is much higher than it used to be. Thus people can afford more debt because
they need less of their income for the necessities of life.

Problems of underemployment also occur when the goods produced are
not the ones people wish to buy. A large number of families may want new
housing, and builders may erect many new small homes as a result. However,
the majority of families in a particular area may desire apartments rather than
houses, or they may prefer to live in one area rather than another. In either
case, many of these newly built homes may go unsold. A few years ago,
automobile makers produced cars in abundance, but the widespread preference for small foreign cars cut sharply into the sales of American-made
automobiles.

Modern technology and machinery, which have contributed so greatly to
our high standard of living, are also contributing to unemployment. In many
industries men are being replaced by machines. Automation makes it possible
for fewer men to do more work. Unskilled and semiskilled workers are losing
their jobs, while at the same time there is a shortage of people with the technical training to operate the more intricate automatic equipment. While the
long-range answer probably lies in more education and training for most
people, the immediate problem is to meet the needs of workers without
jobs and of families without adequate incomes. These immediate needs are
particularly acute in the case of culturally deprived groups who, because of
lack of education and training, have been employed primarily in unskilled
occupations.

The Potentialities for Families in Consumption Choices

Now as never before we have the possibility of having every American
family well fed, healthy, and well housed. Our present plentiful resources put
opportunities for education, leisure, and constructive work within the grasp
of everyone. The real problem is to turn these potentialities into actuality.

Many necessary community projects are not in the control of individual
families or even small groups of families. Such things as slum clearance require large-scale planning, organization, and financing to be effective. However, there are many things individual families can do to utilize more effectively their community resources and family income.

Today's high school and college students are the homemakers and parents
of tomorrow. Upon them will rest the responsibility for the growth and development of the families of the future. Wise habits of consumption and
the ability and skill to make effective choices among many goods and services
can strengthen and improve the lives of families, and through this, the life of
the nation.

SELECTED REFERENCES

ALPERT, PAUL. *Economic Development: Objectives and Methods.* New York: Free Press, 1963.

BURNS, EVELINE M. *Social Security and Public Policy.* New York: McGraw-Hill, 1956.

CLARK, LINCOLN (ED.) *Consumer Behavior: The Life Cycle and Consumer Behavior,* Vol. II, Consumer Behavior Series. New York: New York U.P., 1955.

FOOTE, NELSON (ED.) *Household Decision-Making.* New York: New York U.P., 1961.

GALBRAITH, J. K. *The Affluent Society.* Boston: Houghton Mifflin, 1958.

GORDON, LELAND J. *The Function of the Consumer in a Free Choice Economy.* Westport, Conn.: The Calvin K. Kazanjian Economics Foundation, Inc., 1957.

HOYT, ELIZABETH. *The Consumption of Wealth.* New York: Macmillan, 1928.

MILLS, C. WRIGHT. *The Power Elite.* London: Oxford U.P., 1956.

OGBURN, W.F., and M. F. NIMKOFF. *Technology and the Changing Family.* Boston: Houghton Mifflin, 1955.

PACKARD, VANCE. *The Status Seekers.* New York: David McKay, 1959.

POLANYI, KARL. *The Great Transformation.* New York: Holt, Rinehart & Winston, 1947.

RIESMAN, DAVID, NATHAN GLAZER, and REUEL DENNEY. *The Lonely Crowd,* New Haven, Conn.: Yale U. P., 1950.

VEBLEN, THORNSTEIN. *Theory of the Leisure Class.* New York: Viking, 1918.

2

FAMILY DECISION-MAKING

> The course of action that a family takes rarely just happens; it is based on decisions. . . . The opportunity and obligation to make intelligent decisions is one of the concepts basic to any democratic situation.[1]

FROM THE dawn of civilization until the Industrial Revolution, man could do little more than produce enough for the subsistence of himself and his family. Modern mechanization, however, now enables him to produce with less effort and in less time much more than he and his family can use. In fact, so abundant has this production become that we in the United States are faced with the problem of overproduction. We are capable of raising more food than we can eat and of making more goods than we can sell.

Today's family has a wide range of commodities from which to choose. Food, clothing, and shelter come in an almost confusing array of choices. In the supermarket alone the family faces the task of selecting from over 6,000 products. Among these are foods which must be prepared from the raw stage, foods which are partially prepared, and those which are ready to eat. Foods also come in packages of different sizes, at several price levels. and with varied flavorings. A similar situation exists with respect to both clothing and shelter: clothing can be made at home, purchased cheaply, or ordered from a custom designer; shelter can range from a tenement apartment to a modern trailer or a luxurious home in an upper-income suburb.

This rise in productivity has also been accompanied by an increased appetite for the goods and services that make life easier and pleasanter. People in much of the Western world have wonderful choices: labor-saving equipment, attractive and interesting food, good education, and varied leisure pursuits. (See Figure 6.) In the quest to accumulate these appurtenances of the "good life," however, some families overextend themselves, so that purchases run ahead of family income and funds and jeopardize important family needs. The challenge facing modern families is to how to make wise use of resources, to make choices in the marketplace that reflect their real needs and desires.

[1] Beatrice Paolucci and Carol B. O'Brien, "Decision-Making: The Crux of Management," *Forecast* (November 1959), p. 29.

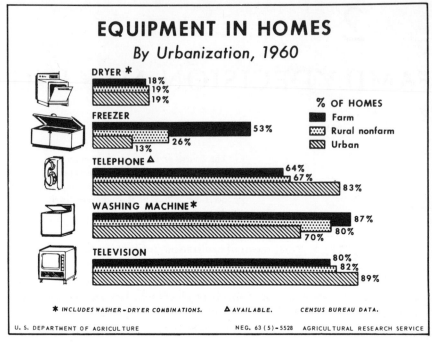

FIGURE 6. *(Courtesy of USDA.)*

What Is Decision-Making?

Where shall we live? How shall we dress? Can we afford a new car, and if so, should it be a large car or a compact? Should Susie take dancing lessons? Shall we buy a new bike for Bob? These are the kinds of economic decisions which families must make.

An understanding of how families reach the decision to buy is of importance to many people: the family itself, the people who produce goods and sell services, and those who work with families in an attempt to help them. This understanding is also basic to the evaluation of family spending in terms of family goals.

Katona describes decision-making or problem-solving behavior as having four parts: the arousal of a problem, deliberation which includes psychological reorganization of the situation, the weighing of alternatives, and finally the choosing among the possible courses of action.[2]

When decision-making occurs is difficult to locate at some specific point in

[2] George Katona, "A study of Purchase Decisions: Part I," in Lincoln H. Clark, ed., *Consumer Behavior: The Dynamics of Consumer Reaction.* Consumer Behavior Series, Vol. I (New York: New York U. P., 1955), p. 31.

time, since many decisions are reached slowly over a long period. According to one definition, a decision is said to take place at the point between tendency and action.[3]

Decision-making occurs only when strong motivating forces or circumstances are present. Habitual behavior is used for many recurring and routine purchases such as groceries, drug items, cigarettes, and other convenience goods. [4] The busy housewife does not stop to analyze each individual purchase; she buys what has proved satisfactory in the past. Thus she relies heavily on advertising, brand loyalty, store loyalty, and past experience. A reinforcing factor for habitual buying is the assurance that one is buying something that is socially acceptable and similar to what others in the same circle of friends are purchasing.

In a study done at the University of Michigan, Katona found some conditions under which people tended to purchase large household goods without carefully considering the alternatives:

(a) when the income of the purchaser was fairly high or the purchase price quite low;
(b) when the education of the buyer was limited;
(c) when there was a special opportunity to buy through friends, a special sale, or a very persuasive salesman;
(d) when the item was urgently needed; and
(e) when previous satisfaction with the item was very great.[5]

Reliance on habit in buying is broken when the situation changes or if a problem arises. The move of a family from one community to another would present a new situation; a change in family income would represent a problem. (In the former case, however, the similarity of living standards and stores in both the old and the new communities might not constitute enough of a change to result in a change of buying habits. Stores are rapidly losing regional and rural-urban differences; Sears, Roebuck, for example, no longer puts out regional catalogs.) Decision-making is also made necessary when the item in question has not been purchased for a long time or when the previously purchased item has proved unsatisfactory.

Who Makes the Decision?

The question of who actually makes the decision to buy or not to buy a particular item is subject to many factors. Culturally accepted roles and patterns

[3] Nelson N. Foote (ed.), *Household Decision-Making*, Consumer Behavior Series, Vol. IV (New York: New York U. P., 1961), Introduction, p. 3.

[4] George Katona, *The Powerful Consumer* (New York: McGraw-Hill, 1960), p. 143.

[5] George Katona, "A study of Purchase Decisions: Part I," in Lincoln H. Clark, ed., *Consumer Behavior: The Dynamics of Consumer Reaction*, Consumer Behavior Series, Vol. I (New York: New York U. P., 1955), pp. 30–36.

of behavior may dictate that the husband decide on the family car and the wife on home furnishings. The roles of the members within the family—who handles the money or who sets the style of living—also affect the decision-making process. The present trend seems to be for husbands and wives to do more things together and to make more decisions jointly. This is probably partly related to the less sharply differentiated roles of men and women in today's society. However, this is partially a middle- and upper-class phenomenon; we shall consider the effects of social status on family decision-making later in this chapter.

Some Factors Influencing Decision-Making

People exhibit a wide range of behavior when purchasing any item, and it is obviously impossible to isolate or even measure accurately any one of the many forces which might influence a decision. Mueller found, for example, that less than one fourth of the 360 purchasers in the sample of 1,000 families who bought durable goods were careful buyers, seeking information and deliberating over their purchases. About an equal proportion displayed no care, making purchases quickly and without information. The balance, comprising about half of the purchasers, fell into an intermediate group, deliberating casually or only on some aspects of the purchase decision.

The same study found that the buying of sport shirts was even less deliberate: fewer people planned carefully for the purchase or sought information before buying. There was less awareness of brands, people tending to choose more freely among available ones. However, buyers paid attention to prices and to specific features, just as in larger purchases.[6]

This wide variety of purchasing styles might be accounted for by many things. Only a few of them can be discussed here.

AGE. Age does appear to have an influence on the purchasing of durable goods (see Figure 7). The older the head of the family and his wife (up to retirement), the less deliberate the purchase decisions. This would indicate that the motivation to use resources carefully decreases in later years. Up to retirement this may be due to several reasons. The family may now be grown and self-supporting, which would lessen the feeling of need to save for the future. Also, incomes may be larger.

INCOME AND EDUCATION. These factors are difficult to separate, since the income a person earns is usually related to the amount of education he has received.

6 Eva Mueller, "A Study of Purchase Decisions: Part II," in Lincoln H. Clark, ed., *Consumer Behavior: The Dynamics of Consumer Reaction*, Consumer Behavior Series, Vol. I (New York: New York U. P., 1955), pp. 36–87.

LIFE STAGE CYCLE: AGE OF HOUSEHOLD HEAD

	% SHARE OF TOTAL SPENDING	% SHARE OF 7-CITY SAMPLE
Under 25 years	3.75	4.86
25–34 years old	19.88	19.96
35–44	27.33	23.38
45–54	24.42	20.65
55–64	15.13	15.19
65–74	7.51	11.69
75 and over	1.98	4.27

HOW FAMILY STATUS INFLUENCES SPENDING PATTERNS

	ALL FAMILIES IN SURVEY	FAMILIES IN $7,500–$9,999 INCOME RANGE	HOUSEHOLD WITH HEAD 65–74 YEARS OLD
	ALLOCATION OF TOTAL OUTLAYS		
Food	24.3%	23.9%	26.7%
Eating Out	5.4	5.1	4.2
Tobacco	1.7	1.6	1.2
Alcoholic Beverages	1.9	1.7	1.8
Housing	30.0	28.3	34.1
Home Operations	6.0	5.4	7.4
Home Furnishings	5.1	5.4	3.1
Clothing	10.4	10.9	7.2
Personal Care	2.8	2.9	2.7
Medical Care	6.3	6.5	9.7
Recreation	3.8	4.1	2.3
Reading	0.9	0.9	1.1
Education	1.3	1.3	0.4
Transportation	14.4	16.3	9.7
Automobile	12.27	14.6	7.8
Miscellaneous	2.2	1.6	3.1

FIGURE 7. (*Data: Bureau of Labor Statistics; reprinted from* Sales Management, *March 1, 1963.*)

Increased education has been found to result in increased deliberation about large purchases; however, in the group with incomes above $7,500, which was composed largely of families where the husband had a college education, there were two tendencies: (1) a greater degree of circumspectness and (2) a greater tendency to regard the decision as less important, requiring less careful consideration. The indication here is that those people who need to plan most carefully were the least likely to do so. Presumably the better-educated people with larger incomes were more highly motivated to use their resources wisely.

OCCUPATION. Since occupation, education, and income are closely related, it might be expected that occupations in which people with little education were predominant would show little deliberation on purchase decisions and that those in which people with more education were preponderant would show more. In the University of Michigan study cited earlier unskilled and service workers did seem least apt to deliberate carefully in buying, while businessmen and professional workers were more deliberate. However, clerical workers and people in sales occupations, who might be expected to rank in the middle group of purchasers, were the most careful buyers of durable goods. This raises the question of motivation: clerical and sales people's salaries have not kept pace with other jobs, and therefore people employed in these fields might feel a greater need for careful use of their income.

In the matter of buying a sport shirt, however, production or blue-collar workers were found to be more deliberate than white-collar workers. This might be due to the fact that a sport shirt represents a larger investment to the lower income groups and is a more important part of their work and play attire.

THE STAGE OF FAMILY LIFE. Young families buy more household equipment. The newly married middle-class couple spends a great deal to accumulate household goods such as furniture, a vacuum cleaner and appliances for the kitchen. A move to suburbia, which usually comes at the point when the family is expanding, stimulates further buying of laundry equipment, garden furniture and equipment, more house furnishings, and perhaps a second car.

The age of the family is an important factor in predicting potential buying proclivity for furnishings and equipment.[7] (See Figure 7.) Expenditures of older families are much lower; presumably they have either already acquired their major furnishings and equipment or have less need for them. After retirement, however, the principal reason for this lowered consumption is that many families have a sharply curtailed income, which reduces their purchasing power.

SOCIAL CLASS DIFFERENCES. There is an increasing tendency for the better-paid working class and the lower ranks of the professional, managerial, and business groups to have the same type of possessions. The plumber and the lawyer may have similar homes, furnishings, and equipment. However, there are certain patterns of social class differences as to who in the family makes the purchase decision. Komarovsky points out that low-income and high-income groups show greater individual autonomy in making purchase decisions than the middle classes, where more frequently the husband and wife decide together.[8]

[7] Vernon G. Lippitt, *Determinants of Consumer Demand for House Furnishings and Equipment* (Cambridge, Mass.: Harvard U. P., 1959).

[8] Mirra Komarovsky, "Class Differences in Family Decision-Making on Expenditures," in Nelson N. Foote, ed., *Household Decision-Making*, Consumer Behavior Series, Vol. IV (New York: New York U. P., 1961), pp. 255-65.

Komarovsky also indicates some other social factors which also help account for variations in family communication about purchase decisions.

1. The higher the aspirations of the couple for themselves and their children, the greater the communication.

2. When the roles of the husband and wife are more formalized—for example, as in the paternalistic family—there is less communication.

3. The closer the ties of the couple to their parents and sibling, the greater the likelihood these relatives will be consulted in making a purchase decision.

4. When a couple lives in the neighborhood or small town in which they grew up, the influence of peers of their own sex and their parental family is very great. The reverse is also true: when couples move away from the place of their origin, their dependence on each other is increased.

5. When a purchase decision involves a large amount of money, there is more frequently discussion between the spouses.

In a study of low-income families in New York City, Caplowitz found that "the popular image of the American as striving for the material possessions which bestow upon him both comfort and prestige in the eyes of his fellows does not hold only for the ever-increasing middle class."[9] Low-income families as well as those with larger incomes buy many major consumer goods.

Consumption for the low-income family is often one way of compensating for an inability to improve their social standing through occupational mobility. New and expensive models of household equipment provide "compensatory consumption." Another good example of this phenomenon is the high rate of automobile ownership among the poorer segments of our society.

The reasons why people buy cars are often unspoken and deep rooted. Cars offer an escape "for adolescents from parental planning and supervision; for the Negro from Jim Crow; for married people from their spouses; for a single woman, from the need for male escorts."[10] The large well-polished car is a status symbol to many Negroes, since this group finds good jobs and housing difficult to attain.

These more expensive items can be sold in low-income areas only because of the adaptations of the credit system made by merchants in these areas. Customers buy on terms that are close to the "dollar down, a dollar a week" phrase. Many do not qualify for credit from regular lending institutions because they do not have a regular job or tangible cash assets. The willingness of the local merchant to extend credit often depends on whether the family has the reputation of paying its debts.

The cost of buying in this manner is not low. Poor quality merchandise is

[9] David Caplowitz, *The Poor Pay More* (New York: Free Press, 1963), p. 12.

[10] David Riesman and Eric Larrabee, "Autos in America," in Lincoln H. Clark, ed., *Consumer Behavior: Research on Consumer Reactions* (New York: Harper, 1958), p. 77.

sold at or above the price of first-rate items, and the credit charges are often very high, reflecting the risk involved in such loans. Often door-to-door salesmen refer the customer to a local merchant; they receive a bonus for each sale made, which is reflected in the price of the article.

In spite of the high cost, low-income families generally shop in their local neighborhoods for durable goods because this is where they are known and can get credit. For the same reason they often buy food in the small corner grocery rather than the supermarket, where the prices are usually lower.

THE PROPORTION OF CREDIT OUTSTANDING. In the last fifteen years consumer debt has grown enormously. (For a fuller discussion, see Chapter 4, "Financing Family Spending.") At the same time recognition of the relationship between consumer buying and the amount of debt families already have has increased. While it is unclear at what point families feel overextended and stop buying, national interest is focused on the extent of credit purchases outstanding as a possible indicator of future family buying intentions.

Subjective Factors Affecting Decision-Making

In a large number of cases the underlying rationale for a purchase decision is not the objective one of need nor the ability to afford the item in question. Sometimes the view a family has of its own situation plays a much more important part in the decision than any more tangible criterion.

FINANCIAL PRESSURE. People buy more when they feel prosperous. Frequently, when one item is almost paid for, they will contract to buy another. A raise in salary often means the purchase of a bigger car or a new television set.

However, measuring financial pressure on a family is difficult. Larger incomes are not necessarily associated with lower pressure. A man with three children earning $7,500 may feel more pressed than one with an annual salary of $5,000 and no family. A man whose income has decreased from $7,500 to $6,000 might feel more pressed than one whose income has just increased to $6,000. The family with $6,000 annual income and a $20,000 house will feel more pinched than one with the same income and a less costly house.

OPTIMISM ABOUT THE FUTURE. People tend to buy more if they feel that their personal future is going to be rosy and that the nation's economic health is good. The family that expects a rising income is less concerned about saving, and the worker who feels that his job situation is secure feels freer to buy. In such cases, fairly weak motivations may result in purchases.

THE INFLUENCE OF FAMILY MEMBERS ON EACH OTHER. It is

difficult to isolate the influence of family members on a decision-making process. One member may feel so strongly about family peace that he will compromise on almost any question to maintain it. Another may feel that his ideas must prevail in any purchase decision. If the father suggests buying a new car and the mother insists on a certain model, it might be considered that both had participated in the purchase decision.

Further, as Becker noted, the influence of family members on each other varies at different times.[11] Parents can influence their children's career choices at some stages of development and not others. The father of a teen-age boy may have a great deal of influence over the choice of his occupation; the mother of a 30-year-old may not be consulted about a job change.

Children actively influence buying decisions. They learn at home from parents and the mass media what to want, and their desires for soda instead of drinking water, for cereal with toys and premiums, and the like, are strong influences. As they get older, they learn from their friends what is accepted, whether it be khaki slacks, a wraparound skirt, or hero sandwiches for lunch. By the time they reach high school, their desires are even more clear-cut and often very insistent; keeping up with the crowd is an essential part of being socially accepted. This requires clothes, spending money, and time to do what the others are doing.[12]

There is also the question of how conflicting family desires are resolved. Most families want more than one thing at a time—a new car, a vacation trip, a new couch, or new clothes. Who is responsible for a compromise as a decision?

THE INFLUENCE OF THE SOCIAL SITUATION. Buying pressure is also exerted by our own standard of living and that of our friends. "Keeping up with the Joneses" is often referred to as a joke, but it is not a factor to underestimate. Most people are very responsive to social pressures, since individuals are members of groups whose opinions they value. Mueller found that more than half of the buyers of large household appliances sought advice from acquaintances and usually looked at appliances owned by them. One third bought a brand or model they had seen in the home of a friend or relative.[13]

Whyte makes the point that word of mouth has always existed as a potent force. In earlier years it exerted less effect on family purchases than it does

[11] Howard S. Becker, "The Implications of Research on Occupational Careers for a Model of Household Decision-Making," in Nelson N. Foote, ed., *Household Decision-Making.* Consumer Behavior Series, Vol. IV (New York, New York U. P., 1961), pp. 239-65.

[12] David Riesman and Howard Roseborough, "Careers and Consumer Behavior," *Consumer Behavior: The Life Cycle and Consumer Behavior,* Consumer Behavior Series, Vol. II (New York: New York U. P., 1955), p. 4. Cf. David Riesman, Nathan Glazer, and Reuel Denney, *The Lonely Crowd* (New Haven: Yale U. P., 1950), and Vance Packard, *The Hidden Persuaders* (New York: Pocket Books, 1958), pp. 135-43.

[13] Eva Mueller, *loc. cit.*

FIGURE 8.   (Courtesy of Fortune Magazine; photography by Aero Service Corporation.)

today because there were fewer commodities available to families and less disposable income in most families. The women who chatted over the clothesline 25 years ago were as tightly knit as the group who talk over coffee today, but their influence on family buying was more limited.[14]

Communication among residents of the same area influences purchase decisions. Whyte notes this in his study of who owned air conditioners in Philadelphia. There seemed to be a heavier concentration of ownership in row housing areas than in upper-income sections; moreover, the pattern of air-conditioner ownership seemed to indicate a clustering of air conditioners in neighboring houses or houses located on the same street.[15] (See Figure 8.)

Suburbia—mass-produced, "precut, pre-engineered, and prelandscaped"[16] —has become a way of life. In these suburbs with their homogeneity of ap-

[14] William H. Whyte, Jr., "The Web of Word of Mouth," *Consumer Behavior: The Life Cycle and Consumer Behavior, op. cit.,* pp. 113-22.

[15] *Ibid.*

[16] William H. Whyte, Jr., "The Consumer in the New Suburbia," *Consumer Behavior: The Dynamics of Consumer Reaction,* Consumer Behavior Series, (New York: New York U. P., 1955), p. 1.

pearance, the buying of goods also has certain homogeneous features. Note the grills in the backyards, the pair of chairs in the living room, and the appliances in the kitchen and utility room.

Whyte suggests several indications of social change in suburbia that have importance in consumer decision-making.

1. In this age of large organizations, the family that moves from one part of the country to another is no longer the exception. Mobility is becoming a more important factor in the buying of household goods. Portable dishwashers have become popular because they can move with the family.

2. Many of these new suburbs are transient communities. Park Forest, which is outside Chicago, has a turnover of one third of the rental apartments annually and almost one quarter of the homes.

3. The traditional image of the small community with its stratified social structure is no longer valid. Class structure in 'the traditional sense does not exist in the new suburbs. But the feeling of transiency divides the population into two groups—those who are on their way to something better and those who have come as far as they can.

4. Social life in these new suburbs is primarily within the group in the development. Sharing of household goods, baby-sitting, and private problems are part of the outgoing life. Privacy is limited or nonexistent.

5. Family life revolves around the children. Parents make friends with their children's friends and their parents. The suburban development is often a difficult place for the couple with no children.

A Representative Study

In a study of 101 people who bought houses near New London, Connecticut, Norris reported that the most frequent reason for buying a house was because these people could not rent or could not rent at a reasonable price.[17] Most of the group weighed renting against buying, but only 17 people considered the problem as having four major alternatives: renting an apartment, renting a house, buying a new house, or buying an old house.

The majority of the group interviewed spent one to three months looking seriously for a house. However, 16 bought a house without any serious looking, and very few considered more than one house.

Katona points out that the market for housing is not satisfied just because people already own a house. Wants and desires change.[18] This is

[17] Ruby T. Norris, "Processes and Objective of House Purchasing in the New London Area," *Consumer Behavior: The Dynamics of Consumer Reaction,* Consumer Behavior Series (New York: New York U. P., 1955), pp. 25–29.

[18] George Katona, *The Powerful Consumer* (New York: McGraw-Hill, 1960), p. 124.

similar to the situation which prevails with regard to household goods: most of the present demand for refrigerators, television sets, kitchen ranges, and washing machines is for replacements by families already owning these things.

Advertising: An Important Influence on Family Buying

"Advertising is any form of public announcement to aid directly or indirectly in the sale of a commodity."[19] It is promoted through many media: radio, television, magazines, newspapers, posters, direct mail, placards, circulars, and menus.

The purpose of advertising is to stimulate the sale of goods. In our industrialized economy, where the producer and processor are far removed from the ultimate purchaser and often unknown to them, advertising is the method of informing prospective purchasers about commodities and services.

Often it is claimed that "good advertising does not try to sell; it aims to help people buy intelligently."[20] Advertising is thought to help raise the standard of living by giving the consumer information to purchase exactly what he needs and wants.

Advertising is a means of mass communication aimed at mass persuasion. It is a way of reaching many people with a message. Persuasive and high-powered advertising has become part of the modern way of life. In a sense advertising is characteristic of an abundant economy and could not exist without prosperity. When people eked out a living, working very hard just to provide the bare necessities, there was little need for advertising. People had no use for information about new products or new variations of existing ones, since all their energies and money were devoted to providing food, clothing, and shelter. However, with the high productivity of much of the Western world, people have money to spend and an interest in spending it on many types of new products and services.

The chief function of advertising is that of a salesman. It can reach millions of people more effectively and efficiently than can personal selling. The cost per dollar of sales is usually less than it was with the old-fashioned method of a salesman trying to reach an individual customer. As a salesman, its purpose is to convince people that they need something, usually a particular brand of a commodity.

Not all advertising is for direct selling. Multimillion-dollar corporations that sell only to other manufacturers also advertise to the public to promote

[19] *Webster's New International Dictionary*, second edition (Springfield, Mass.: Merriam Co., 1956), p. 39.

[20] Harry W. Hepner, *Modern Advertising* (New York: McGraw-Hill, 1956), p. 20.

an image of their company. Du Pont, for example, has changed its image through advertising from that of a munitions maker to that of a pioneer in consumer research—"Better Things for Better Living Through Chemistry."

Another type of advertising which does not aim at direct selling is used by some clothing manufacturers. They advertise so that their salesmen and wholesale customers will believe that the garments are presold to the retail purchaser.

Among the advertisers who do so for direct selling, there is a wide diversity. One company may manufacture a headache remedy, so it will advertise in an attempt to persuade people to try the remedy. A government may want to promote itself or a national product, such as Jamaican rum. Another concern may sell a patented kitchen gadget by mail. By advertising in the Sunday editions of newspapers, book clubs have greatly increased their membership.

Much of the advertising on radio and television and in national magazines is done because companies want to build an image or franchise with the public; they want to develop brand loyalty. From the producers' point of view, brand loyalty helps to ensure that they are not dependent on the personal selling effectiveness of individuals in the corporation, that the company will outlast individuals. Brand-name advertising tries to reach below the level of consciousness so that the customer will not stop to analyze his action at the moment of purchase but will buy the advertiser's brand.

At present, great importance is attached to the consumers' subconscious thoughts. Motivational research attempts to probe the subconscious reasons for purchasing, to find the real reason why people buy or don't buy. Advertising campaigns are geared to these subconscious desires: deodorants are advertised as sex symbols, very expensive cold cream as enhancing one's special attractiveness to men, tea as the drink for virile men.

The largest dollar volume for national advertising is spent on products with high profit margins, items where the number of units used by each customer is large and the production expenses fixed at a high level. Among the most widely advertised products are food and soft drinks; automobiles; soaps, drugs, and toilet articles; beer and alcoholic beverages; tobacco; and electrical appliances.

Decision-Making and Today's Family

While we still have a great deal to learn about how buying decisions are made in families, we are becoming much more aware of the factors that influence these decisions. Companies that wish to sell goods or services make use of this knowledge to sell their wares. Families who wish to use their assets wisely should examine their buying habits and evaluate their purchase decisions carefully to get the things they want most for their money.

SELECTED REFERENCES

BAILEY, BETTY W. *Food Management Practices of Employed and Non-Employed Homemaker Families*, Bulletin No. 98, Georgia Agricultural Experiment Stations, University of Georgia, College of Agriculture, June 1962.

BAUER, RAYMOND A. "Limits of Persuasion," *Harvard Business Review* (September-October 1958), pp. 105-110.

BURSK, EDWARD C. "Opportunities for Persuasion." *Harvard Business Review* (September-October 1958), pp. 111-119.

CAPLOWITZ, DAVID. *The Poor Pay More*. New York: Free Press, 1963.

EDITORS OF *Fortune* MAGAZINE. *The Changing American Market*, Garden City, N. Y.: Hanover House, 1955.

FERBER, ROBERT. "Research on Household Behavior," *American Economic Review*, Vol. 52, No. 1 (March 1962), pp. 19-63.

FOOTE, NELSON N. "The Autonomy of the Consumer," in Lincoln H. Clark (ed.) *Consumer Behavior: The Dynamics of Consumer Reaction*, Consumer Behavior Series. New York: New York U. P.

―――― (ed.) *Household Decision-Making*. Consumer Behavior Series. New York: New York U. P., 1961.

HEPNER, HARRY W. *Modern Advertising*. New York: McGraw-Hill, 1956.

KATONA, GEORGE. *The Powerful Consumer*. New York: McGraw-Hill, 1960.

――――, and EVA MUELLER. "A Study of Purchase Decisions," in Lincoln H. Clark (ed.) *Consumer Behavior: The Dynamics of Consumer Reaction*, Consumer Behavior Series. New York: New York U. P., 1955, pp. 30-87.

LEVY, SIDNEY. "Symbols for Sale," *Harvard Business Review* (July-August 1959), pp. 117-124.

MAYER, MARTIN. *Madison Avenue, U.S.A.* New York: Harper, 1958.

NORRIS, RUBY T. "Processes and Objectives of House Purchasing in the New London Area," *Consumer Behavior: The Dynamics of Consumer Reaction*, Consumer Behavior Series. New York: New York U.P., 1955, pp. 25-29.

PACKARD, VANCE. *The Hidden Persuaders*. New York: Pocket Books, 1958.

――――. *The Waste Makers*. New York: Van Rees, 1960.

PAOLUCCI, BEATRICE, AND CAROL B. O'BRIEN, "Decision-Making: The Crux of Management," *Forecast* (November 1959), pp. 29-30, 48.

RIESMAN, DAVID, and HOWARD ROSEBOROUGH. "Careers and Consumer Behavior," in Lincoln H. Clark (ed.) *Consumer Behavior: The Life Cycle and Consumer Behavior*, Consumer Behavior Series. New York: New York U. P., 1955, pp. 1-18.

――――, NATHAN GLAZER, and REUEL DENNEY. *The Lonely Crowd*. New Haven, Conn.: Yale U. P., 1950, pp. 54-85.

ROBINSON, DWIGHT E. "Fashion Theory and Product Design," *Harvard Business Review* (November-December 1958), pp. 126-138.

SMITH, RALPH LEE. *The Bargain Hucksters*. New York: Crowell, 1962.

STRYKER, PERRIN. "What's The Motive?" in *The Amazing Advertising Business*. New York: Simon & Schuster, 1957.

U.S. DEPARTMENT OF AGRICULTURE. *Marketing, The Yearbook of Agriculture*. Washington, D.C.: Government Printing Office, 1954.

WHITE, IRVING S. "The Functions of Advertising in Our Culture," *Journal of Marketing* (July 1959), pp. 8-14.

WHYTE, WILLIAM H., JR., "The Web of Word of Mouth," *Fortune* (November 1954), pp. 140-147.

———. "The Consumer in the New Suburbia," in Lincoln H. Clark (ed.) *Consumer Behavior: The Dynamics of Consumer Reaction*, Consumer Behavior Series. New York: New York U. P., 1955, pp. 1-14.

WOLFF, JANET L. *What Makes Women Buy?* New York: McGraw-Hill, 1958.

ZELOMAK, A. W. "Profile of the New Consumer," *Challenge* (April 1961), pp. 9-13.

3

DIRECTING DOLLARS

> Scarcity of resources makes it necessary to sacrifice
> some things desired in order to obtain those for
> which the desire is greater. The exactness and divi-
> sibility of money income, the postponability of
> its use . . . all tend to force a consciousness that
> spending is an either-or process.[1]

FOR MOST people, wants and desires outpace available income.
Like the child in the candy store with only a nickel to spend,
most adults and families face a vast array of attractive goods
and services with only a limited amount of money in hand. How much satisfaction and pleasure they achieve with their spending depends on how closely
they harmonize their real desires with their purchases.

To make oneself "master of his money" means learning how to apportion
funds to obtain what is most important. Unless it is carefully directed, money
has a way of dribbling away on frivolous little things. Consider the high
school girl who wants a new skirt, but uses her allowance for ice cream and
Cokes; the housewife who needs a new pair of shoes but, instead, buys expensive convenience foods. Perhaps Dad would feel better with a quiet lunch to
break his busy day, but splurges instead on fancy hardware and tools.

Peoples' wants differ, but most of us would like to have certain things that
always seem a little bit out of reach. Perhaps this is something much too big
for our income, like a yacht, but often it is something we could have if we
planned carefully and gave up some other things.

This calls for organization to direct money where we really want it to go.
Most of us are trained in the business of earning money. We have skills in
wage earning, education to help us understand the world we live in, but little or no training in using the money we earn to help us achieve the goals we
want. Confronted by an ever-expanding array of very attractive personal and
household goods, we often buy before we plan, without considering whether
these items are what we really want.

[1] Hazel Kyrk, *The Family in the American Economy* (Chicago, Illinois: University of Chicago
Press, 1953), p. 322.

Planning Expenditures

Directing your money through preplanning and organizing your expenditures does not mean that you must follow a plan outlined by some "expert," or a set of figures telling what the average family does. This "average" family is probably a composite of lots of different families who vary greatly; the average may exist only on paper.

Each individual and family should formulate a framework for spending that suits their needs, interests, and desires. A simple plan is easier to follow than a complex one, and a written form is easy to refer to. The type of plan you will find useful will depend on the frequency and regularity with which you receive your money. You may have a regular income that is exactly the same every week of the year. If you are a teacher, you may be paid once a month and not at all during the summer. If the wage earner is employed in a seasonal outdoor occupation, he may have heavy earnings two thirds of the year and only unemployment insurance in the midwinter. Four types of information are useful to most families (1) an estimate of income for the coming year; (2) the amount needed for fixed expenses or those items that you are already committed to pay for; (3) the amount of money left for daily living; and (4) a plan for daily expenditures.

If you are a member of a family, then the overall plan should be a family one, in which each member shares in planning and thus has a feeling of a responsibility to make it work. What part the children should play in the planning depends both on their ages and on how the family handles its affairs. Many parents plan the large living expenditures, such as housing, and expect teenage children to share in planning for flexible expenditures. Others discuss all family financial planning with their children.

Estimating Yearly Income

Make an estimate of your anticipated income per month for the coming year. Include interest on savings accounts, dividends if you own stock, a Christmas bonus if your firm regularly pays one, and any additional income you might expect to have. (See Figure 10, p. 36.)

Calculating Fixed Expenses

The next step is to list the expenses you know you will have to pay. List them under the month in which they will have to be paid. They should include:

1. *Taxes.* Itemize federal, state, and city income taxes you will have to pay in addition to whatever is withheld from your salary. List real estate taxes, personal property taxes, and any others that might apply to your family.
2. *Rent or fixed housing expenses.* If you are in a house, this might include your mortgage payment and any insurance that is paid through the bank.
3. *Debts.* List all outstanding debts: the amount due on household equipment, bank loans, or any other obligations.

Housing 29.6%

Food 24.4%

FIGURE 9. The use of family income. *(Photographs courtesy of Du Pont Company: Photograph of operating room, courtesy of Montefiore Hospital, N.Y., Publications.)*

Transportation 14.7%

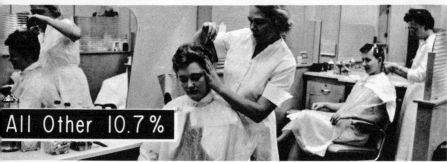

All Other 10.7%

Clothing 10.2%

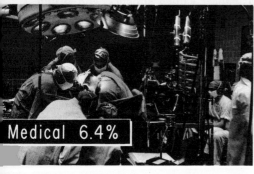

Medical 6.4%

Recreation 4.0%

Estimated Money Income for _____
                                    (period)

Item	Amount
Wage or salary of:	
Member A _____	$_____
Member B _____	_____
Member C _____	_____
Other_____	_____
Other money income	
_____	_____
_____	_____
Total money income _____	$_____

FIGURE 10. *(U.S. Department of Agriculture.)*

4. *Insurance premiums.* Include life insurance, health and accident policies, liability insurance, fire insurance, and any other policies your family presently carries.

Planning Daily Expenditures

If you have carefully estimated income for each month and listed your fixed expenses for each month, then you can just subtract to find out how much is left for day-to-day expenses. This is a good time to sit down with the family to hear their ideas. By discussing expenditures with the family, each one will have a better awareness of what is available and how he can modify his own desires and needs to fit family funds.

The first time you formulate plans, don't try to plan a whole year's expenses —just consider a couple of months ahead. (See Figure 11.) As you gain experience, your plans can be made further in advance.

The principal categories of expenditure that should be included in planning daily expenses are the following:

1. *Food.* Meat, poultry, vegetables, baked products, and all items necessary to the home preparation of meals; meals eaten away from home, including the taxes and tips; carbonated and alcoholic beverages; and snacks, including candy.

2. *Housing.* Include any expenditures not already listed under fixed expenses, such as repairs, painting, insurance, garden supplies, and maintenance costs. If you provide your own heat, this is also a housing expense.

3. *Household operation.* This includes gas, electricity, telephone, cleaning supplies, the purchase of major appliances such as a washing machine, equipment for maintaining the house such as a vacuum, painting the inside of the house or apartment, expenditures for household help, and laundry and cleaning costs for household items.

4. *Clothing.* Include outer clothing, underwear, hats, hose, shoes, acces-

Detailed Plan for Personal Allowances and Requirements for One Person

Item or category	Expense last year or period	Planned expense this year												Remarks
		Jan.	Feb.	Mar.	Apr.	May	June	July	Aug.	Sept.	Oct.	Nov.	Dec.	
Meals, snacks, refreshments away from home.	$	$	$	$	$	$	$	$	$	$	$	$	$	
Clothing														
Personal care														
Medical and dental care and supplies														
Busfare, gasoline, auto upkeep														
Other transportation														
Admissions, other entertainment, and recreation away from home.														
Toys, hobby, sports supplies.														
School supplies, tuition, special lessons.														
Other reading materials, stationery, musical supplies.														
Dues and contributions														
Gifts outside the family														
Gifts within the family														
Future education fund														
Other														
Total	$	$	$	$	$	$	$	$	$	$	$	$	$	

FIGURE 11. (*U.S. Department of Agriculture.*)

sories, material for making garments, sewing supplies, the alteration and repair of garments, and upkeep such as dry cleaning and laundering of sheets.

5. *Automobile and transportation costs.* Include all car expenses except those for vacations: the cost of insurance, repairs, and maintenance, as well as gasoline and oil. Also include expenditures for public transportation such as train, bus, taxi, or subway.

6. *Medical care.* This category covers health insurance, the services of physicians and dentists, medical supplies, the cost of eyeglasses and dental appliances, drugs, and any hospital expenses not covered by insurance.

7. *Home furnishings.* Include all expenditures for furnishings, draperies, curtains, and carpets as well as their maintenance and repair costs.

8. *Personal allowances.* It is conducive to the development of personal pride and the learning of good financial habits if each member of the family receives an allowance for which he does not need to give an accounting to the other members. This includes children. The size of the allowance should be based on the needs of the individual and with cognizance of the maturity of the person. As children get older, they are able to assume more responsibility for personal expenditures. What items an allowance covers needs to be clearly defined, since this can become a source of friction in families.

9. *Family development and recreation.* This includes equipment for sports, music lessons, television and radio (including repairs), expenditures for movies, vacations, and other leisure activities.

10. *Education.* This may be a separate category, or it may be included under savings or family development. In any case a plan should be made that includes planning for the education of the children.

11. *Savings.* Include a definite amount for savings. This should be large enough to cover both emergency funds and long-term goals. An emergency fund of at least two months' income is wise; more, of course, is better. Long-term goals might be a trip to Europe, money to put your children through college, funds for your retirement. Other things that might be included in the savings plan are vacations, Christmas and large outlays for household equipment, building a patio, or braces for someone's teeth. Regular saving helps a family achieve a sense of security.

Some Cautions in Planning Expenditures

1. Don't use someone else's plan. Make one to fit your situation.

2. Don't be overly ambitious; set reasonable amounts for each category of expenditure. If the plan calls for a reduction in expenditures, this needs to be accompanied by a change in the manner of using money before savings will be effected.

3. Don't give up personal allowances. In many families these are very important to family happiness.

```
One family's budget . . .
                                       the big picture
    Here's the master budget worked out by one
family . . . two adults, two children . . . no in-
come but the breadwinner's salary . . . take-
home pay $6,000 a year.
    This budget won't fit your family, so don't
try to use it. You need to figure out your own,
using your own income and your own experi-
ence with expenses.
    But do look this over for inspiration. It shows
how simple a year's financial plan can be yet
still provide practical guidelines for spending
and saving.
```

fixed expenses	per month	per year
mortgage	$100	$1,200
savings account	15	180
life insurance	20	240
taxes	15	180
personal allowances		
Jim	25	300
Sally	10	120
Dot	5	60
Little Jim	1	12
church, charities	5	60
variable expenses		
food and household operations	150	1,800
clothing	25	300
medical and dental	15	180
car upkeep and repair	15	180
house upkeep and repair	20	240
fuel	20	240
light	6	72
water	4	48
recreation, entertainment	14	168
accumulating funds		
Christmas	10	120
vacation	15	180
new furniture	10	120
total	$500	$6,000

FIGURE 12. (*Adapted by permission from* Changing Times, *The Kiplinger Magazine.*)

4. Do plan for some unexpected expenses. There may be an emergency—the roof develops a leak, the car motor gives its last gurgle, Susie spilled ink on her new dress and needs another one for church.

Unexpected expenses and unplanned expenditures are usually the things that knock holes in the family budget. An unplanned expenditure might be a social event that is important to your job, but one you had not planned on attending. Perhaps you have to buy theater tickets and an evening dress. Other types of unplanned expenditures, such as the dress in the store window that you couldn't live without, or the new car which you wanted but couldn't afford, need to be held to a minimum. A portion of the regular savings should be allocated for emergencies and unexpected expenses.

Making the Spending Plan Work

Once you have a plan worked out on paper, the next step is to implement it. An expenditure plan provides the framework within which to plan your expenditures, but actual control over the outgo is also needed. Simple records are very helpful, but detailed records are too much of a chore for most people. Occasionally, a family may wish to keep detailed records of some area of expenditure, such as food, to analyze how money is being allocated among the various foodstuffs.

In addition to records to tell where money is going, most people also need some brakes on their spending, some actual control over outgo. A major problem for families is the job of removing from actual spending funds the amount needed for savings, insurance, investments, and other big long-term items. Many business firms will help their employees save by depositing funds directly in a savings bank, government bonds, or an employee-managed credit union. Some families like to deposit in the bank all the money allocated for long-term goals and big expenses that occur during the year. It is possible to have more than one account at a bank to further separate funds for long-term savings from those which you wish to accumulate for insurance or other big predictable expenses.

Deposits in savings banks accumulate interest, which is an advantage. Moreover, many banks will write bank checks without charge for you to pay occasional large bills. However, if you write a lot of checks, a checking account is more convenient. Both savings and checking accounts can be arranged to allow both the husband and wife to deposit and withdraw. (See Chapter 10.)

In handling the day-to-day expenses three methods seem to be helpful to families: the allowance, the envelope plan, and a checking account.

The Allowance

This is a relatively simple system. Usually the husband gives the wife a certain amount per week from which she pays for food, small household items, and clothing for herself and the children. In some families the wife handles most of the money, and the husband keeps only a personal allowance. This method may work very well for some people, but for others it provides only a loose control over funds.

The Envelope Plan

Some families find it convenient to divide their funds into envelopes with headings: Food, Clothing, Rent, Electricity, and other items. Then they take money from each envelope for purchases or expenses in a particular category. If they are paid weekly and the rent is paid monthly, then they usually accumulate four weeks' money for the rent in that envelope. This method provides a constant check on what is spent and what is left in each category, but has the disadvantage of making cash readily available. Some people find it too

tempting to have money handy when they have an impulse to buy something. It may also be a temptation to other people if they know you keep
money around the house.

The Checking Account

Many families find it easy to deposit their money in a checking account and
write checks against it. The stubs provide a convenient check on what the
remaining balance is and how much has been spent for each type of thing.
However, there is usually a charge for each check or a required minimum
balance that must be maintained.

Assessing Financial Progress

Once a year the family should take stock of its assets and debts. This is helpful in determining whether they have made any economic progress and in
considering future changes in family spending. It is also useful when one is applying for a loan from a bank or other lending institution. (See Figure 13.)

You may find that too much is being put into buying a house and too
little into a savings account; or the family is caught short without ready cash.
Perhaps you should increase your insurance coverage because your family has
grown. A regular check on financial progress shows many people they need
to cut expenses in some areas. The following are some suggestions to cut
spending:

1. Reduce impulse buying by sticking to a plan. Some people find that it
helps to carry less money, to cancel charge accounts and always pay cash.
One is then limited by the amount of money one has in one's pocket when
the urge to buy arises.

2. Study your food bills. Most families could save by substituting lower-
cost foods for some items: less expensive cuts of meat for steak; dried milk
instead of fresh, for cooking; a main dish of macaroni and cheese for meat;
canned fruit instead of fresh in the winter. Also, eating at home is less expensive than a restaurant meal; a packed lunch costs less than a bought one.

3. Examine your housing expenditures. Perhaps you should consider moving to a less expensive apartment or house. Maybe you could rent part of
your house to someone else.

4. Household operation costs should be checked. If your fuel consumption
is very high, perhaps storm windows and weather stripping would be effective.
Maybe it would be worthwhile to insulate the attic floor. Watch your light
and hot water consumption. Most people can cut their utility bills just by
being careful.

5. Reduce expenditures for recreation. This is frequently one of the easiest
places to cut down. Substitute low-cost and free activities for those requiring

Year-end Recap, Comparison and Review

for financial year ending _____

This is what we did with our money during the past 12 months

Income for the 12 months, including investment income .... $ _____

Spent on living a total of .... $ _____

Added to savings and investments, and/or
repaid on general debts .... _____

Paid in income taxes, social security ...... _____

total $ _____

Average monthly expenses, not including savings or taxes, were:

	ACTUALLY SPENT	COMPARED WITH SPENDING PLAN
Food		
Housing..............		
Clothing		
Medical care		
Transportation		
Advancement		
Gifts		
Personal care		
Entertainment		
Allowances, misc.		
Life insurance..........		
totals $		$

Year-end Inventory of Family Net Worth

CASH and SECURITIES

Cash on hand and in accounts .... $ _____

Current insurance cash-surrender value
(as shown on policies) .... _____

Cash value in retirement and other funds..... _____

Government bonds (current cash-in value).... _____

Stocks, mutual fund shares (market value) ... _____

PROPERTY

Equity in house and other real estate
(estimated market value less mortgage
balance......................... _____

Equity in car* .... _____

Other valuable marketable possessions, as
boat, etc. (at estimated market value) ...... _____

Total assets $ _____

LESS DEBT BALANCE (excluding mortgage)

(Creditor) _____

(Creditor) _____

(Creditor) _____

(Creditor) _____

(Creditor) _____

Total debts $ _____

NET WORTH $ _____
(assets less debts)

*Previous year's value less 29% for past year's depreciation.

FIGURE 13. (*From Better Homes and Gardens, Money Management for Your Family. Used with permission.*)

costly expenditures. Free park concerts and television might be substituted for the movies or theater. Swimming at a public beach in the summer could replace bowling or roller skating. Such substitutions not only reduce expenditures for recreation, but also help reduce clothing expenditures for specialized activities—the skating dress, evening clothes, bowling shoes.

6. Reduce expenditures for services. Repair and press more of your own clothing, wash and set your own hair. Do as many things for yourself as possible. Fix and maintain as many things around the house as you can.

Who Should Manage the Family Funds?

There is no one right way to share responsibility for the handling of funds. What is good for your family will depend on the personalities of the members and their feelings about the use of money as well as their experience in handling funds.

Ideally both husband and wife should share in the planning and management of funds, with children participating as they are able to assume such responsibility.

The system used to divide responsibility for handling family funds is not nearly so important as developing the feeling that the planning and use of funds is a family affair, every member has an obligation to promote family happiness through the way in which he uses money.

Financial Management for the Working Wife

One out of every four couples has a working wife. For these working women, the question of sharing responsibility for earning as well as spending is no longer merely academic. Since most women work because they need the money, there is usually no question that the second income will be spent. It is important to family happiness that the working wife help create family harmony in the handling of money. The following principles for working women can contribute to family happiness:

1. From the very beginning, figure your income as part of the family income. Plan with your husband for its use.

2. Put at least part of your salary into a common fund or bank account. Frequently the working wife takes care of the extra expenses that may be associated with her working, such as baby-sitting, extra clothing for the job, transportation to and from work, and her lunches. However, the feeling should be created that both husband and wife are working together for a common goal.

3. Share responsibilities for paying bills from this common fund. The hus-

band might pay the rent or house expenses, insurance, taxes, and automobile expenses. The wife could pay for food, clothing, household operation, and the cost of entertaining at home.

4. Set personal allowances for each family member. These are to be used without accounting to anyone else.

5. Young married couples who are hoping to start a family should try to live on only one income, preferably that of the husband, or assign a portion of the wife's income for savings. Children are costly; the doctor and the hospital expenses need to be paid. Often, the arrival of children is accompanied by a decrease in family income since the wife must give up her work outside the home.

6. When a financial crisis arises, try to select a quiet time for a calm discussion. A common problem is that both persons feel that the family savings belong exclusively to them—the woman because she has worked or the husband because he has the larger income. If the problem can be worked out on the basis that this is a mutual problem and a joint income, then there is less likely to be a feeling of resentment.

The Need for Shopping Skills

Modern merchandising techniques are designed to interest people in buying particular goods and services, and for this purpose items are displayed attractively, packaged conveniently in eye-catching colors, and advertised extensively. These techniques are enhanced by the facts that families in modern America have more money to spend, more goods to choose from, and less tradition to guide them in their choices; for example, many of the items they now buy were not even on the market twenty-five years ago. Despite this growing affluence, many families are over their heads in debt, without sufficient financial resources to feel secure. The highest rate of personal bankruptcy in our history prevails today.

Effective shopping, then, is selecting those things the family really wants and needs and buying them at a price it can afford. It also means buying goods that are serviceable and satisfactory for the use intended.

A great many families could improve their personal situation by improving their skills in purchasing. A dollar saved in buying meat each week is a $52 saving in a year, enough to pay for a weekend holiday or a new vacuum cleaner. Five hundred dollars saved on the purchase of a new car, or a thousand saved on the financing of a mortgage, would help to pay for a child's college education.

Good purchases don't just happen; they require skill, thought, and planning. Careful shopping begins at home, free from the distractions and temptations of a store. Planning before shopping can pay the dividend of helping families have more money for the things they really want. The following are some suggestions to sharpen your shopping skills. (See Figure 14.)

1. Make an expenditure plan and stick to it whenever possible. If you

FIGURE 14. *(Courtesy of Money Management Institute of Household Finance Corporation.)*

find that you do not have enough money in one category, see where you can take money from another to balance the extra outlay.

2. Formulate specific requirements for big and little purchases. This is a tried and tested technique used by businesses as a means of controlling expenditures. In buying a coat, for example, decide what type of coat you need, consider what color will harmonize with your present clothes and those you are planning to buy, and also decide on the maximum amount you can spend.

If you are considering a toaster, consider the type of toaster that would serve your needs best; for example, a two-slice toaster or a combination toaster-broiler. Study the reports of the tests made on various makes and models by testing organizations to ascertain the quality of construction. Read the advertisements to acquaint yourself with what is available at various price levels.

If you are shopping for food, make a list at home to reduce the number of impulse purchases. Supermarkets abound with attractive displays strategically placed to tempt the shopper and her family. Have you noticed the number of people who pick up items on stands at the ends of aisles or just in front of the checkout counter? Add up the number of purchases you made the last time you went shopping. Did you buy some things that were not in your original plan? These extra items are classified as impulse purchases.

If you are going to buy a car, decide what you can spend (which includes how much you can carry per month as well as the amount of the down payment). Then the type of transportation needed should be examined. Perhaps the car will only be used to go to and from the railroad station; maybe you need a vehicle that will hold a large family, plus a dog and the groceries. Gather information about the various makes and models of new and used cars. Some have better histories of trouble-free service. Your insurance agent can furnish you with information about the cost of insuring models and makes of different years. Armed with definite specifications of what you need, what you want, and how much you can afford, comparison shopping at automobile agencies and used car lots becomes much more meaningful.

3. Know the best time to buy various household and family articles. (See Figure 15.) There is a definite pattern of sales in most commodities. Cars are cheaper when the new models come out, houses often cost less in the winter, toys are cheaper after Christmas, and spring clothes are on sale after Easter.

4. Compare prices. Use newspapers, magazines, and advertisements. Check the various types of stores: the department store, the small retailer, the chain store, the mail-order house, and the discount store. The discount store is not always the cheapest; local and department stores sometimes match the prices of discount stores.

Check service plans and guarantees. Local and department stores generally give better service to their customers but may charge higher prices for their merchandise. Price is the outstanding advantage of many discount firms. The small storekeeper and the department store generally are dependent on repeat business and more inclined to make adjustments. However, there is no hard-and-fast rule. The value of a guarantee depends on the group who is making it: some guarantees are very good, but others are worthless.

If you are buying a large item, find out whether delivery and installation are part of the price. Many stores, particularly the low-cost ones, do not include these in the price.

Comparative shopping is often complicated by an inability to make direct comparison. For example, how do you compare a dress at $9.95 with one at $39.95, or Model A of the ABC washing machine with last year's model that has been reduced in price. The most reasonable basis for comparison shopping when goods are not exactly comparable is to select the least costly one that will meet your needs. This should include consideration of the expected length of service of the article. It is poor economy to buy the cheapest carpet sweeper if it will not stand up under regular usage. On the other hand, a party dress that will only be worn for a very few occasions need not be durable.

5. Select items that will not be out of fashion in a short time. This applies to clothing, furniture, household accessories, and even cars. Unless you are willing to pay a high price for the newest and most popular thing and are also willing to replace it frequently, buy things that will stay in style a long time. Clothing in classic styles—the shirtwaist dress, the single-breasted suit in a

Shopping calendar

Stores follow a fairly standard schedule for their "promotions." Some of these are sales. Others are new displays of merchandise on which prices may or may not be a bargain. Here's a month-by-month rundown.

January	February	March	April
white sales, storewide clearances, resort wear, fur sales, furniture sales (late in month)	furniture, home furnishings sales, Washington Birthday sales	housewares, china, silver, garden supplies, luggage	Easter merchandise, spring cleaning supplies, paints, fur storage campaigns, garden supplies, men's & boys' clothing
May	June	July	August
white goods, television, lingerie, handbags	sportswear, camp clothes, lumber, storm windows, refrigerators, rug cleaning	furniture sales (late in month), floor coverings, July 4th summer goods clearances (through month)	summer clothing clearances, fur sales, back-to-school specials, garden equipment sales, camping supplies, fall fashions, furniture
September	October	November	December
back-to-school specials, housewares & home furnishings, china & glassware	Columbus Day specials, fur fashions	Veterans Day specials, Thanksgiving weekend sales, pre-Christmas specials, table linens, blankets	winter clothing specials (late in month), toy and gift items (after Dec. 21)

When they cut prices

Department stores mark down prices on one item or another all during the year. This list shows the price cuts as a percentage of sales, first for the year (1961) as a whole, and then for the months when the markdown ratios equaled or exceeded the annual average.

	annual average	months with greatest markdowns											
		Jan.	Feb.	Mar.	Apr.	May	June	July	Aug.	Sept.	Oct.	Nov.	Dec.
linens and towels	4.9%	6.8%			4.9%			5.1%					
cosmetics	2.2%	4.2%					2.2%	2.5%					
silverware	4.7%	9.5%						4.7%					
corsets, brassieres	3.0%	4.2%	8.0%					3.5%					
negligees, robes	6.7%	26.4%	8.5%					8.3%	7.6%				
children's shoes	7.6%	18.0%					9.0%	9.9%		8.1%			8.1%
women's and misses' coats	11.5%	15.3%	12.3%		16.9%	13.9%	16.9%	14.5%					14.8%
girls' wear	9.6%	29.2%	11.4%		14.2%			18.6%					
furs	6.4%	11.7%	6.8%	7.1%		7.1%	9.4%	7.0%					
men's and boys' shoes	6.7%	14.7%						12.4%					
mattresses, springs, studio beds	5.6%	8.3%											7.4%
luggage	4.1%	5.4%	5.4%	4.2%				4.5%					

FIGURE 15. *(Source of "When They Cut Prices": National Retail Merchants Association. Reprinted from* Changing Times, *the Kiplinger Magazine.)*

conservative color—tends to be fashionable year after year. Living room furniture which is simple in design and color does not become "dated." The principle of classic design applies even to automobiles. The Volkswagen, which has not changed much since the 1930's, has remained in fashion. This is reflected in its continued popularity and high resale value.

6. Buy in quantity if you have storage room and the price is cheaper. Bulk purchases are not always cheaper. In one metropolitan area a nationally advertised laundry detergent weighing twenty pounds costs $4.49 at the supermarket; a fifty-pound bag can be bought from a commercial firm for $7.50 delivered to the door. This is fifteen cents a pound versus twenty-two cents a pound if purchased at the supermarket.

Staple foods such as flour, sugar, and potatoes are less expensive if bought in bulk. They store well if kept free from insects and cool and dry.

Dried milk can be bought in quantity inexpensively from commercial dairies, but does not store for long periods well under most home conditions, since it tends to take up moisture and become lumpy unless kept airtight. Buying in quantity is not a bargain unless the produce is consumed before it deteriorates.

7. Consider time and energy as well as money in evaluating relative costs. The working wife who is also a part-time homemaker may prefer to buy foods that are ready to serve and do her own housework, rather than do all the cooking and hire someone to help with household duties.

8. Buy things for the purpose for which they are intended. If you are going to use tomatoes for soup, then canned Grade C, which is just as nutritious as Grade A, would be the best buy. If you are buying fresh tomatoes for soup, bruised ones might be less expensive than perfect ones.

9. Pay cash if you can; it is cheaper. While it is often difficult or impossible to pay cash for certain big items, such as a house or car, the cost of credit or borrowing money is considerable. Installment buying adds a great deal to the cost of household expenditures. Stores that operate on a cash basis tend to have lower prices.

10. Beware of bargains. A purchase is a bargain only if you get it cheaply and it is what you want and need. Something bought inexpensively is not a bargain if it isn't what you can use. Many women buy clothing on sale, only to find out later that it doesn't go with the shoes or coats they own. However, if they had selected something which harmonized with the rest of their wardrobe and bought it on sale, it might have been a good buy.

Another common fallacy is to buy very expensive items on sale. In many cases even the sale price is higher than the person would ordinarily pay for that item.

Bait advertising is very common and misleading. Those storm windows for $9.95 or the sewing machine for $19.50 may be nothing more than a scheme to get you into the store for a high-pressure sales talk. The salesman may try to "switch" you to a more expensive item.

11. Take time to shop and consider carefully in making large purchases. Don't succumb to the urge to buy immediately because the duration of the sale is limited. This applies to all sorts of purchases, from vacuum cleaners to roof shingles, house painting, car repairs, and life insurance.

12. If you are buying for credit, shop for the credit as carefully as you shop for the commodity. Credit costs vary considerably, and you can often save as much on the cost of financing by careful shopping as you can on the commodity.

13. Accumulate reserve funds to replace equipment. All household equipment wears out. Clothing, cars, washing machines, refrigerators, and mixers have a limited life. When an important piece of family or household equipment breaks down, the family faces a choice of repairing it or replacing it. If the repair is a major one, it may be advisable to buy new equipment. A reserve fund accumulated for this purpose makes possible a wider range of choices available, including stores which do not offer credit.

14. Don't expect miracles. Cutting family expenditures through careful buying takes time, effort, and persistence. However, a little bit saved on several items may enable you to purchase some items that you really want.

What Financial Records Should a Family Keep?

The management of family income and expenditures is similar to the management of a business. Both need to balance income and outgo, accrue savings, and pay taxes. Like a business, a family has records and documents that are important to the members.

Both husband and wife need to know what they own, where important documents and securities are kept, and how these can be safeguarded for the interest of the family. The typical husband will know where his wife keeps her jewelry, but not where her social security card is. Similarly the wife will often know where her husband keeps his fishing gear, but not where he keeps his insurance policies. Many couples are loath to talk about the need to be prepared for unhappy events such as death or disabling illness, a period in which husband or wife may need to assume more responsibility.

A careful plan should be made to keep family records and papers in good form and available to both husband and wife. Some of the records that are most important are a list of family documents, the social security card and number for both husband and wife, the birth certificates for all family members, the marriage license (divorce papers if there has been a divorce of either partner prior to the marriage), a list of all investments and the certificates indicating ownership, a list of bank accounts and the location of the banks, insurance policies and where they are kept, and the wills of the husband and wife.

Many people feel that the best place to keep all of these documents is in a safe-deposit box or a bank where they are free from danger of fire, theft, or loss. A safe-deposit box can be rented in both the husband's and wife's names, or only in one name with the other having the right of access.

Some documents can be replaced if lost, such as government bonds and social security cards; a record of the certificate numbers facilitates replacement if needed.

Sometimes a wife is unaware of the benefits to which she is entitled or for which her deceased husband was eligible. There may be group insurance, health insurance, a pension, or a profit-sharing plan where her husband works. A list of these benefits should also be included in the list of documents.

The Importance of Planning

For a long time in the Western world, many people tried to improve their living conditions by increasing family income. Today, with the majority of Americans in middle-income status, families can most rapidly improve their level of living through the wise use of their resources. This requires careful thinking in formulating the family goals and in developing plans to fit these goals. It also requires persistent effort on the part of the whole family to control spending and to use time and energy wisely.

SELECTED REFERENCES

BRADLEY, JOSEPH F., and RALPH H. WHERRY. *Personal and Family Finance.* New York: Holt, Rinehart & Winston, 1957.

COHEN, JEROME B., and ARTHUR HANSON. *Personal Finance, Principles and Case Problems.* Homewood, Ill.: Richard D. Irwin, 1958.

DONALDSON, ELVIN F., and JOHN K. PFAHL. *Personal Finance.* New York: Ronald Press, 1961.

FREEMAN, RUTH CRAWFORD, and JEAN DUE. "Influence of Goals on Family Financial Management," *Journal of Home Economics,* Vol. 53, No. 6 (June 1961), pp. 448-452.

FITZSIMMONS, CLEO. *Factors Associated with Farm Family Security.* Research Bulletin No. 702 (August 1960), Agricultural Experiment Station, Purdue University.

MACNAB, MARION MYERS. "Financial Management of Young Families," *Journal of Home Economics,* Vol. 53, No. 10 (December 1961), pp. 832-834.

MONEY MANAGEMENT INSTITUTE, HOUSEHOLD FINANCE CORPORATION. *Money Management—Your Budget.* Chicago, Ill.: Money Management Institute, 1963.

TROELSTRUP, ARCH W. *Consumer Problems.* New York: McGraw-Hill, 1957.

U.S. DEPARTMENT OF AGRICULTURE, AGRICULTURAL RESEARCH SERVICE. *Helping Families Manage their Finances.* Home Economics Research Report No. 21, 1963.

WARREN, JEAN. "Income and Housing Expenditures," *Journal of Home Economics,* Vol. 53, No. 5 (May 1961), pp. 349-351.

4

FINANCING
FAMILY SPENDING

A few short generations ago only a business or a government could be in debt and remain respectable. Family debt was, to the neighbors a sign of profligacy or incompetence and, to the borrowers, a sword over the head.

Today the use of credit is so common that it's a rare family or individual that doesn't owe somebody something.[1]

THE USE of credit has become an accepted part of the American way of life. At any one time almost half of the families in the United States are repaying loans or paying installments on purchases of goods or services. Monthly bills for telephone and utilities are standard practice. Charge accounts are a common way of buying, and credit cards have rapidly gained widespread acceptance.

Family consumption can be financed with cash or credit. The present trend is to use more credit and less cash. Increasingly people want to be able to get things immediately, to have the present enjoyment rather than to anticipate a future pleasure, even though it means paying a higher price for the commodity and continuing to pay for it over a period of time.

Scientific advances and modern methods have enabled industry to produce a wide range of consumer goods in great abundance. Mass markets and mass production have made it possible to sell these goods at prices middle-income families can afford. Credit plans have enabled large numbers of families to buy. Most of these people would find it difficult to accumulate enough cash for the full purchase price.

Defining Consumer Credit

"Consumer credit" refers to the money or purchasing power extended by lending agencies to individuals. The term is ordinarily used to describe short-

[1] "All about Credit," *Changing Times* (March 1963), p. 25

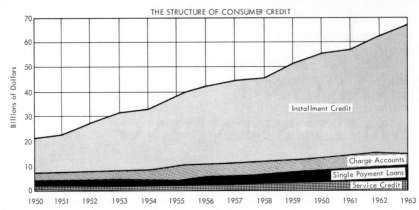

FIGURE 16. *(Reproduced from* A Graphic Guide to Consumer Markets, *1964, prepared by the National Industrial Conference Board under the sponsorship of* Life *magazine.)*

term commitments, payable within thirty-six months. However, it may also include longer commitments, such as mortgages.

Short-term consumer credit may be divided into two parts: installment credit and noninstallment credit. (See Figure 16.) Installment credit refers to loans that are repaid at regular intervals for such things as automobiles, refrigerators, furniture, home repair and modernization, and personal loans. (Installment loans are also frequently used to cover medical expenses or refinance a number of smaller debts.) Noninstallment consumer credit includes thirty-day charge accounts carried by department stores for their customers, single payment loans (loans repaid in a lump sum at the end of the specified time period) extended by banks, and credit extended by service groups such as doctors, dentists, utility companies, and drugstores.

Who Uses Consumer Credit?

Over 45 per cent of all families had some installment debt in 1961. Heads of families under age 45 used credit most frequently. The age group 25 to 34 had the highest percentage using installment credit. These are young families who are establishing new households and growing rapidly in size.

Almost half of the major household appliances and furniture purchased in 1962 was bought on credit plans. Fifty per cent of the refrigerators and washing machines, 60 per cent of the television sets, and over 40 per cent of the household furniture were installment credit purchases. Six out of ten new cars and over 50 per cent of the used cars were financed.

More than 50 per cent of the families with incomes between $3,999 and $9,999 had installment debts in 1962. Of the installment-paying group who

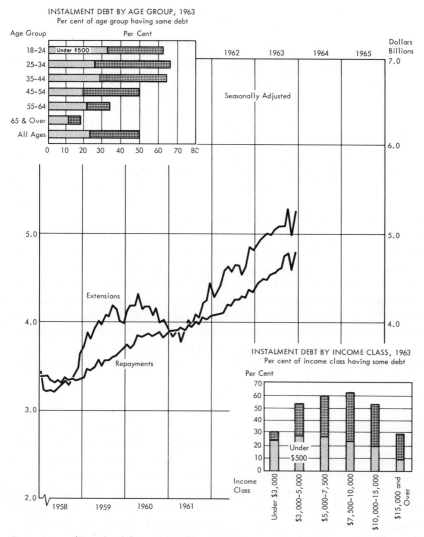

FIGURE 17. *(Reproduced from* A Graphic Guide to Consumer Markets, *1964, prepared by the National Industrial Conference Board under the sponsorship of* Life *magazine. Source of data: from the Surveys of Consumer Finances conducted by the Survey Research Center, University of Michigan.)*

earned between $3,000 and $3,999, the majority owed less than $500. The proportion of families who owed more than $500 increased with the size of the income. Among families earning from $7,500 to $9,999 two thirds of those who used installment credit owed over $500.[2]

[2] National Industrial Conference Board, *A Graphic Guide to Consumer Markets, 1963,* pp. 31, 33. Sources: Survey Research Center, University of Michigan; Federal Reserve Board.

Trends in the Use of Consumer Credit

Consumer surveys and the mounting total of consumer debt indicate that more people are becoming debtors. In 1962 the amount of consumer credit outstanding reached over 57 billion dollars.[3]

Several explanations have been advanced for the rapid growth of consumer credit. Deductions from wages and salaries for federal and state income taxes, social security, hospital and medical insurance, and pension plans have contributed to an attitude of acceptance about committing fixed portions of family income in advance for consumer goods.

Another reason has been the feeling that the government will not let another major depression occur, that job incomes will remain on a high level. William H. Whyte suggests that by buying on the installment plan people avoid decisions about how to spend each paycheck.[4]

The use of consumer credit has multiplied almost ten times from 1940 to 1964.[5] The largest dollar increase has been to finance the purchase of automobiles. People are buying more automobiles at higher prices per car.

The rapid growth of revolving credit plans since 1959 has resulted in installment credit being more widely used for personal and household purchases, whereas formerly it was used almost exclusively for large appliances and automobiles. Many stores permit customers to finance purchases of household supplies, clothing, and services subject to a maximum amount of credit. Long-term credit, to finance mobile homes, boats, and other expensive items, is also being more widely used.

The proportion of disposable income—personal income minus taxes—used for installment and credit purchases has been rising. Consumer buying influences the economic health of the country. When people stop buying consumer goods, factories have to stop producing goods, and the people who work in these factories are out of jobs. Considerable discussion has focused on the question of how much consumer debt in proportion to disposable income is possible before people stop buying goods and services.

Debt repayment of 12 or 13 per cent of disposable income was thought by many economists to be the critical point at which consumers would stop buying. According to the Federal Reserve Board, however, there is no evidence that 13 per cent of disposable income should be a critical point.[6]

The average family finds credit readily available. Thousands of organizations are in the business of lending money or extending sales credit. Young families are the greatest users of installment credit at the present time.

[3] National Industrial Conference Board, *ibid.*, p. 30.

[4] William H. Whyte, Jr., "Budgetism, Opiate of the Middle Class," *Fortune* (May 1956), pp. 133–137.

[5] *Statistical Abstract of the United States, 1964* (Washington, D.C.: Government Printing Office), p. 466. Source: Federal Reserve Board.

[6] Board of Governors of the Federal Reserve System, "Installment Credit Expansion," *Federal Reserve Bulletin* (May 1963), Vol. 49, No. 5, p. 584.

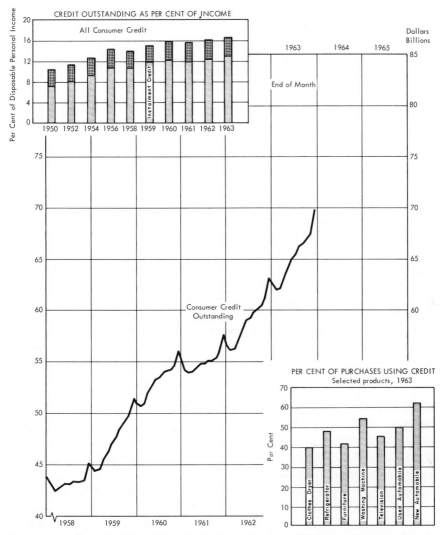

FIGURE 18. *(Reproduced from* A Graphic Guide to Consumer Markets, *1964, prepared by the National Industrial Conference Board under the sponsorship of* Life *magazine. Source of data: from the Surveys of Consumer Finances conducted by the Survey Research Center, University of Michigan.)*

Predictions are that an increased number of families will use installment credit in the next few years. The Bureau of Census population projections indicate that by 1970 there will be a rapid expansion of households with the head under age 25. It seems likely that with more young families, more people will be using installment credit. Also, the recent increase in the use of credit for the purchase of nondurable goods and services seems likely to continue.

Sources of Credit

There are three general types of lenders. One group gives cash—the banks, credit unions, and small loan companies. Another gives sales credit—the department stores, furniture stores, appliance stores, and home improvement companies. The third group provides credit indirectly—sales finance companies and banks. Indirect credit is provided when a store sells an installment contract to a bank or finance company.

Commercial banks are the largest single source of consumer credit. Banks usually offer a wide range of credit facilities, including mortgage and home improvement loans. Their interest rates tend to be the lowest for personal loans, but their credit standards tend to be higher than that of other lenders. Generally, they do not make loans of less than several hundred dollars. Some banks will lend only to their regular customers.

In addition to regular loans, banks and savings and loan associations will give passbook loans. The passbook is collateral and is held by the lending institution until the loan is repaid. Rates are generally from 4 per cent to 5½ per cent. Although it may seem silly to borrow against your own money, many people prefer to do so because they feel they must repay the loan. If they take money out of their savings account, they do not feel compelled to replace it. Also, in certain situations where one needs a loan for a very short period, such as a week or two, it may be more economical to pay the loan charges and get the interest on a savings account. Withdrawals between interest paying dates lose interest from the previous paying date. For instance, a withdrawal on June 1 loses interest from April 1. Thus a loan from June 1 to July 1 may be profitable as illustrated in the following situation. If a bank pays 4 per cent a year, the interest on $1,000 for three months is $10. Withdrawal on June 1 would mean losing the $10 interest. A loan for one month at 6 per cent would cost $5 for the month, giving a profit of $5, if there are no additional charges.

Industrial banks and loan companies were founded to help meet the needs of small borrowers and depositors. Over the years they have evolved to a point where their functions in lending are similar to those of commercial banks. Their credit standards may be a little less strict than commercial banks, but the rate of interest they charge is usually close to that of a commercial bank.

Savings and loan associations operate under federal and state laws. One of their original purposes was to help members buy and build homes, but they now make loans for other purposes. The interest rate on deposits in a savings and loan association tends to be a little higher than that of commercial banks. The amount they will lend on mortgages is usually a higher percentage of the appraised value than a bank would lend.

Credit unions have rapidly become an important source of loans. Approximately 14 million people belong to cooperative savings and credit associations. Membership in a particular credit union is usually confined to a group with a common interest. The members may work for the same company, belong to the same labor union, or belong to the same fraternal organization.

Members make deposits in the credit union which in turn are used to make loans to members. The highest rate of interest, 12 per cent, is less than the rate charged for most installment purchases. Dividends are paid to shareholders just as interest is paid to depositors in a bank.

Life insurance loans can be made against the cash value of a life insurance policy from the insurance company. A loan from a life insurance company can be arranged by the insurance agent, or the borrower may deal directly with the company. Veterans can borrow against permanent GI insurance policies at only 4 per cent. This can be arranged through the local Veterans Administration office.

One of the disadvantages of borrowing against life insurance is that until the loan is repaid the amount of insurance coverage is reduced. On the other hand, if life insurance is used as collateral at a bank for a loan, the face amount of insurance is not reduced.

Consumer finance companies have some of the highest rates of interest of any type of lending institution. Frequently, people who cannot obtain low-rate bank loans, or can get only a very limited amount, find that consumer finance companies will lend them what they need. However, the true annual interest rates usually run over 35 per cent.

Consumer finance companies came into being when various states established regulations to make small loans legal and thus force the loan sharks, or illegal lenders, out of business. Before this time, people who could not qualify for bank loans had no place to borrow money except from illegal lenders at exorbitant rates. Today the existence of consumer finance companies has reduced the number of loan sharks, but some of them are still with us.

Charge accounts were originally a convenience for wealthy customers, but this is no longer the case. Many stores are anxious to sell on credit. The interest on credit sales is a very profitable second business. Customers tend to buy more if they do not have to pay cash. Also, credit customers tend to shop where they have charge accounts.

One of the oldest types of charge accounts is the department store-account which is payable in 30 days, with no extra charge. This is still popular. Frequently charge customers are given extra services: notification of sales before they are advertised, and special consideration if anything is returned.

More recently a variety of short-term credit plans have been promoted that permit payment from 10 weeks to 12 months later. Some give a 90-day period of grace, during which payments can be made without a service charge. These plans are known as the Budget Plan, a Budget Account, a Planned Charge Account, or an All-Purpose Account.

Revolving credit plans are the newest type of charge account, also the fastest-growing. A limit is set on the total amount a customer can charge, and a certain time period stated in which he must pay for his purchases with monthly payments. Whenever the balance owed falls below the upper dollar limit, one can buy more things up to the limit of his credit. For instance a man may buy a television set for $250. His credit limit is $300. When he has paid off $200 of the price of the television set, he may purchase a dishwasher for $250.

Under this arrangement many people stay constantly in debt to the store. As soon as one article is partially paid for, they buy another. They do not need to negotiate a new contract for each purchase, the original one remains in force.

Some stores have a type of charge account that combines the traditional 30-day account and revolving credit. When the monthly bill is sent, the purchaser can pay the whole amount due or just a portion, plus interest, on the remaining balance.

Installment accounts or installment contracts are generally used to buy expensive items such as large appliances or furniture. A separate contract is signed for each item bought.

A variation is the continuous secured account where revolving credit is tied to installment credit. A master contract covers certain types of major items up to a limited amount. Each time a new item is purchased this is added to the agreement.

All of these credit plans permit people to buy without having the money in hand. Many people find it very easy to overbuy if they can "buy now, pay later." When the bills come in, then they find that they have bought more than they can afford.

The Cost of Consumer Credit

Consumer credit is the most expensive kind of credit because it is extended in small amounts. The cost per $100 of a loan is larger for the individual borrower than the charges made to businesses for large amounts of credit. This is much like the difference in cost between buying furniture in wholesale or retail quantities.

Credit charges are usually called interest. People who lend money or extend credit have a markup to cover expenses and return a profit as do merchants of commodities. Shopping for credit, however, is unlike shopping for any other commodity. The prices are stated in many different ways and comparison is complex and difficult.

Methods of Charging for Credit

A lending agency or credit organization can state loan charges in three general ways: (1) simple interest, (2) discount, and (3) dollar charges, or a combination of these. For example, a loan may have both a discount (or point charge) and an interest rate.

SIMPLE INTEREST. This is a percentage of the amount owed during a certain period, usually stated in months or years. Interest is figured by multiplying the rate to be charged times the amount owed for each period. The interest is paid by the borrower when partial or complete repayment is made. On a loan of $100 for one year at 5 per cent there is a charge of $5.00. At the end of the year $105 must be repaid.

Installment contracts often use a variation of simple interest. For example, an installment contract for a television set provides for a loan of $240 for one year at interest of 1 per cent per month of the total amount, to be repaid in equal monthly installments. At the end of each month the purchaser repays $20 plus one month's interest, $2.40, making the total monthly payment $22.40.

When prices of installment loans or contracts are stated, the rates are usually on the amount of the total loan. However, when repayment is made in equal monthly installments, including principal and interest, the borrower (or installment purchaser) really has use of the full amount of money only until the first payment is due.

Payment of 1 per cent interest a month may sound cheaper than it is. Some people think it means 12 per cent a year. However, repayments start in one month. At the first installment $2.40 is paid as interest for one month on $20. This is 12 per cent for one month, or 96 per cent for a year. The second month $2.40 is paid on $20 for two months. This is 72 per cent a year. The average interest charge, using the formula in the next section, "Comparing Credit Costs," is 22 per cent a year.

DISCOUNT. The charge is a percentage of the loan deducted, in advance, from the total loan. For example, if one is borrowing $100 for one year at a 5 per cent discount, the lender will deduct $5.00 and give the borrower $95. At the end of the year the borrower repays $100.

Add-on is a variation of the discount method. In the example given above, the borrower would receive the full $100, but the lender would add $5.00 to the face amount of the loan. By the end of the year $105, plus interest, would be repaid.

DOLLAR CHARGES. The charge is stated as so many dollars for the loan. Percentages are not stated. The credit charges are either paid in advance in cash when the transaction is arranged or added to the loan payments.

A rug is purchased for one-third down and the balance due in equal payments over the year. The price is $99 and the charge $24. The purchaser pays $33 down and $7.50 per month for a year. (The $7.50 charge includes $5.50 for repaying the principal and $2.00 for the credit charge.)

Comparing Credit Costs

There are two ways of comparing credit costs, the dollar price and the true annual interest rate. Dollar cost is figured by adding up everything that is paid and subtracting the cash price of the merchandise. In the rug example above the dollar cost was $24.00.

The "true annual interest rate" is simple interest, which is computed on a yearly basis. The example given before under simple interest is an illustration. Another example would be the charge for revolving credit, which is usually stated as 1½ per cent per month of the unpaid balance. This is actually a "true annual interest rate" of 18 per cent.

It is more difficult to compute the "true annual interest rate" when the charges are expressed in dollars or stated as so many installment payments of a certain size. The following formula, used by the Federal Reserve Board, can be used to find the "true annual interest" on installment contracts.

$$\text{Rate of interest} = \frac{2mD}{P\,(n+1)}$$

m = number of payments in one year
n = number of payments to discharge the debt, excluding the down payment
D = charge for credit in dollars
P = amount of credit (cash price minus down payment)

Example 1

A table costs $50 cash. It can also be bought for $10 down and $5 per month for 9 months. What is the rate of interest charged for the credit?

m = 12
n = 9
D = $ 5 $\text{Rate of interest} = \frac{2 \cdot 3 \cdot 5}{10 \cdot 10} = \frac{30}{100} = 30\%$
P = $40

Example 2

A bank will lend $100 at 6% interest deducted in advance, which is to be repaid in installments of $8.33 per month for 1 year.

m = 12
n = 12
D = $ 6[7] $\text{Rate of interest} = \frac{2 \cdot 12 \cdot 6}{100 \cdot 13} = 11\%$
P = $100

Different types of lending institutions charge different ranges of rates. Generally, banks lend only to the best credit risks and charge the lowest rates. Table 2 gives a rough comparison of credit costs according to the type of lender.

[7] For computational purposes $5.96 has been rounded to $6.00.

TABLE 2
Range of Rates Paid by Consumer Credit Users*

Financing Agency or Type of Loan	RATES PAID BY CONSUMER CREDIT USERS (EQUIVALENT PER CENT PER YEAR ON UNPAID BALANCE) Range of Rates		
	Common Rate	Low	High
A. Cash lenders:	Per cent	Per cent	Per cent
Credit union	12	6	12
Industrial banks	15	12	24
Remedial loan societies—			
Pledge loans	24	9	36
Other loans	18	15	30
Commercial banks—			
Personal loans	12	8	36
Consumer finance companies under small loan laws	30	16	42
Pawnshops	36	24	120
Illegal lenders	260	42	1,200
B. Retail installment financing in 5 states having rate legislation—12-month contract:			
New cars	12	8	24
Used cars under 2 years old	24	9	31
Used cars over 2 years old	30	9	43
Other commodities	24	9	34
C. Retail installment financing in states without rate legislation—12-month contract:			
New cars	12	9	120
Used cars	40	9	275
Other commodities †			

*U.S. Dept. of Agriculture, Agricultural Research Service, *Helping Families Manage Their Finances.* Home Economics Research Report, No. 21 (Washington, D.C.: Government Printing Office, 1963), p. 55.
† Not available.
Source of data: Mors, W. P., *Consumer Credit Facts for You.* Cleveland, Ohio: Western Reserve University, Bureau of Business Research.

True Annual Rate of Interest Varies with the Method
of Stating Installment Credit Charges[8]

When credit charges are added on to the purchase price, and the buyer repays the total in 20 equal monthly payments,

If the quoted rate is—	The buyer pays a true annual interest rate of—
4 per cent per year	7.6 per cent
5 per cent per year	9.5 per cent
6 per cent per year	11.4 per cent
7 per cent per year	13.3 per cent
8 per cent per year	15.2 per cent
1 per cent per month	22.9 per cent

When credit charges are subtracted from the stated amount of the loan at the time of the loan and the buyer repays the stated amount of the loan in 20 equal payments,

If the quoted rate is—	The buyer pays a true annual interest rate of—
4 per cent per year	8.2 per cent
5 per cent per year	10.4 per cent
6 per cent per year	12.7 per cent
7 per cent per year	15.1 per cent
8 per cent per year	17.6 per cent
1 per cent per month	28.6 per cent

When interest is charged on the unpaid balance,

If the quoted rate is—	The buyer pays a true annual interest rate of—
1/2 of 1 per cent per month	6 per cent
3/4 of 1 per cent per month	9 per cent
1 per cent per month	12 per cent
1 1/4 per cent per month	15 per cent
1 1/2 per cent per month	18 per cent
1 3/4 per cent per month	21 per cent
2 per cent per month	24 per cent

Many people do not know what credit costs, how much they are paying in either dollars or rate of interest. They only know how much the payments are per month. Often people shop carefully for large items, comparing various features including price, but neglect to compare the cost of financing

[8] U.S. Dept. of Agriculture, *ibid.*, pp. 55–56.

the item. This is understandable in view of the present difficulty in comparing credit costs. The following is a description of the experience of a shopper in Washington, D.C.

> An advertisement for a gas stove appeared in the newspaper which stated "only $249.50, delivered and installed, no money down, $8.18 per month, plus local sales tax, on your gas bill." I telephoned the extension listed in the ad and asked if $249.50 really was the price if the customer paid for it in monthly installments of $8.18. The salesman's answer, "Oh, no, that is the cash price; there is an extra charge if you pay for it at the rate of $8.18 per month." When I asked the amount of this extra charge he said, "6 per cent on gross." I asked if 6 per cent of $249.50 would be the total extra charge, and he answered, "No, 6 per cent is the annual rate; it would take three years to pay for it at $8.18 per month, so the extra charge for credit would be 18 per cent of $249.50." I asked if the 6 per cent "gross" wasn't an annual rate of about 12 per cent on the unpaid balance. He appeared not to understand the difference; he repeated, "It's 6 per cent gross."
>
> Using this information, I determined that the credit price of this stove, exclusive of tax, is $294.41, the total finance charges $44.91 and the finance charge expressed as a simple annual rate on the average outstanding balance of the obligation is slightly more than 11 per cent.[9]

Other Factors to Consider in Using Credit

The cost of credit is only one of the considerations in shopping for credit. Other factors that are also important may be the speed with which the loan is available. Are there liberal terms to cover a late payment? Must the borrower buy expensive credit life insurance? There may also be less tangible factors to evaluate: privacy, lack of paper work, and the opportunity to establish a credit record that would be useful in the future.

A Credit Rating

Who can borrow and what amount depends on the credit rating one has established. Often the rate of interest a person must pay on a loan is also influenced by his credit rating. Although it is not visible, most people have a credit rating that determines whether they can get a loan from the local bank, a charge account at a department store, or a credit card from a national organization.

An investigation is made into one's background whenever an application for credit is requested. The store, bank, or lending institution will ask some questions, but usually the final answer will depend on the rating given by a credit bureau. Table 3 shows how credit rating is evaluated. There is a whole network of credit bureaus that collects information on people who use credit and exchange information with other credit bureaus. Their data comes from

9 Laura Mae Webb, AHEA Consumer Interest Committee.

member companies, banks, police records, newspapers, and business directories. If you have ever used credit in any form, you probably have a record in a credit bureau. These records will tell whether you pay promptly and what your financial and family situations are.

TABLE 3
How Credit Is Evaluated*

	Favorable	*Unfavorable*
Employment	With good firm two years or more. Job involves skill, education.	Shifts jobs frequently. Employed in seasonal industry such as construction work. Unskilled labor.
Income	Steady, meets all normal needs.	Earnings fluctuate, depend on commissions, tips, one-shot deals. Amount barely covers requirements.
Residence	Owns own home or rents for long periods in good neighborhoods	Lives in furnished rooms in poor neighborhoods. Changes address frequently.
Financial Structure	Has savings account, and checking account that requires minimum balance. Owns property, investments, life insurance.	No bank accounts. Few, if any, assets.
Debt Record	Pays bills promptly. Usually makes large down payment. Borrows infrequently and for constructive purpose.	Slow payer. Tries to put as much on credit as possible. Frequent loans for increasing amounts.
Litigation	No suits by creditors.	Record of suits and other legal action for nonpayment. Bankruptcy.
Personal Characteristics	Family man. Not many dependents relative to income. Mature.	Large number of dependents. Marital difficulties. Young, impulsive.
Application Behavior	Seeks loan from bank with which he regularly deals. Answers all questions fully and truthfully.	Applies for loan at banking office far removed from his residence or place of business. Makes misstatements on application. In great hurry to obtain cash.

*From "All about Credit," *Changing Times* (March 1963), p. 29. Reprinted by permission from *Changing Times*, the Kiplinger magazine.

A good credit rating is a valuable asset. With a good rating a person who finds himself temporarily in financial difficulty because of an emergency or who wishes to borrow for some important purpose can do so at favorable rates. The most important factor in establishing a good credit rating is demonstrating financial responsibility in your personal transactions, holding a regular job, accumulating assets such as a bank account and life insurance, and paying bills promptly. A good credit rating is maintained by the same method as it was established, showing care in paying bills promptly.

Credit ratings follow people as they move from place to place. If you move to a new community and apply for credit, the creditors will probably check your rating with a credit bureau in the community where you used to live. International credit bureaus check the credit of people who have business dealings in other countries or make their home abroad.

What Is a Reasonable Amount of Debt?

Many people try to carry too much debt. Both high- and low-income families have this problem. Spending more than a $20,000 income permits is just as painful as overspending on $5,000. A high-income suburban family can get over its head in debt just as can the workingman's family.

Although personal income has risen in the last ten years, the rate of personal bankruptcies has more than doubled. The ease of obtaining credit seems to make it difficult for some families to keep their spending in line with their income.

There are several rough guides for determining what is a safe or reasonable amount of debt. One is to limit installment debt, exclusive of mortgage payments, to from 10 per cent to 15 per cent of annual income. If the annual family income is $6,000, then the outstanding debt limit should be between $600 and $900.

Dr. Gwen Bymers of the New York State College of Home Economics suggests that families can determine whether they are overextended by asking themselves three questions:

1. Are they committed to installment payments for more than a year?
2. Do they have liquid assets (cash or government bonds) of less than $200?
3. Are they presently making payments that take more than 20 per cent of their disposable income?[10]

Decisions as to how much debt a family can handle cannot be made arbitrarily. The particular family situation is an important factor. A large family with an average income cannot carry as large payments as a small family. A

[10] Gwen J. Bymers, "Time Commitment and Financial Position of Installment Debtors," *Journal of Family Economics—Home Management*, Vol. 2, No. 1 (June 1963), p. 31.

family where the wage earner expects to retire soon should not assume as large a debt as one where the husband is enjoying a rising income.

The purpose for which credit is used also has a bearing on how much debt is reasonable to assume. Education is increasingly being financed by credit plans, the Defense Student Loan Program, and others. In view of the return in dollars and cents of a college education, borrowing for this purpose might warrant assuming more debt than for a new car or a holiday.

The use of credit has become part of our national mores, but it has also become a serious problem to many families. Charging or buying on the installment plan may be easy; meeting the payments may not. How, when, and where credit is used must be decided by each family. In making this decision, consideration needs to be given to how the use of credit can help or hinder family happiness.

Learning to use credit in ways that contribute to individual and family happiness is part of the educative process in our urban monetary society. What should be bought on credit—a house, a car, or clothing? How much of disposable income should be allocated for credit purchases? What should one pay for the use of credit? These are the questions that must be answered.

SELECTED REFERENCES

"All About Credit," *Changing Times* (March 1963), pp. 25–40.

BLACK, HILLEL. *Buy Now, Pay Later*. New York: Pocket Books, 1962.

BOARD OF GOVERNORS OF THE FEDERAL RESERVE SYSTEM. *Consumer Installment Credit*, Part 1, Vol. 1, "Growth and Import," Washington, D.C.: Government Printing Office, 1957.

HOLMES, EMMA. "Who Uses Consumer Credit?" *Journal of Home Economics*, Vol. 49, No. 5 (May 1957), pp. 340–342.

MARGOLIUS, SIDNEY. "Shopping for Credit," Chap. 23, *The Consumer's Guide to Better Buying*. New York: Pocket Books, 1962.

MORS, WALLACE P. *Small Loan Laws*. Cleveland, Ohio: Bureau of Business Research, Western Reserve University, 1961.

———. *Consumer Credit Facts for You*. Cleveland, Ohio: Western Reserve University, 1959.

PHILLIPS, E. BRYANT, and SYLVIA LANE. "Credit and Credit Facilities," Chap. 3, *Personal Finance*. New York: Wiley, 1963.

TROELSTRUP, ARCH W. "Consumer Credit: Charge Accounts, Installment Buying and Small Loans," Chap. 14, *Consumer Problems and Personal Finance*. New York: McGraw-Hill, 1957.

5

FAMILY FOOD

People always have known they must eat to live
—children to grow normally and adults to keep
strong. But food can do more than satisfy physiological hunger and carry psychological and social values. Modern science shows that all of us,
regardless of purse, can add years to our life and
life to our years if we apply knowledge about
nutrition to our selection and use of food.[1]

TODAY it is possible for most families to have attractive,
wholesome, and delicious meals. Good food, at many price
levels, abounds in markets across the nation. Transportation facilities and modern processing, packaging, and storage techniques
make a wide variety of foods available the year round. Several forms, fresh,
canned, dried, and frozen, and several stages of preparation are available to
meet the varied needs of today's homemaker.

As a result of our present abundant productivity, technical development,
and the competitive marketing situation, there has been a rapid expansion
of food items available in the supermarket. We have new food items, such
as dehydrated rice dishes; foods in cans that previously had to be prepared at
home, such as baked apples; and new methods of processing and preserving
foods, such as whole frozen dinners and dried potatoes. Luxury and convenience foods are available as frozen, canned, and dried products in supermarkets across the nation. There has also been a rapid expansion of the
number of package sizes of the same item.

With this great variety of products and choice of sizes, the job of family
marketing has become vastly more complex and much more difficult. Today's
homemaker, who is apt to be a busy lady, must select from over 6,000 products
in the supermarket things which will please her family and which she can afford.

Time, energy, and money, these are the values that the person who plans
and prepares family meals must weigh in organizing her purchasing. If the
buyer has little money, then time and energy must be used to keep costs as
low as possible. If time and energy need to be conserved, then prepared and

---

[1] Hazel K. Stiebeling, "Food in Our Lives," *Food: The Yearbook of Agriculture,* U.S. Dept.
of Agriculture (Washington, D.C.: Government Printing Office, 1959), p. 1.

convenience foods may be the answer. In either case the versatility of the modern food market offers us a wide choice in selecting foods to fit our needs.

Changes in Eating Habits

Our present food habits reflect changes that have taken place in the lives of American families. As families shifted from rural homes to urban and suburban ones, they grew and processed less of their own food and bought more. Fifty years ago, approximately one third of our food was home produced; today that third is reduced to about 8 per cent. For both urban and suburban homes almost all of the baking of bread, preparing of jams and jellies, canning of fruit and vegetables, and churning of butter is done by commercial companies.

What we eat also reflects changes in our way of life. As industrialization took families off the farm and into the city, they found jobs in offices, factories, and stores. Heavy physical labor by men and women was reduced, and consequently the need for large amounts of energy supplied by food was decreased. There has been a sharp reduction in the consumption of carbohydrate foods such as potatoes, cereals, and breads, and an overall reduction in the amount of food eaten. "An American eats just about 100 pounds less food than an American did 50 years ago."[2]

The per capita consumption of dairy products, fruits and vegetables, meat, fish, and poultry has increased. Poultry consumption, which has doubled, accounts for some of the increase in the protein group. Our egg consumption has increased by one fifth, but much of this has been due to the egg content of the prepared foods we purchase. People are consuming about twice as much fluid whole milk as they did fifty years ago, twice as much cheese made from part or whole milk, and ten times as much ice cream. Our use of butter, on the other hand, has decreased. However, the use of margarine has increased. Americans eat more fruit and also more vegetables—except potatoes. The use of white and sweet potatoes has declined to a level of about fifty years ago. Consumption of all forms of sugar and syrup has increased, and also of coffee and cocoa. There has been no increase, however, in the use of tea.

The changes in consumption within food groups have been very great. Although the total use of flour has decreased, the percentage used in prepared bakery products and breads has increased, reflecting the shift from home preparation. The total consumption of fish has been stable, but there has been a shift from salmon to other canned fishes, and from smoked fish to fresh and frozen products. In the meat group, pork consumption is about the same, lamb and mutton less, and beef and veal higher.

[2] Marguerite C. Burk, "Pounds and Percentages," *Food: The Yearbook of Agriculture*, U.S. Dept. of Agriculture (Washington, D.C.: Government Printing Office, 1959), p. 591.

Shifts have occurred among fruits and vegetables. Although use of fresh produce has declined, this is overweighed by the increased consumption of processed forms. The use of tomatoes—fresh, canned, and in sauces—has doubled. More lettuce and less cabbage is being eaten. There has been a marked shift from apples to citrus fruits.

Families are better fed than ever before. Many who left farms now have better incomes and are able to buy a wider variety of foods. Electricity is available in most rural areas so more families now use refrigerators to store perishable foods. Where freezing facilities are available, much more meat is used. The most marked improvement in nutritional level has been in the South.

Several other types of change have taken place in eating habits. About 17 per cent of our food is eaten away from home—for the most part in restaurants, hotels, and at lunch counters. School lunchrooms and industrial feeding facilities have grown rapidly.

Food consumption is also affected by income level. Consumption of beef, poultry, butter, frozen foods, citrus fruits, ice cream, and fresh vegetables for salads increases with higher incomes. In some parts of the country, consumption of pork decreases as the income of urban families rises.

> As families progress from the extremely low to the higher income groups the changes are somewhat in this order: people with very little food increase cereal consumption as the first change; as the income increases, some of the cereals are replaced by additional meat and fat; further additions to the income lead to a decline of cereal consumption, while milk, fruits and vegetables assume more importance. Other changes within the food groups become apparent as incomes grow larger. White bread frequently replaces dark bread, butter replaces cheaper types of fat, and more expensive cuts of meat may be chosen. Thus, the need for protein and niacin are met during prosperity through increased purchase of meat. Calcium and ascorbic acid in adequate amounts appear to be a concern at all economic levels.[3]

The education of the homemaker also influences eating habits. People with more education use larger amounts of dairy products, frozen and canned fruits and vegetables, and less flour and cereal products, potatoes, and dried fruits and vegetables. Whether this is due to a greater knowledge of nutritional principles or a higher income level or both is not wholly clear.

The nutritional level of the families of employed homemakers is as good as that of families where the mother is not employed. Employed homemakers tend to use more meat and bakery products.[4]

---

[3] Henrietta Fleck and Elizabeth D. Munves, *Introduction to Nutrition* (New York: Macmillan, 1962), p. 29.

[4] Data for this section on food habits was drawn from the published material of the U.S. Dept. of Agriculture. Information concerning food consumption and income, education, and employment of the homemaker were from the "Household Food Consumption Survey 1955," by the U.S. Dept. of Agriculture.

The Importance of an Adequate Diet

Food consists of various kinds of nutrients that are necessary for health and growth: protein, carbohydrates, fats, vitamins, minerals, and water. Most foods contain several of these elements, but no one food has all of them in sufficient quantity to supply all our needs. Since the body can store only a small amount of some of these foodstuffs which body processes require, a balanced diet with sufficient amounts of essential nutrients should be eaten daily.

Food guides have been developed that simplify the planning of daily food consumption, including optimal amounts of the essential nutrients. The "Daily Food Guide" developed by the United States Department of Agriculture or the "Food Rules" approved by the Canadian Council on Nutrition serve the same purpose; they are useful as a framework for planning daily meals.

A Daily Food Guide

Milk group: some milk for everyone; children, 3–4 cups; teen-agers, 4 or more cups; adults, 2 or more cups. (Cheese and other milk products can replace some of the milk.)

Meat group: 2 or more servings of beef, veal, pork, lamb, poultry, fish, or eggs. (As a partial substitute, dried beans and peas or nuts may be used.)

Bread and cereal group: 4 or more servings of whole grain, enriched or restored products.

Vegetable and fruit group: 4 or more servings including a citrus fruit or vegetable important for vitamin C (such as tomato); a dark-green or deep yellow vegetable for vitamin A at least every other day; and other fruits and vegetables, including potatoes.

Other foods: as needed to complete meals and to provide additional food energy and other food values.

Canadian Food Rules

Milk: children up to age 12, a minimum of 1 pint; adolescents, at least 1½ pints; adults, at least ½ pint. (The Imperial pint which is used in Canada has 20 fluid ounces instead of 16.)

Meat and fish: 1 serving of meat, fish, poultry, or meat; alternates such as dried beans, eggs and cheese. Eggs and cheese should be served at least 3 times a week, and liver used often.

Cereals and breads: 1 serving of whole grain cereal and at least 4 slices of bread with butter or fortified margarine.

Vegetables: at least 1 serving of potatoes and at least 2 servings of other vegetables, preferably leafy green and yellow ones, and some raw.

Fruit: 1 serving of citrus fruit or tomatoes or their juice and 1 serving of another fruit.

Vitamin D: at least 400 International Units daily for all growing youngsters.

Habits of healthful living, which include good food habits, are established early in life. Therefore, it is important that children learn to enjoy eating wholesome meals to ensure their future health and development.

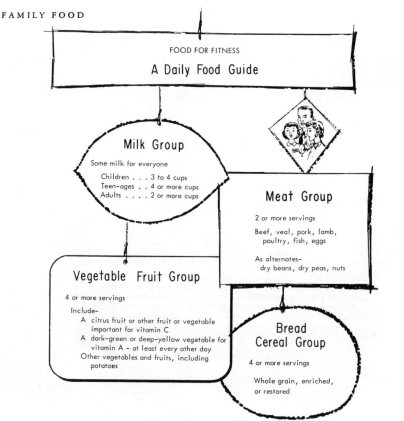

FOOD FOR FITNESS
A Daily Food Guide

Milk Group

Some milk for everyone

Children . . . 3 to 4 cups
Teen-ages . . 4 or more cups
Adults . . . . 2 or more cups

Meat Group

2 or more servings

Beef, veal, pork, lamb,
poultry, fish, eggs

As alternates-
dry beans, dry peas, nuts

Vegetable Fruit Group

4 or more servings

Include-
A citrus fruit or other fruit or vegetable
important for vitamin C
A dark-green or deep-yellow vegetable for
vitamin A - at least every other day
Other vegetables and fruits, including
potatoes

Bread Cereal Group

4 or more servings

Whole grain, enriched,
or restored

Plus other foods as needed to complete meals
and to provide additional food energy and other
food values

FIGURE 19. (*U.S. Department of Agriculture.*)

The Food Budget

The decision as to how much money should be spent on food depends on the family's income, their needs, and their tastes. Nutritious and attractive meals can be prepared at various price levels. Two families of equal income may choose to allocate money very differently. One may put a high value on gourmet foods or eating in fine restaurants, another on travel or education.

The planning of food expenditures should also consider the time and energy available for the preparation and purchasing of meals. A working mother may have little time and energy available; one with small children may have little money and also not much time. Another woman may have grown children, many community obligations, and plenty of money to spend on food. What each of these families buys and serves will be quite different. Their choices will also be influenced by their religious and ethnic back-

FIGURE 20. Family needs must be considered in buying food. (*Courtesy of Du Pont Company.*)

ground; for instance, smoked fish is popular among Scandinavians, and spaghetti among Italians.

The following are some suggestions for planning a food budget:

1. Be realistic in your planning. Consider the number of family members to be fed. Allow for their special needs—the growing boy with a bottomless stomach, Grandpa who cannot eat rich foods, or Baby and the cost of prepared baby foods.

2. Allow for personal preferences; base your plans on what is acceptable to family members. Do not plan to economize by serving veal kidney if no one likes it. Use lots of chopped meat if they enjoy it.

3. Plan for entertaining and eating out if this is important to you. School lunches and Dad's noontime meal at a restaurant are important expenditures for many people. Allow a little leeway to have guests for dinner. The regular

food budget for the family cannot always be stretched to include extra people.

4. Consider food costs in the neighborhood where you shop. It varies at different times of the year and in the part of the country where you live. Fresh fruit and vegetables are cheapest when they are available from local farms. Small private markets may carry fine quality food and give many desirable services, but their prices are often higher. Some parts of the country are far removed from most food supplies, so food necessarily becomes more expensive. Alaska is an example of this type of situation.

5. Keep a constant check on your food spending. It is often easy to confuse food spending with other household purchases in the supermarket, such as soap powder and paper towels. Some people like to keep food money in one purse and use this fund every time they make a food purchase. Another way is to separate your food and nonfood items when you are checking out of the market, so you will have separate receipts covering only food items.

If you are inexperienced in handling food money or wish to analyze your food expenditures carefully, it is helpful to keep a list of all foods purchased and their cost for a period of two weeks. Some people do this by writing on their market receipt the name of the food next to the amount it cost. At the end of the two weeks regroup your expenditures under the headings: (1) meat, (2) bread and cereals, (3) milk, (4) vegetables and fruit, and (5) extras. This will show you how you are spending your food dollars.

6. Have patience. It takes time to learn to manage food money well, but, with practice, you will find that it becomes easier. As a guide to evaluating your spending, you might like to compare your expenditures with estimated food costs compiled by the United States Department of Agriculture (see Table 4).

Stretching the Food Dollar

With careful planning most families can cut down on food expenditures without impairing family health. It is possible to provide a wholesome diet on several levels of expenditure; both steak and stew can be the basis for balanced meals. The basic food patterns described in a preceding section can be adapted to the varied needs of family members on low-cost budgets as well as high. However, it does take careful planning, knowledge about food buying and its preparation, and some effort. The results can be better nutrition at lower cost.

Planning Meals in Advance

Managing food dollars effectively means using the resources available in the best possible way. Time, energy, money, and facilities for food storage

TABLE 4

Cost of One Week's Food at Home* (Estimated for Food Plans
at Three Cost Levels, July 1963—U.S.A. Average)

Sex-Age Groups	Low-Cost Plan	Moderate-Cost Plan	Liberal Plan
Families	*Dollars*	*Dollars*	*Dollars*
Family of two, 20–34 years	14.40	19.60	22.10
Family of two, 55–74 years	12.80	17.60	19.70
Family of four, preschool children†	21.40	28.50	32.50
Family of four, school children‡	24.80	33.30	37.90
Individuals #			
Children, under 1 year	3.10	3.90	4.20
1–3 years	3.80	4.80	5.40
4–6 years	4.50	5.90	7.00
7–9 years	5.40	7.00	8.10
10–12 years	6.30	8.50	9.70
Girls, 13–15 years	6.60	9.00	10.30
16–19 years	6.70	8.90	10.20
Boys, 13–15 years	7.20	9.90	11.30
16–19 years	8.50	11.50	13.10
Women, 20–34 years	5.70	7.80	8.80
35–54 years	5.50	7.60	8.60
55–74 years	5.10	7.10	8.00
75 years and over	5.00	6.60	7.50
Pregnant	7.00	9.20	10.20
Nursing	8.80	11.30	12.50
Men, 20–34 years	7.40	10.00	11.30
35–54 years	6.90	9.30	10.40
55–74 years	6.50	8.90	9.90
75 years and over	6.30	8.50	9.40

* U.S. Dept. of Agriculture, Consumer and Food Economics Research Division, Agricultural Research Service, "Estimated Cost of 1 Week's Food—U.S.A. Average and Four Regions," *Family Economics Review* (September 1963), p. 18.

† Man and woman 20–34 years; children, 1–3 and 4–6 years.

‡ Man and woman 20–34 years; children, 7–9 and 10–12.

The costs given are for individuals in 4-person families. Changes in the amount needed for each individual in other size families, the following adjustments are: 1-person families—add 20 per cent; 2-person families—add 10 per cent; 3-person families—add 5 per cent; 5-person families—subtract 5 per cent; 6-or-more-person families—subtract 10 per cent.

and preparation are what most people have to work with. Skill in planning, organizing, and preparing can enhance them.

The first step is to plan meals carefully in advance. A plan that is made for only one meal or one day is simple, but frequently expensive. Plan meals for a week in advance, if possible, or at least for several days if this is a convenient spacing of shopping trips.

Before making a plan of meals, take a survey of what is on hand in the refrigerator and kitchen cupboards. Perhaps there is some leftover meat which could be used for a lunch.

Study the food advertisements in newspapers before making your plan. Most communities have heavy advertising of foods on Wednesday, Thursday, or Friday. Comparison of advertisements will often indicate a choice of the best buys in several stores. The circulars of food stores give news of food sales. Utilize other sources of information about food buying, such as bulletins of your state extension service, newspaper articles, and radio or television programs in your local area.

Take advantage of sales. Sometimes there is an oversupply of a certain kind of canned or frozen produce when the new crop is being harvested, and the price is reduced. Other sales are loss leaders to induce you to come into a store. One estimate is that the average housewife can save $200 per year by careful shopping for family food.

Make written plans for meals. Hasty or haphazard shopping often fails to take advantage of good buys. List your menus and then make a shopping list. Substitutions can be made in the market if something looks particularly fresh or is on sale, but you are less likely to splurge on expensive foods if you have a written plan.

Select the main course first in planning meals. Then add the other foods. Try to have a variety of flavors, textures, and colors. Consider both the nutritional value as well as the taste and attractiveness of the meal.

Then make out a market list. Be specific and include the quantity needed of each food; for example, 2 pounds of chuck steak, boneless and cut in cubes. Table 6 in this chapter which indicates the servings per market unit will be helpful in figuring how much to buy of each food. Group your market list according to the kinds of items. Put all meats together, vegetables together. This will save you time and energy in marketing and will also make it easier to compare costs.

An exploratory study of the patterns of shopping of 3,200 customers in 13 retail food supermarkets in a northeastern city revealed that customers were exposed to about 64 per cent of the store's display locations, spent less than 23 minutes shopping, made 13 purchases per store visit at an average value of 56 cents per purchase. Purchases on the average, increased at the rate of about 6 per 15 minutes in the store.[5]

It was also noted that about 30 per cent of the shoppers used a prepared shopping list. These buyers averaged 4 more purchases and spent a longer time in the store. Moreover, they spent about 4 to 6 cents more per minute than did shoppers without lists.

[5] Nick Havas, *Customers' Shopping Patterns in Retail Food Stores*, U.S. Dept. of Agriculture, Agricultural Marketing Service (Washington, D.C.: Government Printing Office, 1960), p. 3.

Below are a week's menus for a moderate-cost food plan for a family of four in the Washington, D.C., area. Following is a list of food needed for these meals.[6]

Moderate Cost Meals

SUNDAY

Breakfast

Grapefruit Halves
Waffles—Syrup
Bacon
Milk for children

Dinner

Braised Chuck Roast and Onions
Broccoli   Browned Potatoes
Lettuce Wedges—Cheese Dressing
Rolls
Sliced Peaches   Cake
Milk for children

Supper

Peanut Butter Sandwiches
Asparagus Salad—French Dressing
Baked Apple with Vanilla Ice Cream
Milk

MONDAY

Breakfast

Orange Juice
Poached Eggs on Toast
Milk for children

Lunch

Vegetable Soup
Toasted Cheese Sandwiches
Coleslaw
Milk

Dinner

Casserole of Beef and Lima Beans
Mashed Potatoes
Cucumber-Onion Salad
Bread
Fruit Gelatin   Cake
Milk for children

TUESDAY

Breakfast

Grapefruit Juice
Ready-to-Eat Cereal
Raisin Bread Toast
Milk for children

Lunch

Hamburgers—Buns
Celery Sticks
Oatmeal Cookies
Milk

Dinner

Fried Chicken—Gravy
Parsley Potatoes   Carrots
Waldorf Salad
Bread
Cherry Cobbler
Milk for children

WEDNESDAY

Breakfast

Grapefruit-Orange Juice
Fried Eggs—Bacon
Raisin Bread Toast
Milk for children

Lunch

Chicken-Rice Soup
Green Salad—Cheese Dressing
Jelly Sandwiches
Apples
Milk

Dinner

Sautéed Liver
Mashed Potatoes
Marinated Green Bean Salad
Cornbread
Bananas and Raspberries
Milk for children

[6] Eloise Cofer and Faith Clark, "Food Plans at Different Costs," *Food: The Yearbook of Agriculture*, U.S. Dept. of Agriculture (Washington, D.C.: Government Printing Office, 1959), pp. 583–587.

THURSDAY

Breakfast

Orange Slices
Oatmeal with Raisins
Toast
Milk for children

Lunch

Scrambled Eggs
Hashed-Brown Potatoes
Toasted Cornbread
Fresh Fruit in Season
Milk

Dinner

Swiss Steak—Gravy
Potatoes Boiled in Jackets
Greens
Raw Vegetable Relishes
(Celery, Carrots, Peppers)
Bread
Frozen Peppermint Pudding
Milk for children

FRIDAY

Breakfast

Tomato Juice
Omelet
Toast—Jelly
Milk for children

Lunch

Cubed Swiss Steak and Gravy
(leftover)
on toast
Green Beans
Tomato and Shredded Cheese Salad
Bread
Milk

Dinner

Fish
Creamed Potatoes Peas and Celery
Tossed Green Salad
Bread
Lemon Pie
Milk for children

SATURDAY

Breakfast

Orange Juice
Ready-to-Eat Cereal
Toast
Milk for children

Lunch

Luncheon Meat Sandwiches
(with lettuce)
Celery and Carrot Sticks
Lemon Tarts
Milk

Dinner

Sweet-Sour Spareribs Chinese Style
Rice   Buttered Beets
Green Salad
Bread
Cookies
Milk for children

Food for the Week's Meals

Milk, Cheese, Ice Cream
19 quarts fluid whole milk
½ pound cheddar cheese
1 ounce blue cheese
1 pint vanilla ice cream

Meats, Poultry, Fish
4 pounds beef chuck
2 pounds round steak
1 pound ground beef
3 pounds pork spareribs
¾ pound bacon
1 pound liver
3-4 pounds chicken
1 pound fish, fillet
½ pound luncheon meat

Eggs
2½ dozen

Dried Beans, Peas, Nuts
⅓ pound dried lima beans
⅓ pound peanut butter
1 ounce walnuts (pieces)

Dark-Green, Deep-Yellow Vegetables
1 bunch broccoli
1-1½ pounds carrots,
½ bunch parsley
½ pound green peppers
1 pound salad greens
2 pounds greens

Potatoes
8-9 pounds white potatoes

Fats and Oils
1 pound table fat
1 pound shortening
1 pint salad dressing
½ cup salad oil

Citrus Fruit, Tomatoes
2 grapefruit
1-1½ pounds oranges
¾ pound tomatoes
1 No. 2 can grapefruit juice

1 No. 2 can grapefruit-orange juice
1 No. 2 can tomato juice
1 No. 203 can tomatoes
2 6-ounce cans frozen orange juice

Other Vegetables and Fruit
2 pounds green beans
1 bunch beets
⅓ pound cabbage
1 bunch celery
½ pound cucumbers
2 heads lettuce
1 pound onions
1 14½ ounce can green asparagus
1 can condensed vegetable soup
1 package frozen peas
3 pounds apples
1 pound bananas
1-1½ pounds fresh fruit in season
1 No. 303 can cherries
1 No. 2½ can sliced peaches
½ pound raisins
1 package raspberries (frozen)

Sugar and Sweets
1½-2 pounds granulated sugar
½ pint syrup
½ pound jelly
1 package flavored gelatin
1 package lemon filling mix
1 ounce peppermint candy

Baked Goods, Flour, Cereals
2 loaves enriched white bread
1 loaf whole wheat bread
1 loaf cracked wheat bread
1 loaf rye bread
1 loaf raisin bread
4 hamburger rolls
6 brown-and-serve rolls
5 ounces plain chocolate cookies
2½ pounds all-purpose flour
⅔ pound oatmeal
10 ounces ready-to-eat cereal
⅔ pound cornmeal
½ pound rice

Use the Calendar as a Guide to Purchasing

In many regions of the country there is a seasonal variation in price for meats, vegetables, eggs, and other foods. Fish is usually least expensive in the late spring and summer, beef in the late winter, and many fresh fruits and vegetables in the summer when they are plentiful and available from local producers.

Since most of our large markets carry fresh, frozen, and canned fruits and vegetables, the purchaser can buy whichever form is most reasonably priced at a particular season. Although it is not a hard-and-fast rule, canned or frozen forms of foods are apt to be less expensive than fresh ones except when the fresh food is at the peak of supply. However, some fresh foods have so much waste that they are expensive to ship—peas are a good example; the canned or frozen forms that are packed without waste may be cheaper even in the peak of the season.

Compare Costs

Top quality generally commands the highest price. Often the quality rated top is the largest and most attractive-looking food, which is not always what one needs. For example, large, perfect, bright red apples command a higher price than medium-sized, slightly bruised ones. However, for applesauce or pie the less expensive ones would be fine. Try to estimate the amount of waste in considering whether a lower grade would be a good buy.

Size is often confused with quality. Small eggs or small fruit may be of top quality, but usually the larger size is preferred. Consider how much waste is involved in purchasing a smaller size (skin and seeds or eggshells). Frequently, it is less expensive to buy small sizes. In the early fall, pullet eggs often cost less per pound of usable portion than large eggs.

Top quality is not necessarily more nutritious. Grade B eggs are just as nourishing as Grade A; Grade C canned tomatoes are just as wholesome as Grade A. The difference in the case of eggs is in the degree of freshness, which would not matter if you were using them in scrambled eggs or most cakes. The biggest difference is in the firmness of the whites. In the case of canned tomatoes, Grade A are perfect whole tomatoes and Grade C cut-up tomatoes. If you were planning to use the canned tomatoes for spaghetti sauce, Grade C would be an economical choice, but you might prefer Grade A if you were serving stewed tomatoes as a vegetable.

Quantity purchases usually cost less per unit. Flour, sugar, potatoes, onions, and apples cost less when bought in quantity. Maple syrup, shortening, coffee, and ice cream are lower priced per serving when bought in bulk. Bulk, or quantity buying, however, is only useful when there are adequate facilities for storage and the food can be used before it deteriorates. It is not good economy to buy in quantity unless foods can be stored under good conditions, for example, the freezing compartment of the home refrigerator

FIGURE 21. U.S. grades on canned foods. *(Courtesy of USDA.)*

is usually not cold enough or large enough for anything except short-term storage. A deep freezer that can maintain food at 0°F. is necessary.

Know Your Food Grades

Most stores carry such a wide variety of products that wise selection is difficult. Some companies label foods according to the grade, which is very helpful in intelligent selection because it specifies the quality of the contents. (See Figure 21.) Although some processors have their own system of grading, the most widely used grades are USDA (United States Department of Agriculture). The use of these grades for food products sold in retail stores is strictly voluntary. However, if USDA grades are used, the product must meet their standards. The food processor, handler, or producer who wishes to use U.S. grades must request the services from the Agricultural Marketing Service of the United States Department of Agriculture and pay for it.

The grades apply to the quality at the time the food is graded. All USDA grades are preceded by the letters "U.S." and enclosed in a shield-shaped mark. Except for meat, consumer grades are commonly designated by the letters Grade A, B, or C. Foods graded by a processor according to his own standards are not labeled with "U.S." preceding the grade and do not have to conform to federal standards. (See Figure 21.)

Grades of Beef[7]

Federal grades of meat appear as a purple ribbonlike stamp on retail cuts of meat. United States Grades of beef, established in 1951, are:

USDA Prime—Beef with this label comes from young, well-fed beef-type cattle. The generous amounts of fat that run in streaks through the lean make this meat tender, juicy, and flavorsome. About 30 per cent of all beef from steers and heifers makes this grade. Steaks and roasts are tender and adapted to cooking with dry heat.

USDA Choice—This grade of beef has less fat than Prime beef, and is more economical. More beef of this grade is produced than of any other grade—usually around 50 per cent of all beef that comes from steers.

USDA Good—As the name implies, this grade of beef pleases many families. "Good" beef is less juicy than "Choice" or "Prime" but it may be preferred by beef-eaters who like their meat lean.

USDA Commercial—Older animals and some young ones fall into this grade. Cuts of meat of this grade have a very thin covering of fat and practically no fat through the lean. Slow cooking with moisture helps make the meat tender.

USDA Utility—Beef from animals that are well along in years is usually of this grade. There is very little fat on any cuts of Utility beef. It is used for ground meat, pot roasts, and stews.

USDA Cutter and *Canner* grades seldom go to retail stores; usually they are made into processed meat products.

Lamb and veal also have five grades, but for these meats the last two grades are USDA Utility and USDA Cull instead of Commercial and Utility. (See Figures 22, 23, and 24.)

Federal grading is not the same as inspection. All meat and poultry shipped in interstate commerce must be inspected. Since most beef, veal, and lamb is shipped in interstate commerce, the large majority is inspected. The inspection stamp is placed on the meat or the label if it is packaged or canned. It is also placed on ready-to-cook poultry and poultry products, but may not appear on each individual bird. Fresh chicken is usually shipped in boxes, and the boxes are stamped. In some states a large proportion of the poultry consumed is produced locally and may not be federally inspected.

Read the Label on the Package

Federal law requires that the ingredients of food products in interstate commerce be listed on the label or container in a way that is not misleading. If a product has more than one ingredient, the contents must be listed in order of amount, the most plentiful ingredient listed first.

In those cases where there is a standard of identity, that is, the ingredients are those included in a formula or recipe filed with the Food and Drug Ad-

[7] Extension Service, State Colleges of Agriculture and Home Economics, New York, New Jersey, and Connecticut, *Food Marketing Handbook* (Ithaca, N.Y.: Cornell University, [n.d.]), pp. 2–4, 5.

ministration, the producer is not required to list them on the label. The standard of identity insures uniformity in production so that the buyer can be sure the product is the same each time she buys it. For instance, there are standards of identity for bread, rolls, margarine, evaporated milk, many cheeses, ketchup, jelly, and noodles.

Food products must also list the net contents of the food in terms of weight or liquid measure and the name and address of the producer or distributor. In addition, many canners add descriptive labeling that may include the brand name, an illustration of the product, the size of the product, the maturity of the food, the seasoning, the contents of the can measured in cups or number of pieces, the number of servings, and recipe suggestions for use of the product.

In our self-service, pick-it-yourself supermarket the package or container has become the salesman. It beckons in bright colors from locations designed

U.S. GRADES AT A GLANCE

Product	1st Grade	2d Grade	3d Grade	4th Grade	5th Grade
Beef	USDA Prime	USDA Choice	USDA Good	USDA Standard	USDA Commercial *
Veal	USDA Prime	USDA Choice	USDA Good	USDA Standard	USDA Utility †
Calf	USDA Prime	USDA Choice	USDA Good	USDA Standard	USDA Utility ‡
Lamb	USDA Prime	USDA Choice	USDA Good	USDA Utility	USDA Cull
Yearling Mutton	USDA Prime	USDA Choice	USDA Good	USDA Utility	USDA Cull
Mutton		USDA Choice	USDA Good	USDA Utility	USDA Cull
Butter	U.S. Grade AA (U.S. 93 Score)	U.S. Grade A (U.S. 92 Score)	U.S. Grade B (U.S. 90 Score)		
Cheddar Cheese	U.S. Grade AA	U.S. Grade A	U.S. Grade B		
Swiss Cheese	U.S. Grade A	U.S. Grade B	U.S. Grade C	U.S. Grade D	
Nonfat Dry Milk	U.S. Extra Grade	U.S. Standard Grade			
Cottage Cheese	No Grades -- May be marked USDA "Quality Approved"				
Poultry	U.S. Grade A	U.S. Grade B	U.S. Grade C		
Eggs	U.S. Grade AA	U.S. Grade A	U.S. Grade B	U.S. Grade C	
Milled Rice	U.S. No. 1	U.S. No. 2	U.S. No. 3	U.S. No. 4	U.S. No. 5
Brown Rice	U.S. No. 1	U.S. No. 2	U.S. No. 3	U.S. No. 4	
Dried Beans	U.S. Choice Handpicked U.S. No. 1	U.S. No. 1 Handpicked U.S. No. 2	U.S. No. 2 Handpicked U.S. No. 3	U.S. No. 3 Handpicked	
Dried Peas	U.S. No. 1	U.S. No. 2	U.S. No. 3		
(and related products)	U.S. Grade A (Fancy)	U.S. Grade B (Choice or Ex. Std.)	U.S. Grade C (Standard)		

* Three lowest grades are USDA Utility, Cutter, and Canner.
† Lowest grade is USDA Cull.
‡ Grades used for these products are usually as listed here, but there are some exceptions.

U.S. GRADES AT A GLANCE (cont.)					
Product	Consumer Grades		Wholesale Grades			
	1st Grade	2d Grade	1st Grade	2d Grade	3d Grade	4th Grade
Potatoes	U.S. Grade A Large U.S. Grade A Medium to Large U.S. Grade A Medium U.S. Grade A Small	U.S. Grade B Large U.S. Grade B Medium to Large U.S. Grade B Medium U.S. Grade B Small	U.S. Fancy	U.S. No. 1	U.S. Commercial	U.S. No. 2
Broccoli (Italian Sprouting)	U.S. Grade A	U.S. Grade B	U.S. Fancy	U.S. No. 1	U.S. No. 2	
Brussels Sprouts	U.S. Grade A	U.S. Grade B	U.S. No. 1	U.S. No. 2		
Carrots	U.S. Grade A	U.S. Grade B	(Topped carrots) U.S. Extra No. 1	U.S. No. 1	U.S. No. 2	
Corn (Husked, on the cob)	U.S. Grade A	U.S. Grade B	(Green corn) U.S. Fancy	U.S. No. 1	U.S. No. 2	
Cranberries	U.S. Grade A					
Kale	U.S. Grade A	U.S. Grade B	U.S. No. 1	U.S. Commercial		
Parsnips	U.S. Grade A	U.S. Grade B	U.S. No. 1	U.S. No. 2		
Spinach Leaves	U.S. Grade A	U.S. Grade B	U.S. Extra No. 1	U.S. No. 1	U.S. Commercial	
Tomatoes	U.S. Grade A	U.S. Grade B	U.S. No. 1	U.S. Combination	U.S. No. 2	U.S. No. 3
Turnips	U.S. Grade A	U.S. Grade B	(Topped turnips U.S. No. 1	U.S. No. 2		
Celery	U.S. Grade AA	U.S. Grade A (3d Grade – U.S. Grade B)	U.S. Extra No. 1	U.S. No. 1	U.S. No. 2	
Apples	None	None	U.S. Extra Fancy	U.S. Fancy	U.S. No. 1 U.S. No. 1[1] Cookers U.S. No. 1[2] Early U.S. Hail Grade[3]	U.S. Utility

[1] Same as U.S. No. 1 except for color.
[2] Same as U.S. No. 1 except for color, maturity and size.
[3] Same as U.S. No. 1 except for hail injury.

FIGURE 22. *(U.S. Department of Agriculture.)*

to increase sales. Mandatory grade labeling and standards that define what constitutes a serving would be useful for intelligent choice. Also a uniform practice of indicating clearly the net contents would make it easier to determine what is in a container. Some industries now do a fine job of labeling the contents. Under the Cereal Institute's new labeling code, net content on cereal products is clearly stated.

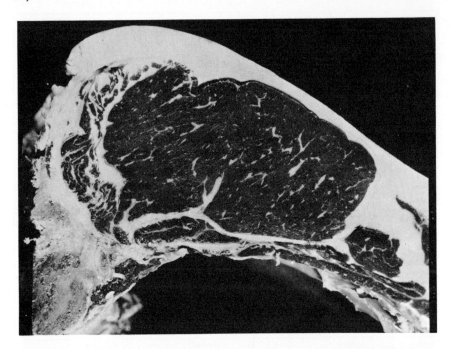

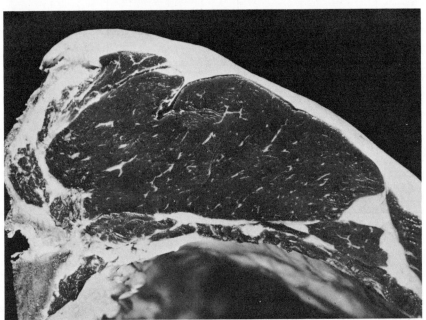

FIGURE 23. Meat grades take into consideration the amount of fat marbled throughout the meat and the tenderness of the meat. "Choice" meat (above) is jucier and more tender than meat graded "good" (below). (*Courtesy of USDA.*)

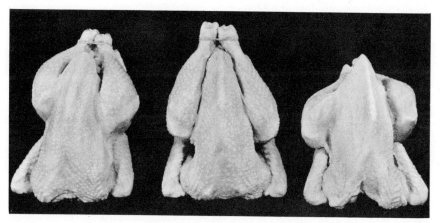

FIGURE 24. Three grades of poultry. (*Courtesy of USDA.*)

The Impact of Trading Stamps

The rapid growth of stamp plans has been due largely to their widespread use by retail food stores, chiefly supermarkets, that is, departmentalized food stores, with a sales volume of one million dollars per year and at least a fully self-service grocery department.

According to a survey made by the Department of Agriculture, retailers paid 375 million dollars for trading stamps in 1956. This is approximately a thousand trading stamps for every man, woman, and child in the United States.[8] Stores subscribe to stamp plans because they believe that stamps help to attract and retain customers. Stamps appeal to people as a way of obtaining items without direct outlays of money.

The trading stamp companies, which sell the stamps to the retail stores, really are engaged in selling products commonly sold by nonfood retail stores, but instead of actual merchandise, they sell prepaid merchandise certificates—stamps—to stores, which offer the stamps to their customers as a premium on purchases.

Most stamps are redeemed for merchandise, but some companies redeem stamps in trade or cash. In a few states, stamps are redeemed in cash because other methods are illegal. The same company may redeem stamps for merchandise in one state and for cash in another.

The merchandise which the customer receives by redeeming stamps is worth approximately 2 per cent of the dollars which must be spent to get it.

[8] U.S. Dept. of Agriculture, Agricultural Marketing Service, *Trading Stamps and Their Impact on Food Prices,* Marketing Research Report No. 295 (Washington, D.C.: Government Printing Office, 1958), p. 1.

In the study reported by the Department of Agriculture[9] the average prices in stores giving stamps increased 0.6 per cent, or about 30 per cent of the average merchandise value of the stamps.

Trading stamp plans have brought an enormous increase in sales to some stores, but little or no change to others. A retailer may cover the cost of stamp plans by having fewer sales and increasing the number of high-profit nonfood items. In general, the small profit margin per dollar of sales in supermarkets is not sufficient to cover the cost of stamp plans, and the retail price must reflect the cost of the plan.

Forms of Food

Since all of the available forms of a food—fresh, canned, and frozen—have similar nutritive value if they are correctly processed, stored and prepared, the wise choice must be based on individual family requirements. In comparing the prices of fresh and processed fruits and vegetables, it is important to consider that most of the waste is removed from processed foods; compare the cost per serving rather than cost per weight.

Canned Foods

Canned foods are fresh products processed with heat and permanently sealed in containers. In the process the food is cooked. Canned foods can keep indefinitely as long as they remain tightly sealed.

Commercially canned foods are packaged in cans and jars in a variety of sizes. In planning food shopping it is helpful to know approximately how much is in each size can. (See Figure 25.)

Frozen Foods

Frozen foods are usually prepared in a form that reduces the amount of home preparation. The following is a brief summary of how some of the most popular frozen foods are packed.

MEAT. The excess fat is trimmed off, and some cuts are deboned.

POULTRY. It is cut up in parts, packed in halves or quarters, or made into boneless rolls. Sometimes a package is made up of only one part of the fowl—that is, chicken breasts. The newest trend is to sell poultry with the stuffing inside, ready for roasting. (Birds that are stuffed are very perishable and should be kept frozen until ready to be cooked.) Another new trend is to sell rolled boneless poultry.

FISH. It comes in the whole range of cuts and stages of dressing just as fresh fish does. Some very popular prepared fish items are fish sticks, codfish cakes and bite-size portions.

[9] U.S. Dept. of Agriculture, *ibid.*, p. 28.

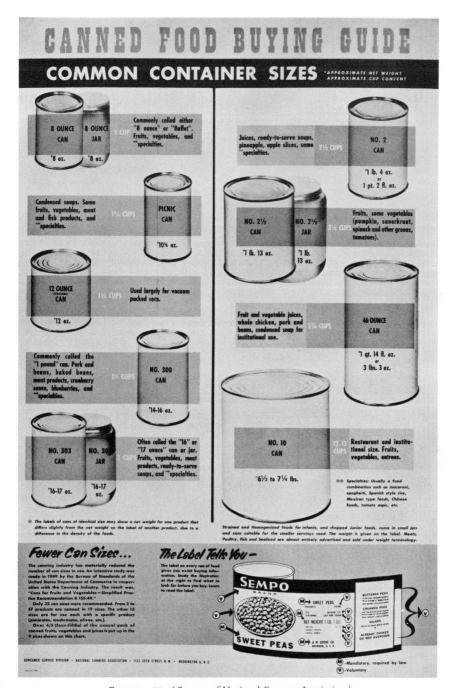

FIGURE 25. (Courtesy of National Canners Association.)

LOBSTER AND SHRIMP. These are sold both cooked and uncooked, in and out of the shell. Recently, precleaned shrimp has been marketed in large pliofilm bags.

FRUITS. These are usually fully prepared, uncooked, and packed with a heavy sugar syrup. Vitamin C is added to some fruits, such as peaches, to maintain color.

VEGETABLES. These are usually trimmed of all waste and parboiled (dipped in boiling water) before being packed. Thus they are partially cooked and require a shorter cooking period than do fresh vegetables of the same type.

FRUIT JUICES. These are packed in concentrated form; part of the water is removed, which must be replaced before use. In some cases sugar is added to juices and punches.

DINNERS. These usually require only heating. They are packed on divided plates in which they can be heated and served. Some of the newest ones also include dessert and soup, really a full dinner.

SPECIALTY FOODS. These include foods such as pizza, manicotti, and many others; they are becoming more widely available. Most of them just require heating.

BAKED PRODUCTS. These include cooked and uncooked cakes and pies as well as cookies and piecrusts. Some need only be defrosted, such as waffles, pancakes, doughnuts, turnovers, rolls, and buns; others require baking.

ICE CREAM. This is made from milk, milk solids, milk fat, and flavoring, and usually contains a stabilizer such as gelatine. State regulations in the United States and federal codes in Canada control the composition.

OTHER FROZEN DESSERTS. These include ice milk, sherbet, ice cream cakes, and specialty ice cream products like tortoni and spumoni.

Packaged Foods

Packaged goods are one of the fast-growing areas of prepared foods. In addition to mixes for baked goods such as cakes, rolls, muffins, biscuits, bread, coffee cakes, waffles, pancakes, corn bread, popovers, cream puffs, and cookies there are mixes for ice cream, pie fillings, frostings, meringues, macaroni and cheese, potatoes au gratin, and other things.

Packaged mixes are time-savers and most of them have a reputation of high quality. The decision on whether to use one and how to do so will have to depend on individual needs and tastes. Does the family like the product? Is it economical? Does it save preparation and clean-up time?

Dried Foods

Drying foods is one of the oldest ways of preservation. Moisture is removed by either sundrying or mechanical dehydration. The most widely used dried foods are fruits such as apricots, prunes, and peaches. Next are meat, milk, and vegetables such as peas and beans. Dried soup mixes are quite popular.

Food Buying Guide

Meat

Meat takes about one third of the family food dollar. Americans are very fond of beef, and in periods of prosperity the demand for beef is strong and the price stays high.

The food value of different cuts of meat does not vary as much as the price. The premium for high-priced meats is paid for flavor and tenderness, not food value.

The cost of meat depends on several factors: the desirability of the cut, the grade, and the seasonal variation in price. The cuts that command the premium prices are those that are most tender; they come from the part of the animal that had the least exercise. In beef these are the loin, which includes the steaks, and the rib or chest area.

Price per pound alone is not a good guide to meat value. Many cuts have a high percentage of waste. Cost per serving is a better way to compare prices. Table 5 shows the amount of waste in some of the popular cuts of beef.

STRETCHING THE MEAT DOLLAR. Here are some ways to cut costs:

1. Buy some of the less popular cuts that require longer cooking. Meat in a pot roast or stew is just as nutritious as that in a steak, and much less costly. Lamb ribs can be as tasty as pork ribs. Try fixing them the same way. They are delicious broiled, barbecued, or baked.

2. Substitute other foods for meat. Occasionally, use a cheese dish as the main course. This is also a good source of protein.

3. Pay attention to seasonal price variations, particularly those of beef and pork, which we use more plentifully than lamb or veal. Buy more pork in December and January and more beef in February and March to take advantage of seasonally low prices. These are also good times to buy for the freezer. Use more lamb in March and April.

4. Shop for the specials. In many areas the supermarkets have sales before the weekend. Frequently, a particular cut of meat is reduced. Go to several markets to take advantage of sales.

5. Use more fresh or frozen fish. With the exclusion of shellfish, many fish entrees cost less than meat. And they are usually quick cooking. Buy frozen fish from a reliable store; sometimes it is not kept cold enough and deteriorates.

Poultry

This includes chicken, turkey, duck, goose, and guinea hen. The 1961 consumption of chicken and turkey was approximately 38 pounds per person.[10]

[10] Edward Karpoff, "Postwar Changes in Poultry Consumption," *National Food Situation* (July 1961), p. 17.

TABLE 5

Percentage of Lean Meat in Various Cuts of Beef*
U.S. Grade Choice†

Cuts of Beef	Percentage of Lean Meat
Roasts	
Chuck or shoulder, bone in	74
Chuck or shoulder, boneless	89
Chuck arm pot roast	69
Chuck blade pot roast	65
Rib, standing 10″ cut (7th & 8th ribs)	59
Rib, rolled and tied	75
Round tip, boneless	85
Rump, bone in	59
Rump, boneless	71
Steaks	
Chuck blade	65
Club	58
Flank	100
Porterhouse	61
Round tip, boneless	85
Round, full cut	83
Sirloin, hip bone	54
Sirloin, double bone	61
Sirloin, wedge and round bone	69
T-bone	59
Stews	
Brisket, bone in	51
Brisket, boneless	60
Flank meat	41
Heal of round, boneless	85
Neck, bone in	62
Neck, boneless	79
Plate, bone in	53
Plate, boneless	63
Fore shank, bone in	44
Fore shank, boneless	81
Hind shank, bone in	29
Hind shank, boneless	75

*Extension Service, State Colleges of Agriculture and Home Economics, *Food Marketing Handbook, ibid.*, pp. 2-7. Sources: University of Illinois, Animal Husbandry Department, Beef Division, "The Economy of Retail Cuts of Different Grades of Beef."
†Adjusted to 1951 U.S. Grades of Beef.

In selecting poultry (see Figure 24) look for the following:
1. Short legs and a plump body, which is a sign of meatiness.
2. A good covering of fat, which is a sign of tender meat.
3. Clean, smooth skin free from pinfeathers, bruises, and discolorations.
4. If the poultry has been frozen, avoid buying a bird with damaged wrapper; exposure to air dehydrates the fowl and encourages rancidity.

The amount to buy per serving varies with the bird. Chickens range in size from broilers, which weigh about 2 pounds, to roasting and stewing chickens, which may be 6 to 8 pounds. Allow one-quarter to one-half a bird per serving for broiling chickens and ducks; one-half pound ready-to-cook weight for other types of chickens, turkey, and goose; and one guinea hen per person. Large birds have more meat in proportion to bone and yield more servings per pound. For example, a 22-pound turkey has more edible meat per pound than an 8-pound turkey.

Dairy Products

EGGS. The average American eats over 350 eggs per year, or about one per day. Many of these are eaten in prepared products such as baked goods and combination dishes such as casseroles.

Eggs are graded by candling, a procedure in which eggs are held up to a light to determine the amount of air space between the shell and the white of the egg. The smaller the air space, the fresher the egg. (See Figure 27.)

Which size egg is the best buy? In one quality grade you may find two or more sizes of eggs side by side in the store. The important comparison is how much edible egg do you get. The color of the shell is not an indication of nutritive value.

MILK. Milk is often called our most perfect food. It is a rich source of protein, calcium, Vitamin A, riboflavin, and other minerals.

"If all the dairy products we consume yearly were in the form of fluid milk, the amount would be about 302 quarts each. On the average, we consume annually less than one-half that, or 133 quarts, as fresh fluid milk and the rest as other dairy products."[11]

The cost of milk varies considerably with the form purchased. Dry skim milk is much less expensive than fresh whole liquid milk. Consumers Union estimated that if a family of five drank the amount of milk recommended by most nutrition guides—one pint each day for the parents, and one quart each day for the children—substitution of dry milk for one half of this amount would save more than $100 a year.[12]

Fruits and Vegetables

The price of fruits and vegetables varies with the seasons. Quality is usually best and prices lowest when fruits and vegetables are available from nearby

[11] New York State Cooperative Extension Service, *Focus on the Food Markets,* (May 22, 1961), p. 1.
[12] *Consumers Reports* (January 1962), p. 18.

farms. Fruits like tomatoes and cantaloupe are often half the price in peak seasons. The following chart indicates the times of peak supply for some of the fruits and vegetables in the New York City area:

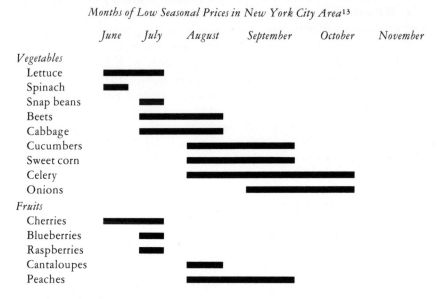

Months of Low Seasonal Prices in New York City Area[13]

	June	July	August	September	October	November
Vegetables						
Lettuce						
Spinach						
Snap beans						
Beets						
Cabbage						
Cucumbers						
Sweet corn						
Celery						
Onions						
Fruits						
Cherries						
Blueberries						
Raspberries						
Cantaloupes						
Peaches						

The following buying hints are useful in selecting fresh fruits and vegetables.

1. Vegetables and fruits are very perishable. Leaves wilt and flavor deteriorates quickly. Look for firm smooth fruits and vegetables, ripe but not mushy.

2. Size is not a reliable guide to quality, although one may pay a premium price for large fruit and vegetables. Good quality comes in most sizes. In some cases oversized products may be tasteless or woody. Buy vegetables of the same or similar size so that they will cook in the same length of time. In selecting asparagus, try to select stalks of uniform thickness so that the thin ones are not overcooked before the thick ones are done.

3. Select fruits and vegetables with a bright, fresh color. This is often a sign of freshness and nutritive value.

4. Buy the quantity needed. Some fruits and vegetables have very little waste, others a good deal.[14]

Table 6 is helpful in determining how much fresh vegetables to buy at one time.

[13] New York State Cooperative Extension Service, "Buying and Preparing Food for Institutions," *Highlights on the Food Markets* (June 26, 1961), p. 1. Source: *Extension Food Marketing Handbook.*

[14] Adapted from "General Buying Hints," Chapter 28, "Buying Food for Good Nutrition," *Introduction to Nutrition,* by Henrietta Fleck and Elizabeth D. Munves (New York: Macmillan, 1962), p. 491.

TABLE 6
How Much Fresh Vegetables to Buy at One Time*

One Pound as Purchased	Servings
Asparagus	3 to 4
Beets	3
Beet tops, mustard and turnip	3 to 4
Broccoli	4 to 5
Cabbage	5 to 6
Carrots	3 to 4
Eggplant	5 to 6
Kale	5 to 6
Lima beans in pod	2 to 3
Onions	2 to 3
Peas in pod	2 to 3
Potatoes	3 to 5
Spinach	4 to 5
Squash, Hubbard	2 to 3
Squash, summer	3 to 4
String beans	6
Turnips	3 to 4

* Henrietta Fleck and Elizabeth D. Munves, *ibid.*, pp. 492-493. (Order of items was changed.)

Cereals and Grain Products

Cereals, rice, flour, and macaroni, and bread, rolls, and other baked foods are made from grain. Wheat is the most widely used grain, but barley, corn, rye, oats, and rice are also important. Much of the outer shell is removed in

FIGURE 26. Attractive and tasty vegetables. *(Courtesy of The Wesson People.)*

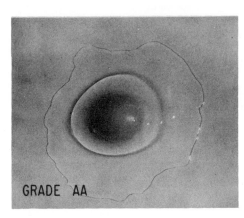
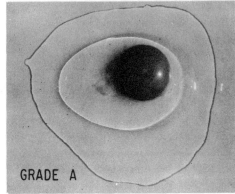

GRADE AA

GRADE A

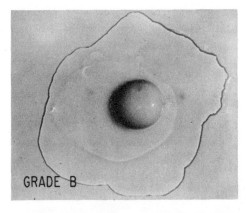
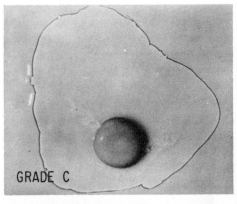

GRADE B

GRADE C

JUMBO	EXTRA LARGE	LARGE	MEDIUM	SMALL	PEEWEE
30 oz.	27 oz.	24 oz.	21 oz.	18 oz.	15 oz.

the milling and processing of grains, particularly in the preparation of white flours. These outer layers contain important nutrients which are frequently replaced through a process known as "enriching."

Enriched bread must have a specified amount of iron and three B vitamins, thiamine, riboflavin, and niacin. The addition of these nutrients does not change the flavor, color, or cooking quality of the food. But it makes the nutritive value of enriched white bread very similar to that of whole wheat bread. At present thirty states and Puerto Rico require enrichment of bread. New York State, for example, requires all-white bread, rolls, and buns, including French, Vienna and Italian, to be enriched.

CEREALS. Three types of cereals are on the market: (1) Instant, which are cooked, then canned or dried and packaged. These need only hot milk or hot water added to them. Many baby cereals are prepared in this way. (2) Cereals requiring cooking. There are both regular and quick-cooking

FIGURE 27. *(Facing page)* U.S. Department of Agriculture grades for shell eggs. *(Courtesy of USDA.)*

MARKS ON THE PACKAGE
The marks on the package show both the grade, or quality, of the egg and the size. Remember that quality and size are not related in any way. The USDA mark is in the form of a shield *(four typical examples shown, top row)*, which always shows the grade. It may also show the size. If the size is not included on the shield, this will appear near it on the package. The shield may be printed on the top of the carton, or it may appear on the paper tape sealing the carton. The name and address of the distributor or packer will also be shown, usually on the carton.

QUALITY
The differences in quality among eggs are seen in their spread when they are broken. (All the broken eggs shown are the same size.)
U.S. GRADE AA *(second row, left)* shows small spread, thick high white, and a firm, high yoke. This is the best egg to fry, poach, or cook in the shell.
U.S. GRADE A *(second row, right)* shows more spread than Grade AA, and less thick, high white. The yoke is firm and high. Good to fry, poach, or shell-cook.
U.S. GRADE B *(third row, left)* shows wide spread, little thick white, and rather flat, enlarged yoke. Fine for scrambling and general cooking.
U.S. GRADE C *(third row, right)* shows great spread, thin, watery white, and a flat, easily broken yoke. Good for scrambling and general cooking.

SIZE
Eggs are graded into six standard sizes *(bottom row)*. The minimum weights per dozen for these sizes are as follows:
JUMBO: 30 ounces per dozen. This size comes in out-size cartons.
EXTRA LARGE: 27 ounces per dozen.
LARGE: 24 ounces per dozen. This is the most common size, fine for a single serving.
MEDIUM: 21 ounces per dozen. Fine for general use.
SMALL: 18 ounces per dozen. Plentiful in late summer and fall; sometimes called "pullet eggs."
PEEWEE: 15 ounces per dozen. This size comes in special small cartons. A fine size for serving small children. The sizes that appear most often in retail stores are Large, Medium, and Small. Any size may be of any quality grade.

FIGURE 28. A wide variety of ready-to-eat breakfast cereals are available. *(Reproduced by permission from Consumer Bulletin, published by Consumers' Research, Washington, New Jersey.)*

forms. Quick-cooking cereals are partially precooked. The difference in cooking time between oatmeal that is precooked and the regular form is about twenty-five minutes. This difference may be important to a busy family. (3) Ready-to-eat cereals. These are light, dry cereals which need no preparation. Some are even packaged in individual foil-lined boxes which can be used as serving dishes. (See Figure 28.)

Generally, the more highly processed a cereal is, the more it costs per serving, and the less time it takes to prepare at home. The following is a comparison for a wheat cereal:

	Cost Per Family of Four	Preparation Time
Regular	.02	25 minutes
Quick-cooking	.06	10 minutes
Instant	.05	1 minute
Ready-to-eat	.10	0 minutes

RICE. Rice is prepared as a cereal and also used separately. The common forms of rice are white, brown, and converted. Wild rice is not really a rice, but the seed of a wild grass. It is darker in color and stronger in flavor than rice.

White rice is regular rice, polished after removal of the hulls and bran. Brown rice has only the hulls and outer coatings of bran removed. Converted rice is white rice that is specially processed to improve cooking qualities. The food value of brown rice is generally greater than that of white rice, but some white rice is enriched similarly to bread.

MACARONI PRODUCTS. These include macaroni, spaghetti, and noodles. Macaroni comes in a tubular shape, in the shape of shells and rings, and in a wide variety of other shapes. Spaghetti is a solid, rod-shaped product, available in several thicknesses, such as thin spaghetti or regular spaghetti, which is slightly thicker. Noodles are made flat, ribbon-shaped in various widths or in fancy shapes such as alphabets, shells, and bows. In the United States, egg noodles must contain 5.5 per cent of egg-yolk solids; in Canada, 4 per cent.

Good quality macaroni products are pale cream in color, hold their shape in cooking, have a delicate flavor, and do not cloud the cooking water.

Storage of Food

Careful storage of food is important to get the greatest value from your food dollar. Staples and canned goods require little care. A cool, dry place is most desirable for dry staples such as flour and sugar. Sealed jars or metal containers are good for cereal products that may attract insects.

Fresh fruits and vegetables deteriorate quickly; most of them have a limited storage life. Low temperature, about 40 degrees F., which is the desirable temperature for the refrigerator, prolongs their storage life. A few foods, such as potatoes and bananas, store better in a cool, dry place outside the refrigerator. Moisture helps most vegetables maintain their crispness, but excess moisture causes decay. Since carrots and green vegetables for salads wilt easily without moisture a covered container in the refrigerator is the best place to store them.

Frozen food deteriorates quickly unless maintained at 0 degree F. or lower. Stores try to transfer frozen foods quickly from the containers in which they are shipped to the storage case. The same care is needed in bringing frozen foods home from the store. It is often helpful to select frozen foods last in the market.

The Usefulness of Food Additives

Food additives date back to the time when man first tried to store food for periods of scarcity. Salt was used to preserve food in biblical times, and so, too, were spices. But the varied uses of modern food additives are new. Additives are substances other than those that occur naturally in food. They are usually chemicals used in crop production or added during food processing to preserve quality in getting food to market.

Some Common Food Additives

Perhaps it is easier to understand why additives are used if we examine some of their purposes.

NUTRIENT SUPPLEMENTS. These are vitamins and minerals added to food to improve its nutritive value. For example, Vitamin A is added to margarine and Vitamin D to milk. Thiamin, riboflavin, niacin (another B vitamin), and iron are added to "enriched" bread. Iodine added to salt makes it "iodized."

NONNUTRITIVE SWEETENERS. These are sugar substitutes for people who must restrict their intake of ordinary sugar because of diabetes or prefer to do so as a reducing aid. Saccharin and the calcium and sodium cyclamates are the most frequently used substitutes.

PRESERVATIVES. Preservatives are used to prevent spoilage and other undesirable chemical changes. The preservatives in fat are called antioxidants; those in bread are called mold or rope inhibitors or antimycotic agents. Additives to dairy products help to prevent changes that spoil the color, flavor, texture, or appearance of dairy foods. Some of the other common preservatives are benzoic acid, sugar, salt, and vinegar.

EMULSIFIERS. These help to improve the uniformity of volume, the fineness of grain, smoothness, homogeneity, and keeping quality of foods. Many baked products, ice creams, cake mixes, and frozen desserts contain emulsifiers.

STABILIZERS AND THICKENERS. These help to add smoothness and evenness as well as to thicken such foods as ice cream, candy, frozen desserts, chocolate milk, sweet beverages, and some fruit juices.

ACIDS, ALKALIS, BUFFERS, AND NEUTRALIZING AGENTS. These are important in many processed foods. Soft drinks are often flavored by the addition of an organic acid. The acidity of cream to be used for butter is controlled with organic acids.

OTHER TYPES OF ADDITIVES. Flavoring agents are added to bakery goods and ice cream. Bread is improved in color by the addition of oxidizing agents that whiten the flour and prevent caking, hardening, and drying.

Recent Changes in Laws Concerning Food Additives

Regulations covering food additives were part of the original federal Food, Drug and Cosmetic Act of 1906, and of the later one of 1938. Both Acts prohibited the sale of any food containing harmful ingredients. Under these laws the Food and Drug Administration had to prove an additive harmful before it could be removed from the market. Since 1938, so many new additives have been developed that it has been difficult for the Food and Drug Administration to keep up with checking on their safety before they were widely used.

A new law was passed in 1958, which took effect fully in 1960. This shifted the burden of proving food additives harmless from the FDA to the food processors and chemical manufacturers. Now food processors and chemical manufacturers must run extensive tests on new additives and have them approved by the Food and Drug Administration before the additive may be used. This new law better insures the safety of the American food supply.

Another problem arose when pesticidal residues remained on fresh fruits and vegetables. The Miller Amendment of 1954 established procedures for the setting of safe limits or tolerances for pesticidal residues remaining on fruits and vegetables. Registered tolerances are established that are small enough, so that there is little chance of harm from a cumulative effect because a large margin of safety is specified. Processed food can contain a specified amount which never exceeds the tolerance allowed on raw products. Some foods, such as milk, are not permitted to have any pesticidal residue.

A new concern has been added by our atomic age. Radioactive fallout can contaminate our food supply. Extensive study is now going on to watch its effects and control it.

Food Fads, Facts, and Fallacies

"Magical qualities have been attributed to certain foods since the earliest days of history. The early Greeks compelled criminals to eat garlic to purify themselves of the crimes they had committed."[15]

Food fads are usually short-lived ideas about certain foods or food combinations as the means to cure diseases or help an individual's health. Reducing diets are recurrent fads. Most of these rest on the use of one or only a few foods: grapefruit, yogurt, wheat germ, or others. Usually they have little to recommend them.

Fallacious information is also circulated about food to promote certain products. According to the Food and Drug Administration:

> Notwithstanding the abundance and quality of the American food supply, a persistent campaign is being carried on to undermine public confidence in the nutritional value of staple foods. False ideas about food are circulated by food faddists and by fringe promoters of vitamin and mineral products. Such products are sometimes offered as cure-alls for serious disease conditions. This may be dangerous to health, especially if ailing people are led to put off getting proper medical attention.[16]

Good nutrition is based on a balanced diet. Reducing usually means eating less food, but still eating a balanced diet. Modified diets for special situations should be prescribed by a qualified member of the medical team.

SELECTED REFERENCES

COFER, ELOISE, and FAITH CLARK. "Food Plans at Different Costs," *Food: The Yearbook of Agriculture.* Washington, D.C.: Government Printing Office, 1959.

[15] Henrietta Fleck and Elizabeth D. Munves, *ibid.*, p. 528.
[16] Food and Drug Administration, U.S. Department of Health, Education and Welfare, "Food Facts vs. Food Fallacies" (Washington, D.C.: Government Printing Office [n.d.]), p. 1.

Consumer Reports. "How to Save $200 a Year at the Supermarket" (February 1961), pp. 64–67.

DAWSON, ELSIE H. "When You Cook," *Food: The Yearbook of Agriculture.* Washington, D.C.: Government Printing Office, 1959.

FLECK, HENRIETTA, and ELIZABETH D. MUNVES. *Introduction to Nutrition.* New York: Macmillan, 1962.

LARRICK, GEORGE. "The Pure Food Law," *Food: The Yearbook of Agriculture.* Washington, D.C.: Government Printing Office, 1959.

LENNARTSON, ROY W. "What Grades Mean," *Food: The Yearbook of Agriculture.* Washington, D.C.: Government Printing Office, 1959.

LEVERTON, RUTH M. *Food Becomes You.* Ames, Iowa: Iowa State University Press, 1961.

MCLEAN, BETH BAILEY. "Planning Meals for the Family," *Food: The Yearbook of Agriculture.* Washington, D.C.: Government Printing Office, 1959.

PAGE, LOUISE, and ELOISE COFER. "Your Money's Worth," *Food: The Yearbook of Agriculture.* Washington, D.C.: Government Printing Office, 1959.

U.S. DEPARTMENT OF AGRICULTURE. *Essentials of an Adequate Diet.* Agriculture Information Bulletin No. 160. Washington, D.C.: Government Printing Office, 1956.

———. *Food Consumption of Households in the United States.* Household Food Consumption Survey 1955. Report No. 1. Washington, D.C.: Government Printing Office, 1955

———. *Food for Families with Young Children.* Home and Garden Bulletin No. 13. Washington, D.C.: Government Printing Office, 1960.

———. *A Fruit and Vegetable Buying Guide for Consumers.* Home and Garden Bulletin No. 21. Washington, D.C.: Government Printing Office. 1955.

———. *Home Care of Purchased Frozen Foods.* Home and Garden Bulletin No. 69. Washington, D.C.: Government Printing Office. 1960.

———. *Nutrition Up to Date, Up to You.* Reprinted from Home and Garden Bulletin No. 1. Washington, D.C.: Government Printing Office, 1955.

———. *Shopper's Guide to U.S. Grades for Foods.* Home and Garden Bulletin No. 58. Washington, D.C.: Government Printing Office, 1958.

U.S. DEPARTMENT OF HEALTH, EDUCATION AND WELFARE, CHILDREN'S BUREAU, *Nutrition and Healthy Growth.* Children's Bureau Publication No. 252. Washington, D.C.: Government Printing Office, 1955.

———. Food and Drug Administration. *Read the Label on Foods, Drugs, Devices, Cosmetics.* Miscellaneous Publication No. 3. Washington, D.C.: Government Printing Office, 1957.

WATT, BERNICE K., and HAZEL K. STIEBELING. "Keeping the Values in Food," *Today's Health,* Vol. 36, No. 48 (April 1958).

WAUGH, FREDERICK V., and KENNETH E. OGREN. "What Your Food Money Buys," *Food: The Yearbook of Agriculture.* Washington, D.C.: Government Printing Office, 1959.

6

FAMILY HOUSING

Naturally, many people who would like to have
better housing will not have the money to afford
it. Others will satisfy their desires by improving,
modernizing, or enlarging the houses they have.
Nevertheless, the findings about the widespread
desires for better housing and the strong under-
pinning of people's felt needs clearly indicate
that housing demand is not a function of income, interest rates, and household formation
alone.[1]

MANY PEOPLE dream of the day when they can afford
a comfortable house surrounded by grass and trees.
Still others want a spacious or luxurious apartment in
a metropolitan area. Families in the United States spend as much as one
fourth of their income on housing and close to one half of their time in
their homes.

Few people are satisfied with four walls and a roof for shelter; most people
want more. Frequently, the purchase of a home is influenced by aspirations
and desires rather than practical considerations. Attitudes about the style of
the desired house, the street on which to live, and the social life of a community evoke strong emotional feelings. People make housing decisions
in haste because of these feelings. If the decision is not a happy one, it is
difficult and expensive to change. The wise selection of a place to live usually
means a compromise that harmonizes important family needs and wishes with
the available funds.

Careful planning for housing is important to family happiness. A house
is also a home, a place for family living, relaxation, and self-expression. Many
families overestimate their ability to finance rental or purchase costs. The
consequence is a strain on the budget and everyone's disposition. Since
housing costs are such a substantial part of the family living expenses, careful
planning and management of them can contribute greatly to family satisfaction and stability.

[1] George Katona, *The Powerful Consumer* (New York: McGraw-Hill, 1960), p. 126.

FIGURE 29. A handsome new house. *(Ben Schnall, photographer.)*

The Stages of Family Life and Housing Needs

The desire for a particular size and type of housing is closely related to the situation of the family. When the family size is increasing, there is often a desire for more space inside and outside a home. When the family size is shrinking, where children are leaving home or going away to college, less space may be desired. If the expectation is for an increased income, people often feel lavish in selecting housing. Attitudes about income expectation are influenced by one's occupation and the forecast of the future of the local and national economy.

Living Alone

Each age and stage has its influence on housing. Many single people, both young and old, desire freedom and flexibility; they enjoy living without the effort and expenditure required to maintain a large home or apartment. Less responsibility for household upkeep leaves them with more time and money for career development, leisure activities, hobbies, or travel. A single room or a small apartment is often sufficient. Some share an apartment or house with one or more people in the same situation.

The Beginning Couple

The majority of newly married couples find that a small apartment or house can serve their needs until their pattern of living is clearly defined or the family grows. During the first few years of their marriage many young couples accumulate funds to provide for future housing and to buy household goods.

The First Child

There is a point at which the pattern of living changes dramatically for most young couples. The family's schedule revolves around the new baby, expenses are increased, and mother spends most of her time at home. Parents spend more evenings at home. The desire for household conveniences and outdoor play space frequently stimulates a reappraisal of the housing situation.

As more children come, there is an even greater desire for mechanical equipment to ease the daily routine of the household, plus room for indoor and outdoor play space and individual privacy. All of these factors stimulate the family's desire for more housing space, either a house of their own or a larger apartment.

The Schooling Years

Home living needs to be organized around the needs of the individual family. Families with working mothers and busy wives may desire an efficient arrangement of household space and equipment; others might want lots of play space and trees or proximity to a good high school. The location of the home in the community begins to assume great importance as the family's life and children's activites spill over into the neighborhood.

The Later Years

At the point where the children are becoming independent many parents begin to reduce their household work and develop other interests. As families' responsibilities decrease and family members leave home, less space is required and fewer things are needed. Older men and women, particularly those who are left alone, often adjust to smaller quarters that require less physical care. Frequently, housing on one level is desired.

How Much Housing Can You Afford?

Some families begin to look for a place to live without a plan or budget in mind. They may rent or buy a home with many attractive features only to discover later they can neither afford the living space nor does it fit their needs. Since most people's desires outrun their income, the problem of shopping for a satisfactory place to live requires a compromise of the important family needs and aspirations with the budget. The ultimate decision of where to live, how to live, and how much to spend should be based on a careful evaluation of what the family can afford to spend for housing. (See Figure 30.)

The housing market has boomed since World War II. New homes and suburban developments have mushroomed. Today there is a diversified selection of homes to choose from, both old and new, at many price levels.

The average buyer of a new home with an FHA mortgage in 1961 got a house costing about twice annual income, before deductions for federal income taxes, and took on monthly costs of about one-fifth of monthly income. That's based on annual income of $7,740, a home costing $15,184, and monthly housing expenses of $134.12—including mortgage payments, taxes, insurance, heating, utilities and maintenance.[2]

[2] *U.S. News and World Report* (May 21, 1962), p. 81.

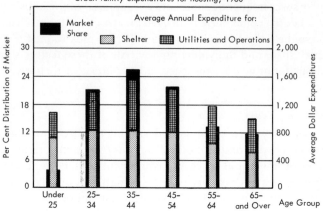

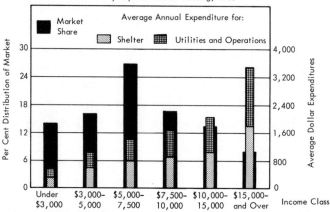

FIGURE 30. The market for houses. (*Reproduced from* A Graphic Guide to Consumer Markets, *1964, prepared by the National Industrial Conference Board under the sponsorship of* Life *magazine. Sources of data: U.S. Department of Labor and The Conference Board.*)

Buying a house means making long-term financial commitments that will take a substantial portion of the family income for many years. Formulas are given as guides to how much money one can afford to spend on a house. One formula is to pay no more than two and a half times the annual income for a house. Another is to spend one week's salary per month for rent or house payments. Still another is that one week's salary should be 1 per cent of the price of the house. These are not really useful because individual family circumstances differ greatly. A number of the factors influence what a family can afford.

Family Size

The number of children in a family can determine how much room they need. The big family will probably have to spend a larger part of their income for housing. The family with only one or two children may not need so much room. Therefore, they will not need to use so much of their income in this way.

Living Standards

The living standards of families vary greatly. One family spends a lot on a fancy car, another on recreation and travel. Still others want to save for special purposes and retirement. The proportion of income spent for housing varies at different income levels. In general, families with smaller incomes spend a larger proportion of their income for housing than those with larger incomes. Even a family with a comfortable income may find that they need to cut down on other enjoyable aspects of living if they spend a great deal on housing. If the children are close to college age, the family might not want to spend a large portion of their income on housing.

The Future Prospects

Formulas encourage people to decide on housing expenditures on the basis of present income, but true buying ability also depends on future prospects. A man who expects to retire in a few years on a sharply reduced income would be foolish to base his ability to buy a house on two and a half times his present income. However, a young man with fine training and good prospects might buy with hopes of a rising income.

A second income in the family is another consideration. If a wife works, should her income be counted as income in considering one's ability to pay?

One lender gives credit for half the wife's income if she is a professional and under 32. If she is over 32—and less likely to "retire" to motherhood—grants full credit. He gives no credit at all for incomes earned by a nonprofessional working wife under 32, half-credit if she is 32 to 38, and full credit if she is older.[3]

Family Savings

While the rules of how expensive a house one can afford are based on income, in actual practice an important consideration is the amount of money the family has saved for the down payment. With a larger down payment, families can afford a more expensive house than can those with the same income and little or no cash for a down payment.

Lending agencies that handle family mortgages are somewhat flexible in defining what a family can afford to carry; they usually attempt to analyze

[3] *Changing Times* (October 1958), p. 2.

the individual cases, considering other family financial commitments such as debts on cars, household furnishings, and personal obligations.

For most people house-buying ability is based on two factors: the amount of money available to make a down payment, and the amount they can borrow with a mortgage. The size of the mortgage it is possible to obtain depends primarily on how much income the family has that can be used as payment of principal and interest.

The Extra Costs of Owning a House

Home ownership brings expenses, in addition to the monthly mortgage payments. If the family has been living in a rented house, they may expect such things as fuel and utility bills; but if they have been in an apartment these costs may have been a part of the rent.

Utility companies can give a rough estimate of bills based on the size and type of house and heating equipment. They will also indicate what deposits are required in advance for gas, electric, and telephone service and what the fees are to turn these utilities on.

Estimates of maintenance are more difficult to determine. If the house is new, little repair may be needed inside; but the grounds may need new grass and shrubs. If it is old, painting, plumbing, and heating repairs may be needed. A figure that has been suggested is to allow 1 per cent of the cost of a new house and 2 per cent for an older house for yearly maintenance. Extras such as garbage collection, lawn repair, and painting are frequently 2½ to 8 per cent of the family income.[4] Other initial expenses are the costs of closing title and moving. The closing costs involved with the financing of a house may be as much as several hundred dollars. These may include adjustments for water bills or taxes that have been paid for part of the coming year by the seller, title insurance, and legal fees.

Moving costs vary with the amount to be moved and the distance involved. Since most young people move from smaller to larger quarters in buying a house, furnishings and equipment may also be needed. In moving from an apartment, there may also be expenses for garden tools and plants. Shower curtains, rugs, and trowels can add up to a considerable figure.

Last, there is the hidden cost of living in a neighborhood. The way of life and standard of living of a neighborhood influence one's own expenditures. This is particularly true if there are children in the family. As Morgan put it,

. . . When you select a place to live . . . You buy a neighborhood, a standard of living, and even a pattern of living unless you are extremely individualistic or have

[4] *Changing Times* (October 1958), p. 3.

no children. . . . The plight of a poor family whose daughter associates with girls who have wardrobes of cashmere sweaters is not a laughing matter.[5]

The choice of a particular home in a particular neighborhood has further financial implications. Few families live in isolation; neighbors, the community group, and the social activities of the area are an important part of family life. Many people feel compelled to spend money on house furnishings, the garden, personal clothing, and recreation to keep up with the standard of the neighbors or friends in the community. Thus, the decision to purchase a house often entails decisions about a way of life as well.

Shopping for Housing: The Range of Choices Available to Families

Fifty years ago American families had the choice of building, buying, or renting a house or an apartment. Today families can also live in a trailer or buy a cooperative apartment. A cooperative apartment house is one held by a group of people either as stockholders in a corporation in which title is vested or as beneficiaries under a trust agreement, with the title vested in the trustee. Generally, each of the stockholders occupies an apartment. When they wish to move they sell their shares to someone else who in turn will occupy the apartment. The owner of a cooperative apartment can deduct his share of the taxes on the property from his income tax as can a homeowner.

Although a few unions had built cooperative apartment houses for their members back in the 1930's, it was not until after World War II that cooperative housing really became common. A recent variation of cooperative apartments, the condominium, limits the liability of cooperative apartment owners.

Garden apartments with numbers of family units have mushroomed in suburban areas in the last fifteen years. The buildings are one to three stories high, and built around a grassy area. These have been fairly moderate in rent and particularly inviting to young families with small children. Most garden apartments provide public laundry facilities and playgrounds.

Trailer living has also grown in the last few years. A modern trailer contains all the comforts of a home in miniature, but the average cost of a new trailer is between $5,000 and $6,000, much less than most houses. Trailers may appeal to mobile families and older couples because they can be hauled from one part of the country to another more inexpensively than families can move from house to house. As a result many servicemen's families and workers in occupations that require frequent moves have bought trailers. Many army bases now have trailer parks on the post.

By 1960 trailers had become a large enough type of housing to be con-

[5] James N. Morgan, *Consumer Economics* (Englewood Cliffs, N.J.: Prentice-Hall, 1955), p. 234.

sidered as a separate category by the Census Bureau. "In 1950, . . . occupied trailers on wheels or on temporary foundations were identified. . . . In 1940, occupied trailers were combined with tents, boats, railroad cars, and shacks."[6] Los Angeles alone had 33,531 trailers in 1960. All but 641 were mobile, not on a permanent foundation.[7]

Large multifamily apartments have been built in urban areas where the land is so expensive that it is cheaper to build apartment units vertically rather than next to each other.

Home Ownership versus Renting

There are a number of advantages to home ownership. Most people feel a definite sense of belonging to a community. Home ownership can also convey a feeling of security to the family members. Such an intangible is very important in building constructive family life. For most families home ownership is a permanent type of life; it provides children with the opportunity for long-term associations with their schoolmates. Often families participate more freely in community activities when they own a home. They are more apt to feel they have a stake in the community.

The homeowner can change his house to meet his changing needs. For example, additions may be made if the family expands, or a play space for children may be provided in an unused area of the house. Homeowners tend to improve their living quarters more than do renters.

Financially, there are some real advantages to renting. There is a definite risk to the financial investment represented by the purchase of a home. In periods of decreased income the failure to meet a mortgage payment may jeopardize the family's entire investment in a house or property. Rental dwellings can be left without sacrificing an investment.

A renter often has fewer overhead or extra expenses. In many cases rents are based on competitive values rather than on maintenance costs. In some cities rent control laws which were initiated during the shortages of World War II are still in effect and keep rentals low. The landlord may have to repair or improve a rental property without the prospect of an adequate return. If it is cheaper to rent than to buy, renting may give the family an opportunity to save for more desirable housing facilities or for other family interests such as education or travel.

Renting also offers flexibility. If the husband's job takes the family to another location, or if the family is unsure of just where they wish to live, renting is wise. A renter is only obligated to payments for the period of a lease. At the end of the lease period the family is free to move.

[6] U.S. Dept. of Commerce, Bureau of the Census, *United States Census of Housing*, 1960, 1962, p. XXI.

[7] U.S. Dept. of Commerce, Bureau of the Census, *ibid.*, pp. 6, 40.

There is no responsibility and less work involved in renting an apartment. Older couples and single people especially enjoy this. Also, it is easier to be away for a week or a month. One doesn't need to check on the furnace, the plumbing, or shovel snow. Many people do not want the work and responsibility of a house.

Another advantage of renting is that if the community changes, it is easy to move. On the other hand, there may be severe economic loss in selling a house when a community is changing.

Facilities as Part of the Cost of Housing

The availability of public facilities in a community is an important thing to consider. For instance, is there nearby transportation? Is it inexpensive, convenient, and dependable? What school facilities are available for children? How good are the schools? Is a car necessary? Will you need a second car? Must one take a railroad or bus to work? Also, what is the distance and accessibility to shopping, recreational facilities, and houses of worship?

What type of services does the community provide—voluntary or paid police and fire protection? Insurance rates for homeowners are highest with volunteer protective services. Garbage collections sometimes require an extra charge. Is bus transportation needed to school? Does the community provide it, or does the homeowner pay for it?

Buying a New House

Once a family have decided what they want in a house and where they want to live and if they have the necessary money for a down payment, then the real job begins. Buying a new house has advantages; everything inside and out is clean and it has the latest modern equipment. One can often select the interior decoration as part of the purchase price. Generally, new houses cost less to heat than older houses of the same size because they are well insulated and compact. Also, maintenance may be low for the first few years. Many new houses are well designed for utilization of space; they include better closets, more attractive kitchens, and more usable yards. However, landscaping costs are often additional and surprisingly expensive. One may also encounter problems and expenses due to faulty construction.

Some facilities are provided in new housing; others are added later. If you are purchasing property where all utilities and services are not installed and services not completed, it is advisable to obtain written information on these and to check at the city or community planning office as to their specific plans. In some developments the builder undertakes to supply the streets and sidewalks; in others it is an obligation of the town and an assessment against the individual household.

If you are buying a new house, it is a good idea to check on the reputation of the builder and investigate whether the house was built in compliance

FIGURE 31. Shopping for a new house. (*Courtesy of Du Pont Company.*)

with the local building code. Is it possible to make additions to the house, or
are these limited by the building code? The income and tastes of families
living in the area are also important. In general, it is not wise to buy in an
area where the income level of the majority of families is considerably more
than your own. Community activities tend to operate at a level related to
the average family income in the community. The family that settles in a
community where the average income is much higher than their own may
be unable to participate in some of the community activities: the Saturday
round of golf, the women's bridge club, or parties for children.

It is also wise to look at the larger community. A house is usually purchased
on a lot; the combination should be harmonious with other houses and lots
in the area. This does not mean they must be duplicates but that they should
look well as part of a community.

A neighborhood can change because an industry develops on the out-
skirts of town or is planning to leave town. Are the types of industry nearby
likely to improve the community, detract from the community, or in other
ways adversely affect the value of the property? Buying a house rarely carries
a guarantee. Therefore, it is the responsibility of the purchaser to be sure he
is making a wise investment.

Looking for an Older House

Sometimes a family can get more space for their housing dollar by buying a used house rather than a new one. The older house may be more substantially built, the type of community established, the schools already built and paid for, and transportation and shopping facilities easily available. Also, an older house may have many improvements such as an extra bathroom or a fully landscaped garden. In any community there are usually a considerable number of used houses to choose from.

One important disadvantage of buying an older house is that it may require considerable work and expense for decorating, painting, and repairing. To determine whether an existing house is a good buy, it is necessary to obtain estimates of the renovation needed.

Renting a Dwelling

Renting a house or an apartment can be done either with a verbal or written agreement. This agreement is known as a lease. A written lease signed by both the landlord and the tenant is a legal document binding on both parties. Verbal understandings are less binding and more easily confused.

It is commonly accepted that it is wise to have certain things stated in the lease. Some of these are:

(a)   The length of the lease. Most written agreements are for a year or more.

(b)   The amount of the rent. Generally the rent is fixed for the period of the lease unless otherwise stated in the written agreement.

(c)   The amount of notice to be given to the landlord before moving or vacating the premises. However, this may vary; the lease can state that no notice automatically renews the lease or increases your rent.

(d)   The date the rent is due, and to whom it should be paid.

(e)   The nature of the payment for rent, such as a check or cash.

(f)   Whether a tenant can sublet the apartment if he must vacate. In some leases if an apartment is sublet, the original tenant must collect the rent and pay it to the landlord. Still other landlords prefer to offer a new lease to the new tenant. A new lease relieves the original tenant from any further financial obligations.

(g)   The amount of security or advanced payment that must be made. Sometimes a deposit of one or two months rent must be made until the expiration of the lease. The cost of repairing damages to the property may be taken from it.

(h)   Who maintains the property and makes normal repairs? This should include such things as decorating, plumbing repairs, and charges for utilities.

CHECKLIST FOR

In looking at either apartments or houses to rent or buy, there are both general and specific points to consider (such as those included in the checklist below) to help you decide whether the facilities will meet your requirements. Answers to many of the questions can be found through careful inspection, trying out equipment and plumbing, and by asking questions of the occupant, owner, or other person in charge. Questions of a technical nature to which you would like the answers may require the help of an expert. To use the checklist, make a check opposite each point that is adequate for your needs, omitting

Exterior

- Is the character of the community:
  to your liking?
  convenient for your activities? _____

- Is the style of the dwelling:
  attractive?
  in keeping with others in the area? _____

- Is exterior construction in good condition? _____

- Are major views pleasant? _____
  Is there sufficient:
  daylight?
  sunlight? _____

- If there is a yard, is it large enough for:
  a play area?
  outdoor living? _____
  a garden? _____

- If it is a house, is it located to take best advantage of:
  sun?
  wind? _____
  shade? _____

- Is property fenced in or enclosed with shrubs for children's safety? _____

- Are the dwellings far enough apart to provide the privacy you want on either side, as well as at the back of the house? _____

- Is yard landscaped, with lawn and shrubs in good condition? _____

- If there is a well instead of a public water system, are the following adequate:
  depth of well?
  quantity of water? _____
  flow of water? _____

- If there is a septic tank instead of a municipal sewer system, is it:
  adequate in size for your family? _____
  properly installed? _____

- Are there improvements on the lot, such as:
  sidewalks and streets?
  grading? _____
  utility connections? _____

- Are there parking facilities, such as:
  a garage or carport?
  24-hour parking on street or in an alley? _____

Entrance

- Are entrances well lighted? _____

- Is there a side or rear entrance for deliveries? _____

- Is there an outside entrance for fuel deliveries? _____

- Is the entrance to inside hallway kept locked? _____

- Are there locked mailboxes? _____

- Are there facilities for accepting packages when you are away? _____

- Are hallways and stairways well lighted and clean? _____

- Is there elevator service that eliminates climbing steps to the apartment? _____

- Are there adequate fire escapes? _____

Interior

- Are the following in good condition:
  windows and doors?
  floors, walls, and ceilings? _____
  roof and gutters? _____
  porches, including railings? _____
  steps? _____

- Is insulation adequate? _____

- Are walls and floors insulated against noise? _____

- Are electric outlets where you will need them for:
  lamps?
  radio and television? _____
  large appliances? _____
  small appliances? _____

Buying a Cooperative Apartment

Buying a cooperative apartment is a business venture. One enters into a partnership agreement with a group of people to purchase a large dwelling in which each family occupies one section. This type of venture has all the advantages and disadvantages of a business venture. For example, is each

RENTING OR BUYING

those which do not apply to the property at which you are looking. Then evaluate the importance to you of the points you have left unchecked. You probably will not find any one location that will measure up to your standards in all respects, but if the features most important to you are included, perhaps you can afford to overlook the less important items. Applying this checklist to each house or apartment in which you are interested may give you a basis for making an intelligent decision, and may save you from dissatisfaction and unnecessary expense later on.

- Is the current adequate for all purposes and appliances? _____

- If there is a basement, is it:

  well ventilated and dry? _____
  well lighted? _____
  without hazards, such as low beams, exposed pipes and wires? _____

Equipment

- If needed, are the following provided: for all windows:

  shades or blinds? _____
  storm windows? _____
  screens? _____

- Are the following adequate and in good condition:

  plumbing? _____
  heating unit? _____
  kitchen appliances? _____
  laundry appliances? _____
  water heater? _____
  Are all of the above operating satisfactorily? _____

- If needed, is there a place for storing:

  screens? _____
  storm windows and doors? _____
  outdoor furniture? _____
  garden and yard tools? _____

- Are there facilities for disposal garbage, such as:

  an incinerator? _____
  disposer in kitchen sink? _____
  city garbage collection? _____

- Is there telephone service? _____

  Must you have a telephone installed? _____

- May you have an outside aerial for television? _____

- Is there a charge for plugging into a common aerial? _____

Arrangement of space

- Can the rooms be adapted to your needs? _____

- Are rooms and wall spaces large enough for your furniture? _____

- Is amount and arrangement of work space in kitchen satisfactory? _____

- Is there space for laundry purposes? _____

- Is placement of bathroom convenient to all areas of house?

- Are closets, cabinets, shelves and all other storage spaces adequate for your needs? _____

- Are windows well placed for satisfactory ventilation in all rooms? _____

- If not, are there fans or an air conditioning system? _____

Responsibility for maintenance when renting

- Is the person responsible for upkeep and taking care of complaints easy to get in touch with? _____

- Is he:
  the owner? _____
  an agent? _____
  a representation of a management firm?

- What maintenance costs are included in the rent, such as for:

  electricity? _____
  gas? _____
  water? _____
  telephone? _____
  repairs and replacement? _____
  decorating? _____

- If needed:
  will the landlord make repairs? _____
  decorate completely before you move in? _____

- Is window washing taken care of by the management? _____

- Are you offered a written lease? _____

FIGURE 32. (*From Money Management,* Your Shelter Dollar, *copyright by Household Finance Corporation. Used with permission.*)

member of the cooperative group financially able to maintain his share? What is your responsibility if a member does not? Would it be necessary to increase your mortgage payment if someone else does not meet his payment? Will you have a share in saying how the building should be run? Is the property likely to increase in value, decrease in value, or at least maintain itself? Can you sell or lease your apartment or withdraw from the cooperative group if you wish to? Will you have any voice in the selection of new occupants?

The usual arrangement in cooperatives is that one pays an initial purchase price and then a monthly carrying charge. The purchase price is a per cent of the cost of the total building; the carrying charge is a per cent of the operating expenses.

Luxury cooperative apartments in major cities have increased in popularity since World War II. One of their great advantages is that each family can deduct some of the interest on the mortgage and some of the real estate tax from their federal income tax, just as if they owned a home. This involves a substantial amount of money for people in high income brackets and has helped to sell luxury cooperatives that cost from $10,000 up.

Moderate-cost cooperatives also have been growing. Often a family must pay a purchase price of only $400-$600 per room and a monthly carrying charge that is less than rent for similar apartments. Some of these are really cooperatives, completely owned and managed by the occupants. In others the occupant pays part of the building cost as a purchase price, but the project is really controlled by the builder.

Financing to Buy or Build a Home

Few families have sufficient money to buy a house outright. Most people make a down payment from savings and borrow against the value of the house for the rest. A loan with a house as security is called a mortgage. This is a legal contract between the borrower and a lender that outlines the conditions under which the money has been lent and the way in which it must be repaid. The term "homeowner" is used loosely to describe all persons having at least partial ownership of a house, but the amount of their share may be very little. In most cases the lender of the funds retains conditional title to the property until the mortgage loan is repaid. This means the lender retains the deed and the right to sell the house if the mortgage is not paid.

If one is planning to finance part of the purchase price of a house, it is wise to shop carefully for a mortgage. The amount of money borrowed, the period for which the money may be borrowed, and the rate of interest on the loan vary considerably in different parts of the country, at different times, and according to the credit rating of the individual or family who wish to borrow money. (See Figure 33.)

If a family does not have sufficient money for a down payment, they may resort to an additional or second mortgage. A family may wish to buy a house valued at $10,000. They have $2,000 in cash and can obtain a first mortgage for $6,000. This leaves a difference of $2,000, which may be financed by a second mortgage. Negotiating more than one mortgage or loan to purchase property is often a very difficult and unhappy venture. Both loans must be paid off at the same time from an income that has not been sufficient for the family to have accrued sizeable savings.

Where to Apply for a Mortgage

There are a variety of institutions that lend money for home purchases: savings and loan associations, life insurance companies, banks, trust companies, and special mortgage loan companies. One may apply directly to any of these financing agencies for a mortgage if he is not purchasing a new house from a builder with a prior mortgage commitment. Nowadays some builders arrange for mortgages for the houses they build through large commitments from lending institutions that cover a group of houses. The bank or institution in turn takes back individual mortgages. In this situation the purchaser then does not have to negotiate his own mortgage.

The amount of money a family can borrow for a mortgage, the length of time over which the money must be repaid, and the rate of interest on the mortgage loan may differ among lending institutions in a community. Mortgage terms also vary in different areas, at different periods, and according to the credit rating of the individual or family who wishes to do the borrowing. Therefore, it pays to shop around. Careful consideration should

MONTHLY PAYMENT TO PRINCIPAL, INTEREST AND MORTGAGE
INSURANCE PREMIUM AND TOTAL MONTHLY PAYMENT AT 5-1/2 PERCENT

Term of Loan	$10,000			$15,000			$20,000		
	Principal and Interest	Mortgage Insurance Premium*	Total Monthly Payment	Principal and Interest	Mortgage Insurance Premium*	Total Monthly Payment	Principal and Interest	Mortgage Insurance Premium*	Total Monthly Payment
20 years	$68.80	$4.11	$72.91	$103.20	$6.17	$109.37	$137.60	$8.23	$145.83
25 "	61.50	4.13	65.63	92.25	6.20	98.45	123.00	8.26	131.26
30 "	56.80	4.14	60.94	85.20	6.21	91.41	113.60	8.28	121.88
35 "	53.80	4.15	57.95	80.70	6.22	86.92	107.60	8.30	115.90
†40 "	51.60	4.15	55.75	77.40	6.23	83.63	103.20	8.31	111.51

TOTAL COST OF INTEREST AT 5-1/2% AND TOTAL MORTGAGE INSURANCE PREMIUMS

Term of Loan	$10,000 LOAN			$15,000 LOAN			$20,000 LOAN		
	Interest	Insurance Premium	Total Payment	Interest	Insurance Premium	Total Payment	Interest	Insurance Premium	Total Payment
20 years	$ 6,507	$ 592	$ 7,099	$ 9,761	$ 887	$10,648	$13,014	$1,184	$14,198
25 "	8,392	763	9,155	12,587	1,145	13,732	16,783	1,526	18,309
30 "	10,429	948	11,377	15,643	1,422	17,065	20,857	1,896	22,753
35 "	12,472	1,134	13,606	18,707	1,701	20,408	24,943	2,268	27,211
†40 "	14,728	1,339	16,067	22,092	2,008	24,100	29,456	2,678	32,134

Taxes and hazard insurance are added to the monthly payments, but not shown in these charts.
* Monthly premium during first year of loan at the rate of 1/2% per annum on average outstanding balance during year.
† Maximum mortgage term limited to 35 years except that the term may be increased to not more than 40 years when authorized by the Commissioner.

FIGURE 33. *(From Federal Housing Administration. Used with permission.)*

be given to the way interest charges are calculated and the extra expenses involved in obtaining the loan. The longer the duration of the mortgage, the larger the total amount of interest to be paid. Before settling on an agency to finance your mortgage, check on its reputation, and be very sure that it offers the least costly method of financing.

BANKS. Savings banks are one of the important sources for individual homes purchase mortgages. The percentage of a house's value that a bank may loan on private property is specified by state law, such as no more than 70 per cent on mortgages that are not insured by the FHA or Veteran's Administration. But these laws generally do not restrict the banks in appraising property. In a state where the home mortgage loans are limited to a small per cent of the value, some banks appraise property considerably higher than market value and thus can lend a larger proportion of the purchase price. In general, however, banks are quite conservative in their appraisals and loans.

SAVINGS AND LOAN ASSOCIATIONS. These are companies whose primary business is lending money for home building. In some large communities they are very active in home financing. They do not operate under the same restrictive laws as banks and therefore may lend on more liberal terms.

PRIVATE SOURCES OF MONEY. Private lenders are not as restricted as institutional lenders. In most states the laws pertaining to lending against property allow for higher interest rates than for personal loans. However, conservative private lenders generally follow the policy of larger institutions and lend only a fixed proportion of the valuation of property. When one borrows money from an individual lender, it is often difficult to rearrange terms or to extend the mortgage if an emergency arises.

Types of Mortgage Arrangements

Several methods of paying off a mortgage are possible. These are as follows:
PRINCIPAL DUE AT EXPIRATION OF MORTGAGE. At one time this was a common type of mortgage. The family paid only taxes and interest on the loan for the duration of the mortgage. On the due date of the mortgage the full amount of the loan was expected to be returned to the lender. However, during the devastating depression of the 1930's so many families lost their homes that this type of mortgage became less popular.

PARTIAL PAYMENT MORTGAGES. Since the 1930's partial-payment mortgages have been widely used. Today the most common type of mortgage is an amortized one—that is, each month regular payments are made on both the principal and interest. The payments are so arranged that at the conclusion of the period of the mortgage the entire principal has been paid back to the lender. Generally, this type of mortgage has fixed monthly payments. Under this type of fixed payment plan, during the first few years of the mortgage a high percentage of the monthly payment is for interest and a low percentage is for principal. Towards the conclusion of the mortgage period this ratio is reversed.

PACKAGE DEALS. Some mortgage contracts include in the monthly payments to the lender the cost of items other than principal and interest on the home loan; these additional items might be insurance on the building, life insurance on the borrower, state and local taxes, and the cost of mechanical equipment in the house. The package mortgage is a variation of the amortized mortgage; it permits the buyer to spread payments for equipment or other items over the period of time the mortgage runs. Many new developments sell houses with mortgages that include payments for refrigerators, stoves, and washing machines which in turn are included as part of the house.

OPEN-END MORTGAGES. An open-end mortgage clause permits the borrower to request additional funds, which are added to the unpaid balance of the mortgage. These additional funds are usually for the purpose of improving, repairing, or renovating the house. The additional amount borrowed is paid back with the regular monthly payments in one of two ways: by extending the period of the payments or by having an additional payment each month. There is usually no refinancing charge if the mortgage was originally written as open-end. For instance, a family purchases a house for $20,000 with an open-end mortgage. After a few years they find they need more room and want to add two more bedrooms. By this time the unpaid amount of their mortgage is $15,000 and has twenty years to go. They might borrow $5,000 in an open-end mortgage for the new addition, raising the amount of the unpaid balance again to $20,000 and increasing the duration of the mortgage to thirty years.

Types of Mortgage Loans

Various types of mortgage loans are made by banks. Often one institution will make several types of loans.

THE CONVENTIONAL MORTGAGE. The conventional mortgage is an arrangement between a borrower and a lending agency. There is no government insurance. The institution or individual lends funds to a borrower at whatever rate of interest is agreed upon for a stated period of time. The lender is not insured against default of payment by the borrower.

The duration of conventional loans usually does not exceed twenty-five years, or an amount in excess of 80 per cent of the appraised value of the property. The rate of interest for conventional loans has varied since 1945 from 4½ per cent to 7½ per cent.

FHA LOANS. These loans are insured by the government, but the government does not make the loan. The Federal Housing Administration insures the lending agency against loss if the borrower defaults. For this insurance, the borrower pays a monthly premium to the government of one-half of 1 per cent on the outstanding unpaid balance during the term of the loan. Private lending agencies, not the federal government, give FHA home loans. The FHA must appraise the house and approve the loan.

FHA regulations have changed several times in the last few years. The maximum rate of interest on FHA loans is 5¼ per cent plus one-half of 1 per cent insurance charge (1964). Loans may be made for up to thirty years. The largest FHA loan is $30,500 on a single family home. FHA loans are amortized loans, with the borrower having the privilege of prepayment.

There is also an FHA home improvement loan program. Families may borrow to make permanent improvements to their homes. Such loans are made by lending institutions and insured by the FHA. There is a maximum of thirty-six months for these loans, and they must be amortized. However, interest rates are not based directly on the unpaid balance. There is a fixed interest charge for the whole loan for the duration of the loan, although the unpaid balance is being reduced monthly. Thus the stated 5 per cent rate of interest is really a true interest rate on the unpaid balance of almost 9 per cent over the period of thirty-six months.

GI, OR VETERANS' LOANS. As part of the Servicemen's Readjustment Act of 1944 Congress included facilities for granting loans to veterans for home buying. A GI loan may be made to male or female veterans of World War II and veterans of the Korean War provided they served ninety days in active service and received an honorable discharge.

These loans are handled by private lending agencies, but are insured at no cost by the federal government. The Veterans Administration insures the loan without charge for up to 60 per cent of the maximum amount of $7,500 for any one veteran. Loans can be made for up to 100 per cent of the purchase price of property up to $12,500 if this is equal to or less than the appraisal by the Veterans Administration. If the property is priced higher than the valuation set by the Veterans Administration, then lending institutions are not permitted to lend any money under the GI Bill. The maximum interest rate (1964) for GI loans is 5¼ per cent, and loans on residential property may be for up to thirty years.

The Legal Mechanics of Mortgages

A real estate mortgage is a legal document in the form of a lien on land, buildings, or other permanent improvements of property. This is given as security by the borrower to the lender to insure repayment of the loan. The borrower gives conditional title of the real estate to the lender. This means that the lending institution would only get title to the property in the event of a foreclosure. The borrower also agrees to assume all obligations as owner of the real estate mortgage, to pay taxes and meet other obligations against the property, to maintain the property, and to meet any additional expenses, such as repairs, that may arise.

In the event of a default of payments, the borrower has further obligations which include paying the cost of the foreclosing. Many lenders also insist that a bond or personal note be signed by the borrower; so in a foreclosure, if the property value does not cover the outstanding debt, the borrower has an obligation to repay the difference.

A mortgage is cancelled by paying off the principal of the loan. At this time the borrower should receive a formal release certifying that the mortgage has been paid. The mortgage and the release are recorded in civil records. A marginal release is simply a statement written by the lender certifying that the mortgage has been repaid.

When property is purchased, a written agreement is usually made which is a legal contract of sale; it includes the purchase price, a complete description of the property, a description of anything extra included in the sale, an understanding as to who will pay the taxes and other charges accrued against the seller, the date the buyer will take possession of property, whether the seller will provide a clear title, the statement that the seller will give the deed to the property at the time of settlement, and any other agreements reached between the buyer and the seller regarding the equipment or personal property to be conveyed. A binding contract must state in writing the conditions and terms of the sale and be signed by both parties. It is always advisable to have a lawyer study the deed, draw up the contract of sale, and read the mortgage terms.

Many people purchase title insurance. This is a form of insurance that states that the title insurance company will pay the purchaser for any loss if anyone has a claim against the property before the new owner purchased it. Title insurance companies usually search legal records carefully before giving this type of insurance. Most title insurance is arranged for by a lawyer.

When contracting for a house purchase, the family might also consider purchasing mortgage insurance. This is really decreasing life insurance on the principal wage earner for the amount owed on the mortgage. If he dies the mortgage would be paid off, and the family would retain the house.

Taxes

Taxes are an important part of the cost of home ownership. The rate of taxes is determined by each community. They are computed on a specific rate of assessed valuation. The following terms that are used in discussing taxes are sometimes unclear to homeowners.

Tax—A compulsory payment for the support of a government.

Real estate—Land, including the buildings or improvements on it and its natural assets as minerals and water.

Real property tax—A tax on real estate.

Personal property tax—A tax on all property other than real estate. Personal property is sometimes called "movable" in contrast to real property which is immovable.

General property tax—Includes real property taxes and personal property taxes.

Assessment—A tax based on an estimated value of property usually for specific improvements such as sewers and sidewalks.

Tax rate—The specific amount of general property taxes per $1,000 assessed valuation to be paid in a given year.

Millage—A rate of taxation expressed in mills per dollar.

Method of Computing Taxes

Local assessors make up a list of taxable property in the area and place a value on the total property. The local and state governments divide their estimated budget requirements by the value of taxable property to determine the total tax rate. This tax rate is generally stated in terms of a certain amount for each $100 of assessed valuation; for instance, if the tax rate is $6.05 on a property assessed at $15,000, then the taxes are $907.50.

The following is an example of how the tax is computed on a house in a New Jersey community. The total tax levy for the community is $1,634,778.36; the total assessed value is $17,769,330.00.

$$\text{The rate of taxation or millage} = \frac{\text{tax levy}}{\text{assessed value}} = \frac{\$\,1,634,778.36}{\$17,769,330.00} = .092$$

The house is appraised according to the *Real Property Appraisal Manual for State of New Jersey.*

House value	= $12,127	Handbook value of house
Additions and Deductions	= $ 395	
Replacement cost as of 1954	= $11,732	
Conversion factor to 1962	1.19	
Replacement cost 1962	$13,961	
Effective age depreciation	17.5%	Determined from State Manual
Net condition of house	82.5%	

The building appraisal is made in the following manner:

(82.5%) × ($13,961) =	$11,517	(The value of land is determined
Property Appraisal	$ 3,000	by what land is selling for in the
Total Appraisal	$14,517	specific town. In this case it is
		about $40.00 a front foot value.
		Plot 75′ × 150′.)

Tax rate   20.6%   Average assessment ratio which
                                               is determined by a sales ratio
                                               study. Per cent of assessment in
                                               relation to market value.

Assessed Value = total appraisal times tax rate for the town.
    ($14,517) × (20.6%) = $2,990

Taxes to be paid by taxpayer = assessed value times millage.
    ($2,990) × (.092) = $275.08

Additional Information about Taxes

1. Tax rates alone are not a good basis to use in comparing the taxes of different localities because the assessed valuation may vary greatly from one community to another. Jonesville may have a tax rate of $2.20 per hundred but assess property at 100 per cent of the total appraisal value. On a $15,000 property at a rate of $2.20 the tax would be $330. Smithville may have a tax rate of $4.20 but assess property at 50 per cent of the total appraisal value. The tax on a $15,000 property, appraised at $7,500 and taxed at a rate of $4.20 tax rate would be $315.

2. Tax rates are determined annually. They reflect the cost of government changes up or down.

3. Tax rolls are open to inspection. A citizen may register a complaint against what he considers a too high evaluation of his property. In most areas he can appear before a local board of review.

4. Many buyers are inclined to underestimate the tax burden. Some economists[8] think that if the taxes exceed 3 per cent of the purchase price, the upkeep of the house is too high.

Useful Kinds of Insurance for Homeowners

Title insurance was discussed earlier in this chapter. Fire insurance provides reimbursement if a house is wholly or partially destroyed by fire. Most lenders who finance home mortgages require that one carry this type of insurance. It is wise to carry fire insurance on the full market value of the house so that in the event of a fire you will get what the damaged property was worth.

Liability insurance protects one against financial loss for injury to another person or the property of someone other than the insured. If a neighbor slips on the sidewalk, the homeowner is responsible in case of injury. How-

[8] Leland Gordon, *Economics for Consumers* (New York: American Book Co., 1961), p. 453.

ever, the neighbor must prove that his accident was the result of negligence on the part of the homeowner. The law imposes upon everyone the duty to use "due care" at all times to prevent injury to others. The failure to do this constitutes negligence.

If a workman is injured while painting a house, the owner is not responsible under normal circumstances if the work was being done by a contractor covered by workmen's compensation or other insurance. If the workman was not covered by insurance, then the employer is responsible for the costs of the injury. If a workman was hired without a contract, such as a friend painting the house on his day off, the homeowner is responsible for any injury.

A common type of household insurance is a comprehensive fire, theft, and personal liability policy. In addition to fire loss protection, this offers liability for bodily injury, illness, death, or property damages suffered on your property by a nonmember of your family. The cost of the policy varies with the specific terms. In 1964 one common type of policy on a house worth $20,000 in New Jersey cost $70.00 per year.

Moving to a New Home

Moving to a new house can be very costly. Some of the major expenses involved are:

1. Lawyer's fees, if you are buying a house. These vary from about $200 to $500.
2. Overlapping rent. Sometimes it is necessary to live in the old house while the new one is being painted, or perhaps the family cannot break their lease or sell their old house immediately.
3. Painting and redecorating the new home.
4. Moving costs. Rates for a local move, within one state and under one hundred miles, vary, In New Jersey they are $5.00 per hundred pounds.

Interstate moving rates are regulated by the Interstate Commerce Commission. Under ICC rates to move 1,000 pounds 100 miles would cost $58.50; to move 1,000 pounds 1,000 miles would be $120.50. However, in addition to these costs there may be charges for packing certain items, special handling for such things as a piano, and other extras. It is wise to get a written estimate of the total cost from several movers before contracting with one.

Cutting Shipping Costs

Some of the ways to save money when you are moving would be:

1. Get rid of everything you don't need.

2. Stock up on cartons and crates; many moving companies charge for these.

3. Take down your own draperies and roll your carpets.

4. Do your own packing. The basic rates for moving do not include packing.

(a) Wrap each glass and dish separately and stuff paper around each one. Pack the glasses with the drinking edge down, the dishes on edge, and the most fragile pieces towards the top.

(b) Books are usually cheaper to ship by parcel post at the special book rate.

(c) Pack records with pieces of cardboard between each one.

(d) Lampshades. Wrap in tissue (not newspaper).

How to Save Time, Money, and Annoyance in Moving

1. Be fully covered by insurance in writing. Insure belongings to their full value. (Some movers will not provide adequate insurance unless the movers do the packing.)

2. Don't overdo anything. Spread the planning and packing over a long period to avoid fatigue.

3. Go easy on your car. Don't turn it into a moving van. It's not built to carry bulky furniture. Use a trailer if you are carrying heavy items.

4. Use a tape measure. Before you move, you want to know where things will go and where they'll fit.

5. Tag everything. Mark the room where it goes. Mark cartons to show which end is up. Mark fragile things. Explain these markings to the moving men.

6. Protect your appliances. They may need special servicing before they can be moved. Consult local distributors or servicemen.

7. Tell movers what not to take. Put special tags on items that don't go with the mover.

8. Be there for the moving van. Delays in unloading may cost money. Record any damage on delivery receipt before you sign. Have money for payment ready; many movers will not unload until they are paid.

9. Let the cleaner help. On a local move, send suits, blankets, and rugs to cleaners if they need servicing and have him deliver them to the new address.

10. Know what your husband's business firm will pay. If your move is the result of transfer, check what expenses will be borne by the company. Many will pay for a few long-distance calls, a wife's advance scouting trip, the family's hotel bills while awaiting the van, and all packing and moving costs.

11. Tell the children early about the move and let them plan it.

12. Tell your neighbors and suppliers about your move in advance. Include the gas, electric, and water companies; bread, milk, egg, and other delivery services; the laundryman; the post office; all stores where you have

an account; the newspaper and magazine to which you subscribe; and the neighbors. Also, have school records transferred for your children.

13. Collect renewable prescriptions currently used by members of the family: eyeglasses, vitamins, and drugs. It will save you money if you have them on hand.

Our Changing Communities

In the early 1900's Americans moved from rural areas to cities. Now middle-class families are rapidly moving to the suburbs surrounding the metropolitan areas. The suburban population is growing at a much faster rate than that of central cities due both to the exodus of the population from cities and to the fact that the largest group leaving the cities is comprised of young families that are constantly expanding in size.

Some of the reasons for the middle-class migration from city to suburbs are:

1. The rise in number of American families. New family units need homes.

2. Prosperity. Families have been able to accumulate savings during recent years. With the accumulation of funds has come the desire to own a home. A house surrounded by grass and a friendly community are part of the modern American dream of good living.

3. The increasing difficulties of living in cities. Cities have become much more densely populated in the last few decades. They are difficult for private transportation; the schools have deteriorated; play facilities for children are poor; and the cost of living has increased sharply. Families are enticed to live in the suburbs where there is play and parking space.

4. The miracle of modern transportation. Fine highways and the wide-spread ownership of one and two cars have enabled people to travel from suburban homes to central cities for employment.

Many of these newer suburb areas are homogeneous in family income and age of the residents. William H. Whyte made a study of the suburbs for *Fortune* in which he discusses this homogeneity. From one community to another "the statistics varied little: average income, about $5,700; average husband's age, 31; children, one born and one on the way; politics, 68 per cent Republican."[9]

In many senses suburban communities are matriarchies, but the focus on

9 William H. Whyte, Jr., "The Consumer in the New Suburbia," *Consumer Behavior: The Dynamics of Consumer Reaction*, Consumer Behavior Series, Vol. I, (New York: New York U. P., 1955), p. 1.

children is so frequently great that in many cases one might say that community life revolves about them. Daily schedules and parental friendships are often outgrowths of children's activities.

As middle-income families moved out of central cities to the suburbs, they have been replaced in many northern cities by Negroes and Puerto Ricans. Of the total of 20,498,000 nonwhite individuals in the United States 72 per cent were urban residents in 1960.[10] "Negroes constitute 92 per cent of all nonwhites."[11]

Low-income families come to the cities with hopes of improving their living conditions and for better job opportunities.

"The census of 1960 showed the population of the five largest cities in the United States totaled about 17½ million . . . nearly one tenth of the entire population of the country."[12] Although four of these five cities had population decreases between 1950 and 1960, the decreases did not bring their size below the 1940 level.

Large cities have been faced with expanding low-income populations and deteriorating housing. Clearly, the people who needed better housing could not afford to pay for privately constructed housing. And so low-cost housing projects have been developed. These are financed with a combination of city, state, and/or federal aid. The rents are low and families must have below a certain income to qualify for admission. Many cities have tried to combine the construction of low-income housing with slum clearance projects. In some cities this has been done on a massive scale; whole neighborhoods of deteriorated housing have been demolished to make way for new modern projects.

Looking Ahead in Housing

The pleasant thought of good housing for everyone seems to be taking hold of our nation. In the last twenty-five years both rural and urban areas have greatly improved their housing. For middle-income families a detached suburban home has become a dream they can realize. However, large segments of our population have been neglected in the general prosperity, particularly subpopulations like the Negroes, Puerto Ricans, and Mexicans, and citizens over age 65. From present indications it appears unlikely that these groups will be able to provide adequate housing for themselves in the near future without government help.

[10] U.S. Dept. of Commerce, Bureau of the Census, *U.S. Census of Population 1960*, United States Summary, 1962, pp. 1-250.

[11] U.S. Dept. of Commerce, Bureau of the Census, *ibid.*, p. XII.

[12] Metropolitan life Insurance Company, "Population Profile of Our Largest Cities," *Statistical Bulletin*, XLII (November 1961), p. 2.

SELECTED REFERENCES

"Apartments Make Sense, Too," *Changing Times* (May 1962), pp. 17-19.
BEYER, GLENN H. *Housing: A Factual Analysis.* New York: Macmillan, 1962.
CHARLTON, MARY FOLSOM. "Effect of Pattern on Sense of Space," *Journal of Home Economics,* Vol. 53, No. 2 (1961), pp. 112-115.
"Different Way to Own an Apartment," *Changing Times* (October 1962), pp. 29-30.
LEWIS, DORA BURNS, and JEAN and ESTHER SEGNER. *Housing and Home Management.* New York: Macmillan, 1961.
LYNES, RUSSELL. *The Tastemakers.* New York: Grosset, 1954.
"Remodeling the House? Don't Get Stuck," *Changing Times* (June 1962), pp. 41-43.
ROGERS, KATE ELLEN. *The Modern House, U.S.A.* New York: Harper & Row, 1962.
WARREN, JEAN. "Income and Housing Expenditures," *Journal of Home Economics,* Vol. 53, No. 5 (1961), pp. 349-351.
WATKINS, A. M. *Building or Buying the High-Quality House at Lowest Cost.* Garden City, N.Y.: Doubleday, 1962.
WIESENDANGER, DELPHA. "Housing Research in Relation to Home Management," *Journal of Home Economics,* Vol. 48, No. 1 (1956), p. 25.
"Yes, Houses Can Cost Less," *Changing Times* (April 1962), pp. 31-34.

7
BUYING
FAMILY CLOTHING

Ever since primitive people began to adorn their naked bodies with colored clays, men and women have been occupying themselves more or less with the attaining, enhancing, and preserving of external beauty in themselves.[1]

CLOTHING does more than protect you from the elements. It is also a means of display, a source of pleasure and an indication of your taste, style, and social position. Although the time has passed when ermine and silk were reserved for those of noble rank, clothing is still a status symbol. The custom made suit and the Mainbocher dress have replaced ermine and silk as symbols of the upper class.

Clothing and grooming contribute significantly to our first impression of people. An attractive appearance is not only a social asset but a requirement for many jobs. Fortunately, today it is possible to be well dressed at many income levels. The stores abound with attractive clothing at various prices. Designers and manufacturers have developed attire to suit varied needs and activities. There are multipurpose garments for work and play, and specialized clothes for sports and parties.

The Revolution in Dress

The most dramatic change in the past thirty years has been the decreasing formality of American clothing, accompanied by a remarkable increase in the use of leisure clothing. This decrease in formality reflects other changes in family life. Not too many years ago most people worked at manual occupations that required heavy-duty working clothes, such as the farmer or factory worker wore. For leisure or festive occasions they "dressed up." Today greater numbers of people are employed in white-collar or semiskilled occupations for which they must be somewhat formally attired; but away from work they are more inclined to relax and dress casually.

[1] Grace Margaret Morton, *The Arts of Costume and Personal Appearance* (New York: Wiley, 1955), p. 1.

Impetus has been given to the trend toward casual dress by the trek to the suburbs. Suburban life is informal, casual, and family centered. The care of larger families and outdoor living and cooking are done more comfortably in low-heeled shoes, shirts without ties, and shorts or slacks. Easy washability and durability are important considerations in children's clothing. Many children up to age seven or eight wear polo shirts and blue jeans for play.

"The clothing needs, desires and demands of American families . . . have changed considerably from that of the days when clothing was either for dress or work, with somewhat worn-out representatives . . . serving as leisure clothing."[2] Today clothing may be purchased for a particular need: work or play or a combination of these uses. Leisure clothing is often new and attractive.

Fashions exist in clothing for the beach such as the cabana set (swim trunks and a matching shirt) for men, the short beach coat for women and, most recently, high-fashion bathing suits for pre-teen girls. One needs special shoes for bowling; skiing is done in stretch pants; and golf calls for a wide selection of special shorts, skirts, jackets, shoes, and even belts to hold tees.

Standards of Dress Vary

Acceptable standards of dress are not the same in all parts of the country. In the Northeast a white or light-colored shirt, tie, and suit are the usual attire for an office position; but in southern California, which may not be any hotter than New York or Washington, D.C., in the summer, a sports shirt and slacks may be worn.

Standards of acceptable dress also change over a period of years. At one time it was not considered good taste to wear a sleeveless dress in an office job.

Factors that Influence Clothing Buying

Income

Increased personal and family income has influenced the amount people can spend for clothing. The first half of the twentieth century has witnessed the rapid growth of per capita real income.

Available statistics indicate that, on the average, the after-tax income of each American, when adjusted for price changes, is now about 2½ times such income at the beginning of the century. In broad terms, this implies that the average person today, through his or her family's income, has command over 2½ times as much in goods or services as the average person 50 years ago.[3]

---

[2] Mildred Thurow Tate and Oris Glisson, *Family Clothing* (New York: Wiley, 1961), p. 10.
[3] Board of Governors of the Federal Reserve System, *Consumer Instalment Credit*, Part I, Vol. I (Washington, D.C.: Government Printing Office, 1957), p. 7.

As income rises, the number of garments purchased increases, and the amount spent for each also increases, a study by the Institute of Home Economics in 1956 showed. For instance, husbands with incomes of from $4,000 to $5,999 purchase 35 per cent more clothing each year than do husbands in families with incomes from $2,000 to $3,000. Not only did husbands in the higher income bracket purchase more articles of clothing, but they spent more than twice as much for clothing. The number of garments purchased by the wives did not increase as much from the lower income bracket to the higher, but the amount spent per garment increased more rapidly. The number of children's garments purchased, and the amount spent for each were less influenced by income than were adult purchases.[4]

The proportion of family income allocated to clothing expenditures in 1963 was 8.7 per cent of disposable income. This average lumps together the frugal and the extravagant, the dowdy and chic dressers, and both young and old. It is a reduction from 1947-49, when the average was 12.6 per cent.

It is interesting to compare how much families in various situations spend on clothing. The Department of Labor estimates that the amount needed to maintain a "modest but adequate" (not minimum) level of clothing for a city worker's family, consisting of a 38-year-old employed husband, a wife not employed outside the home, a 13-year-old boy, and an 8-year-old girl, is $558 per year.[5]

The Use of Consumer Credit

"The widespread use of consumer installment credit is a characteristic of recent decades."[6] Regular and revolving charge accounts of department stores and mail-order houses are one of the common methods of purchasing clothing. How much our present high clothing standards are due to credit and how much to prosperity is difficult to assess, but charge account purchases at holiday seasons such as Easter and Christmas indicate that many people buy more freely on credit.

Family Location and Occupation

The amount of clothing purchased and the amount paid for it depend to some extent on whether you live in the city or country. Farm families usually own smaller and less expensive wardrobes than do city families.[7] But they spend a larger proportion of their income on clothing than do city families. This difference is probably accounted for by two important factors: the larger

[4] Margaret L. Brew, Roxanne R. O'Leary, and Lucile C. Dean, *Family Clothing Inventories and Purchases*, Agricultural Information Bulletin No. 148, U.S. Dept. of Agriculture (Washington, D.C.: Government Printing Office, 1956), pp. 7–11.

[5] Bureau of Labor Statistics, *Monthly Labor Review*, August and November 1960.

[6] Board of Governors of the Federal Reserve System, *Consumer Instalment Credit*, Part I, Vol. I (Washington, D.C.: Government Printing Office, 1957), p. 7.

[7] Brew, and others, *op. cit.*

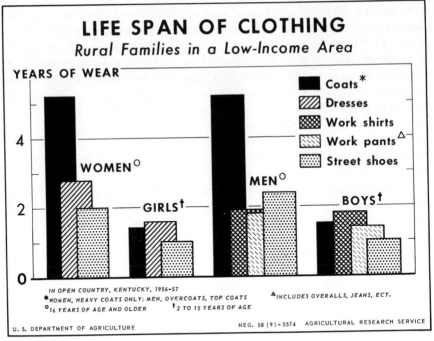

FIGURE 34. *(Courtesy of USDA.)*

size of farm families, and the smaller cash income of farmers. As farm family income has increased, however, and communication and transportation between urban and rural areas have improved, farm families have come closer to the clothing expenditures of city families.

Regional differences in clothing have diminished in this country, and to some extent over the world. Extensive traveling by car and plane, improved methods of communication, national magazines, movies and television, and national chain stores have helped to increase our homogeneity of clothing. Also, the increase in income in some sections of the country has enabled families who previously could not afford much to buy more clothing.

Geographic location naturally affects the type of clothing needed. People in the northern half of the country wear more wool clothing, which costs more than cotton and other lightweight fibers. The combined cost of clothing and upkeep for families in the South is less than in the North and West.[8]

[8] U.S. Dept. of Labor, Bureau of Labor Statistics for the Wharton School of Finance and Commerce, *Study of Consumer Expenditures, Incomes and Savings;* Vol. VI, *Summary of Family Expenditures for Clothing for Women and Girls,* and *Children under Two,* p. 161; Vol. VII, *Summary of Family Expenditures for Clothing for Men and Boys, Clothing Materials and Clothing Services,* 1957, p. 160.

The Family Life Cycle

Family expenses for clothing are greatly influenced by the stage of family life, and particularly by the number and ages of the children. As children get older, they usually need more clothing and more expensive items. The figures from the Community Council of Greater New York (see Table 7) are minimum figures for a New York City family which illustrate how clothing expenditures for children increase with age.

TABLE 7
Clothing Costs for Children*

Age		Annual Cost
Child:	infant	$ 36.40
	1–3	70.20
	4–6	83.20
	7–9	109.20
Girl:	10–12	114.40
	13–15	130.00
	16–20	145.60
Boy:	10–13	119.60
	13–15	137.80
	16–20	158.60

*The Community Council of Greater New York, *Annual Price Survey and Budget Cost, 1962* (New York: Community Council of Greater New York, 1963).

Older, retired couples can usually spend less for clothing. The Bureau of Labor Statistics estimates of clothing needs for a retired couple who participate normally in the life of the community ranges from $197 in Houston to $233 in Cleveland.[9]

Personal Values

Personal philosophies about the importance of clothing, which are derived from one's own experience will greatly influence how money is spent for clothing. Some people feel that clothing is merely a necessity, others that clothing is a means of enhancing their personality.

Being attractive raises a woman's opinion of herself—looking her best makes her feel good and more self-assured.

Others' opinions and attentions are also responsible in part for a woman's concern with her own looks. Being attractive helps a woman in most social situations. It may open doors for her; it may make social contacts easier. Also, a woman

[9] *Statistical Abstract of the United States, 1962* (Washington, D.C.: Government Printing Office), p. 351.

likes to have other women admire her—perhaps even envy her. And very impor-
tantly she wants to be attractive to men.[10]

Many of the same values that influence women's clothing expenditures also
operate with men—the desire to be attractive to others and the realization that
clothing is an asset in social and business situations. The desire to be attractive
to others often leads teen-agers into some bizarre clothing fads.

Societal Values

The pages of history have often reflected the relationship between clothes
and social values. The court of Louis XV indulged in frivolous, fantastic styles;
the Jacobites of the French Revolution were severe in the simplicity of their
clothing. In the United States, the dress of the ladies of Southern plantation
manors prior to the Civil War was that of an ostentatious and wealthy leisure
class. Women's clothing in the 1920's was designed to make it easier for
women to work and move about, an indication of the philosophy of the times.

Social and Psychological Needs

To be part of the group means conforming in clothes as well as in social
activities. "Clothing frequently is important as a means toward acceptance by
the group."[11] In applying for a job or meeting a social group, clothing can
create a favorable or unfavorable impression. It is often stated that looking
successful is the first step toward being successful.

Attractive and appropriate clothing helps one to be accepted by the community. The children's clothes at school and parties, Mother's dress at the
P.T.A. and the supermarket, the whole family's impression at its house of
worship—these can help the family to be comfortable in the community.
Generally, good taste in accordance with group standards and simplicity are
acceptable. Extreme clothes are envied and admired by only a limited circle.

Clothing is often associated with behavior. Girls in shorts and slacks lounge
about more casually than in a dress. Some delinquent teen-agers have certain
styles of dress. As part of a campaign to improve teen-age behavior, many
high schools now have standards of dress—no sneakers, no blue jeans, no
black leather motorcycle jackets, and no men's shirts worn outside.

The individual's and the family's attitude toward clothing expenditures will
also be influenced by the value they place on the need to conform, to be
comfortable, to express themselves through clothing, and to participate in
social activities.

Looking Your Best

Most people are interested in how they look. Just stand in a busy place where
there is a mirror and notice how many people look at themselves. Generally,

---

[10] Janet L. Wolff, *What Makes Women Buy* (New York: McGraw-Hill, 1958), p. 166.
[11] Mildred Thurow Tate and Oris Glisson, *Family Clothing* (New York: Wiley, 1961), p. 22.

people want becoming clothes suited to their way of life and at a price they can afford. An ideal wardrobe need not be large, but it should include becoming clothes for the usual occasions in your life. Some people need a dress for a formal party; others culottes for bowling, white shorts for tennis, or slacks for gardening. To be attractively dressed at a modest expense requires knowing how to: (a) plan a wardrobe, (b) develop skill in selecting becoming clothes, (c) judge quality and construction in buying or making clothing, and (d) care for clothing.

Wardrobe Planning

The basis of a good small wardrobe is a balanced plan, one which includes an adequate variety and number of clothes for the varied activities in your life. Some people accumulate an excess of party clothes and not enough for everyday use. Others never have the right clothes for parties and business occasions.

People's needs differ. The suburban housewife who lives in casual clothing needs a different wardrobe from that of the urban working woman or the college student. The business executive who attends many formal affairs and travels frequently needs different clothing than does the small shopkeeper. Even within the same job category, clothing requirements may vary. The salesgirl in a beach community may wear more casual clothes than one in a city store.

If you are planning clothing purchases for a family, think through the needs of each member. How do they spend most of their time, at work, in school, or at home? What are their social activities? What kind of clothing is suitable for these situations? How many changes are needed? The climate, the neighborhood, where one goes to work and play, and with whom—all will influence clothing needs.

TAKE INVENTORY. The first step in planning a wardrobe is to take inventory of what is on hand. This is similar to the planning procedure in business; existing inventory is evaluated before new orders are placed.

A good procedure is to separate clothing into three groups: those things that are wearable as is; those things that need fixing, cleaning, or alterations; and those that are no longer wearable. Try on anything about which there is a doubt.

Then make a list of what each person owns. Group it under headings such as suits, jackets, slacks, coats, and so on. Another way to make this list is to group clothing as outfits.

The next step is to evaluate your present stock of good, usable clothing. What is needed so that you will have attractive outfits? A red hat is not very useful unless it looks well with your dress, suit, or coat. A print blouse needs to be worn with a plain skirt of a harmonizing color and fabric. Perhaps some of the things you have not worn recently might form the basis for a new outfit.

Consider whether clothing you already own can be used for more than one purpose. Perhaps the white tennis shirt can also be used for gym. The gray spring coat could be waterproofed to also serve as a raincoat.

BUILD A BASIC WARDROBE. Stretching the clothing dollar becomes more possible if each member of the family plans his clothing around a basic wardrobe. A man might select all his clothes to go with brown shoes and a brown tweed topcoat. A woman might plan her wardrobe to go with navy accessories, navy shoes, gloves, and handbag. By planning everything to go with one or two basic colors, the need for duplicating accessories is reduced and more of the clothing dollar is available for other uses.

A basic wardrobe not only utilizes a central harmonizing color scheme, but the clothes themselves are versatile. The coat is simple enough to be worn for both dressy and everyday occasions. This rules out elaborate collars and buttons or very rough, tweedy fabrics. A dark or neutral color of a durable fabric with little design will serve many purposes.

Uncluttered styles with few trimmings or drapings are most adaptable. A plain wool dress can have accessories for a football game or an informal dance. A man's single-breasted suit in a solid dark material can be worn to the office or to a party.

If clothing is to be worn for more than one season, it needs to be of a quality that will last. Both fabric and construction are important. By stretching the life of garments, costs can be cut. A winter coat that costs thirty dollars and is worn for three years costs only ten dollars per year. If it lasts only two years, the cost is fifteen dollars per year.

Two-piece outfits and coordinates lend themselves to many variations. A few clothes can look like a larger wardrobe by changing blouses and skirts. Men can achieve the same versatility with sports jackets and slacks. Ease of upkeep is also important in building the basic wardrobe. This does not mean that everything must be extremely dark in color, but it does mean that city clothing should not be so light in color that it needs to be cleaned after each wearing. Fabrics with a slight texture or design reduce the appearance of soiling.

Table 8 indicates what a group of social agencies considered minimum annual clothing purchases for women in three different situations; Table 9, for an employed man and an elderly retired man. (A fraction indicates that the item is purchased less frequently than once every year—that is, ⅓ means purchased every third year.)

PLAN YOUR SPENDING. Estimate clothing needs for the next year. (See the chart below.) If possible, also list the big items you would like to add during the next three years. Group the items for the next year under the month when they will probably be needed. Put down the approximate cost of the garment. Underline the things which are absolute necessities, such as new underwear or a winter coat for a youngster.

Total the estimated costs for each person. Does the total fit into the amount allocated for clothing? If not, changes will need to be made. Some things will have to be eliminated, or deferred. Perhaps an old garment can be altered or

WHAT'S NEEDED

MOM											
Sept.	*Oct.*	*Nov.*	*Dec.*	*Jan.*	*Feb.*	*March*	*Apr.*	*May*	*June*	*July*	*Aug.*
Slip $4.00	Coat $35.00	Stock-ings $3.00				Suit $25.00		2 blouses $8.00			
Dress $10.00											
Shoes $8.00						Hat $ 5.00					

remodeled. Maybe the skirt of an old suit can be used with a new blouse instead of buying another dress. Study the newspaper advertisements. Perhaps some things can be purchased less expensively than you had planned.

If you are making a family plan, consider whether each person has a fair allotment of money for his needs. The growing adolescent boy may need a whole new wardrobe because nothing fits, but his sister who has not changed in size may be able to manage with fewer new things.

Allow some leeway for emergency expenditures—the boots that tear, the extra pair of gloves to replace those which were lost, or possibly more clothing for a rapidly growing youngster.

Try to space the big family expenditures so that several do not fall in one month.

Keep expenditures for clothing within the range you had planned. Do not get carried away in the store by something that is very nice but far beyond your budget.

Compare values at several stores. Clothing is often offered at different prices in competing stores. Sidney Margolius, the well-known author who writes on consumer problems, has this to say:

> Men's clothing is an area in which definite savings are possible. I have seen Dacron-and-cotton shirts of much the same quality at one store for $5, at a store down the street for $3.95, and a few weeks later at a sale for $2.70. I have seen exactly the same raincoat at a men's shop for $22 and at a self-service store for $18. I have seen a man pay $50 for a coat and two days later walk past the same store and see it on sale for $40.[12]

Shop ahead of actual need where possible. Planning clothing purchases on a long-range basis permits buying without the pressure to get something immediately, so that there is time to do comparison shopping, to study values at sales, and to consider alternatives carefully. A new winter coat for an adult

[12] Sidney Margolius, *The Consumers Guide to Better Buying* (New York: Pocket Books, 1963), p. 114.

TABLE 8
Average Number of Clothing Purchases for Women Per Year*

Item	Employed Woman	Housewife	Elderly Woman
Outer Garments			
Hat	2	1	1
Coat (winter) "dressy"	1/4	—	—
(winter) casual	1/4	1/4	1/7
(spring)	1/4	1/4	1/4
Raincoat	1/2	—	—
Suit, wool	1/2	1/3	1/4
Sweater	1/3	2/3	1/5
Dress—wool, casual	1/2	1/3	1/3
rayon, "dressy"	1	—	1
rayon, casual	2	1	—
cotton, casual	2	1	1
housedress	—	1	1
Skirt, wool	1	3/4	1/5
Blouse	3	3/2	1/3
Slacks	—	1/4	—
Underwear			
Panties	4	4/3	3/4
Brassieres	3	2	1/2
Girdle	3	1	1/4
Slips, nylon tricot	3/2	1/2	1/2
cotton	1/2	1	1
Sleeping garments	2	2/3	1/3
Bathrobe	1/2	1/4	1/4
Footwear			
Shoes, oxford	3	3/4	2/3
casual	1/2	3/4	—
pump	1	1	2/3
Slippers	1/2	1/2	1/3
Galoshes or boots	1/3	1/5	1/5
Anklets	2	1	—
Stockings—nylon	18	11	6
Accessories: Per cent of yearly replacement cost of above items	10%	15%	15%
Dry Cleaning			
Coats	4	2	2
Suits	2	1	1
Dresses	4	2	3
Skirts	2	1	1
Shoe Repairs			
Half soles and heels	3	1	1/2
Lifts	6	5	2

*Budget Standard Service, Research Department, Community Council of Greater New York, *A Family Budget Standard* (New York: Community Council of Greater New York, 1963), p. 26.

TABLE 9
Average Number of Clothing Purchases for Men Per Year*

Item	Employed Man	Elderly Man, Retired
Outer Garments		
Hat, fur felt	1/2	1
Topcoat, wool	1/5	1/10
water repellent	—	1/10
Jacket, winter	—	1/14
Suit, wool, 2-piece	1/2	1/3
Sport jacket	1/10	1/7
Sweater	1/4	1/4
Slacks—wool	1/2	1/2
rayon	1	—
cotton	—	1
Dungarees	1	—
Shirts, dress	7/2	5/2
sport, knit	3/2	1
Underwear		
Shirts, T	3	2
Shorts	4	3/2
Pajamas	1/2	1/5
Bathrobe	1/10	1/10
Footwear		
Shoes	2	1/2
Slippers	1/4	1/4
Rubbers	1/4	1/10
Socks	12	4
Accessories: Per cent of yearly replacement cost of above items	15%	15%
Dry Cleaning		
Hat	1/2	1/2
Coat (overcoat, topcoat or raincoat)	1	2
Jacket, winter	1	1
Suit	3	2
Sport jacket	1	1
Slacks	3	2
Shoe Repairs		
Half soles and heels	2	1/2
Lifts, rubber	2	1

*Budget Standard Service, Research Department, Community Council of Greater New York, *A Family Budget Standard* (New York: Community Council of Greater New York, 1963), p. 26.

can often be found at half price in January or February, and spring clothes are on sale just after Easter. While it is very economical for adults to buy ahead of the season, it is not wise to buy ahead for growing youngsters because of the rapidity with which they change size.

BECOME A SKILLFUL SHOPPER. Learn to select garments that fit into your clothing plan and go with the major items in your present wardrobe. Do not develop "bargain fever." Nothing is a bargain unless it is right for your needs. The stunning dress or the good-looking sports shirt is not a good buy, even on sale, if it does not go with your other clothes or your way of life. Nor is it a bargain if the price is more than you had planned to spend. A couturier dress at a sale may cost much more than a medium-priced dress at its regular price.

Medium-priced clothing usually offers good value. Very expensive clothing often has high-fashion styling which is quickly dated. Usually it is priced high because only a small number are manufactured. Cheap clothing is apt to be flimsy and poorly made. The medium-price lines tend to combine good materials and workmanship with a moderate version of current fashions.

Look for store brands of standard items. Shirts, blouses, underwear, and socks are often sold under more than one brand name. Department stores and mail-order houses that sell under proprietary labels (their own special brand name) can usually buy these articles in such large quantities that they under-sell more widely advertised brands.

Buy for cash or on a 30-day charge account. Credit charges add appreciably to the cost of a garment. Most revolving credit plans cost at least 18 per cent per year. Also, the habit of buying on credit tends to discourage comparison shopping at competing stores and often makes it easy to buy more than one can afford. (For further discussion of credit see Chapter 4, "Financing Family Spending.")

Buy the correct size. This is absolutely essential if clothing is to look well and feel comfortable. The most satisfactory way to be sure of proper fit is to try on the garment. (Allow for shrinkage in the washer and dryer for some items.) If this is not possible, keep a list of sizes for yourself and other family members. Buy where clothing items can be returned if they do not fit well, because the sizes on the label are not always the same in all stores and makes. For mail-order purchasing or the selection of a pattern, take measurements according to the directions in the catalogue or pattern book. Buy the size that is closest to the measurements.

Selecting Becoming Clothes

If a dozen alert, intelligent, young women were asked to express frankly what they most desire in appearance, their replies would most probably be alike: "I should like to have style; to have individuality; to be considered smart."[13]

---

[13] Grace Margaret Morton, *The Arts of Costume and Personal Appearance* (New York: Wiley, 1955), p. 1.

Style is an elusive quality that sets the well-dressed person off from the rest of the crowd. Part of being stylish is to wear the right clothes for the right occasions. Another part lies in simplicity—clothes that enhance the appearance of the wearer but do not draw attention away from the person. Good fit and workmanship make the clothes look as if they belong to the individual. Lastly, there is the personal touch, the certain little extra that makes clothing expressive of the individual's personality. Perhaps it is the smart tie or the distinctive way of wearing a scarf.

Analyze your figure and coloring. Color, line, texture, and style can be used to enhance good points and minimize less desirable ones. To look slimmer and taller, wear cool, dull, dark one color outfits, vertical lines, dull-finished fabrics, fairly smooth but not shiny weaves, and small scale fabric designs. Contrasting colors in shirts and pants or blouses and skirts cut apparent height and make an individual look heavier.

To look shorter or less angular, full skirts and sleeves, contrasting colors, shiny or lustrous fabrics, bulky textures, and rather large scale plaids are effective.

CHOICE OF A FABRIC. Selecting clothing materials is no longer a simple job of choosing between a cotton and a rayon blouse. The wide variety of fibers, blends, weaves, knits and finishes of fabrics offers the opportunity to select the ones that are best for a specific purpose or use. Decide what you need in a fabric when buying clothing and materials. Perhaps you want a shirt that needs little ironing or a dress that will retain the shiny, crisp finish. Generally, tightly woven, firm fabrics wear best and require the least pressing.

Read the label to learn about fabric and finish. (See Figure 35). New fabrics abound, and old ones are being given new finishes to change their properties. Staples like cotton and wool are being combined with man-made fibers. Some wool is treated so that it does not shrink in the washing machine, and cotton is often woven with polyesters such as "Dacron" to reduce wrinkling.

In the United States, under the Textile Fiber Products Act and the Wool Products Labeling Act, all fabrics must be labeled with the generic name (acrylic, acetate) and the percentage, by weight, of each fiber if it exceeds 5 per cent of the total. In Canada, labeling is optional, but if it is used it must give the name of the fibers in decreasing order of the amount present (by weight).

Check to see if the fabric is labeled to indicate whether it is color-fast and preshrunk. "Vat-dyed" cotton, linens, and rayons are most color-fast to washing, cleaning, bleaching, sunlight, perspiration, and rubbing off (crocking). Washable fabrics should be labeled as to shrinkage: less than 1 per cent is most desirable. Some trade names, such as "Sanforized," also indicate that the fabric is preshrunk.

Frequently, information about the care of the fabric is given on a label. Nevertheless, terms such as "drip-dry" or "wash and wear" are not always reliable guides to fabric care. Information is often given about whether the fabric should be washed by hand, put in the washing machine, or dry-cleaned.

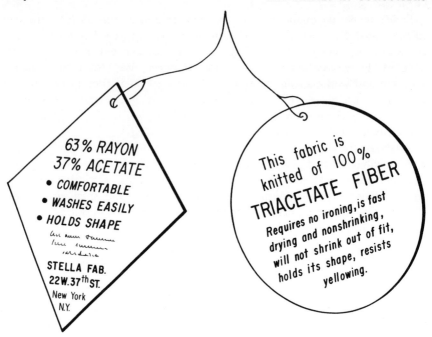

FIGURE 35. The labels on clothing often furnish useful information about how to care for the garment, in addition to telling the generic name of the fiber or fibers.

Satisfaction with a purchase often depends on giving it the right care for the fabric and finish.

EVALUATING WORKMANSHIP. Recognizing good workmanship will help you judge the quality of ready-made clothing. The cut and construction of a garment affect its appearance, fit, and wearing qualities.

Both the visible and invisible qualities of workmanship have an influence on a garment's appearance, as does the quality of materials used in construction, between the outer cloth and the lining. The following pictures show the construction of three qualities of men's suits:

Indications of Good Workmanship

1. The machine stitching is small, even, straight, and secure. Thread should match the garment in color.

2. The design is carefully matched, particularly at the armholes, center front and back seams, pockets and collars.

3. Buttonholes are smooth, flat, and do not ravel. The buttons should fit through easily and without strain.

4. In most cases the principal parts of the garment should be cut "on grain" —that is, the lengthwise thread of the fabric should be perpendicular to the floor.

5. Garments intended for rough usage should be sturdily constructed and reinforced.

Clothing Care

The proper care of clothing will enable garments to look their best and last longer. These are just a few suggestions to extend clothing life.

1. Air clothing immediately after use.
2. Put clothes on hangers, with the shoulders in place and fasteners closed, immediately after wearing.
3. Mend garments promptly and carefully.
4. Launder and clean clothes before they are very dirty.
5. Wear a raincoat and boots to protect clothing in wet weather.
6. Protect out-of-season clothing against moth damage and mildew.

An attractive wardrobe doesn't just happen; it takes time, thought, and continuous care to have becoming and appropriate clothing clean and ready to wear for many different occasions. Wardrobe planning and selection takes effort but pays dividends in making you feel confident that you are well dressed, and within your budget.

SELECTED REFERENCES

ANSPACH, KARLYNE. "Clothing Selection and the Mobility Concept," *Journal of Home Economics,* Vol. 53, No. 6 (June 1961), pp. 428–430.

COWAN, MARY L. *Introduction to Textiles.* New York: Appleton-Century-Crofts, 1962.

EBELING, MALSA, and MARY LOU ROSENCRANZ. "Social and Personal Aspects of Clothing for Older Women," *Journal of Home Economics,* Vol. 53, No. 6 (June 1961), pp. 464-465.

FITZSIMMONS, CLEO. "Buying Clothing," Chap. 12, *Consumer Buying.* New York: Wiley, 1961.

GORDON, LELAND J. "Fashion Made Wants," Chap. 8, *Economics for Consumers.* New York: American Book Co., 1961.

HAWES, ELIZABETH. *It's Still Spinach.* Boston: Little, Brown, 1954.

LINTON, RALPH. "Concepts of Role and Status," *Readings in Social Psychology,* eds. Swanson, Newcomb, and Hartley. New York: Holt, Rinehart & Winston, 1952, pp. 263–266.

MORTON, GRACE MARGARET. *The Arts of Costume and Personal Appearance.* New York: Wiley, 1955.

PACKARD, VANCE. *The Hidden Persuaders.* New York: McKay, 1957.

ROSENCRANZ, MARY LOU. "Clothing Symbolism," *Journal of Home Economics,* Vol. 54, No. 1 (January 1962), pp. 18–22.

RYAN, MARY S. *Psychological Effects of Clothing,* Part I, Part II, Part III, Part IV. New York: Cornell University, Agricultural Experimental Station, 1953.

SMITH, MARGARET. *Clothing Fabrics, Facts for Consumer Education*, Home Economics Research Report No. 1, 1957.

STONE, GREGORY P., and WILLIAM H. FORM. *The Social Significance of Clothing in Occupational Life.* Michigan State College, Agricultural Experimental Station, Technical Bulletin 247, 1955.

SYBERS, RUTH, and MARY ELLEN ROACH, "Clothing and Human Behavior," *Journal of Home Economics*, Vol. 54, No. 3 (March 1962), pp. 184-187.

TATE, MILDRED THUROW, and ORIS GLISSON. "Factors Affecting Clothing Decisions," Chap. 2; "Family Clothing Expenditures," Chap. 6, *Family Clothing*. New York: Wiley, 1961.

U.S. Department of Agriculture. Agricultural Research Service. *Buying Women's Coats and Suits. Home and Garden Bulletin No. 31, 1957.*
———. *Men's Suits: How to Judge Quality*. Home and Garden Bulletin No. 54, 1957.

VEBLEN, THORSTEIN. *Theory of the Leisure Class*. New York: Modern Library, 1912.

8

FAMILY
TRANSPORTATION

Transportation developments since 1900 have been dominated by the acquisition of an automobile by the typical American family.[1]

SINCE 1920 the use of public transportation has been declining and the use of the automobile increasing. Contemporary social patterns have been influenced by the widespread possession of automobiles. Drive-in restaurants, theaters, country inns, and suburban bowling alleys—all are dependent upon patrons with cars. The development of public beaches and parks inaccessible by public transportation has grown because so many people have cars.

Many explanations have been given for this trend. Automobiles became available at moderate prices. As families saw their incomes increasing and their work week decreasing, the possibility of moving farther from their place of work seemed attractive. Many of these outlying areas were not on public transportation lines, or at a considerable distance from them.

Installment financing of automobiles, with payments stretching over several years, brought automobiles within reach of middle-income families. At the same time the number of middle-income families who could afford cars was increasing.

The Automobile as a Status Symbol

Social standing and personal affluence are often judged by the clothes we wear, the house we live in, and the car we drive. While these things are no measure of a man's character, they are symbols of success, and therefore highly prized. Many people stretch themselves financially to buy a late model car which enhances this image.

The car has become such an important indication of status that one can

[1] U.S. Dept. of Labor, *How American Buying Habits Change* (Washington, D.C.: Government Printing Office[n.d.]), p. 177.

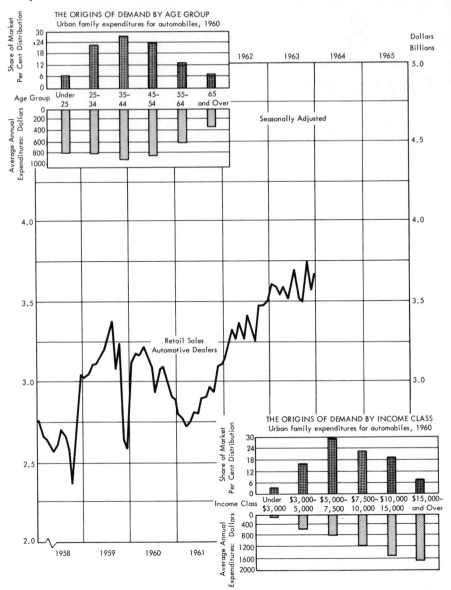

FIGURE 36. The market for automobiles. (*Reproduced from* A Graphic Guide to Consumer Markets, 1964, *prepared by the National Industrial Conference Board under the sponsorship of* Life magazine. *Source of data: U.S. Department of Labor, U.S. Department of Commerce, and The Conference Board.*)

judge the level of an executive in some corporations by the type of company car he drives. Also, it may be considered poor taste for a junior executive to own a more costly car than his boss in many organizations.

Often a car is used to compensate for other symbols of status among culturally deprived groups in urban areas. Families who are unable to find attractive housing in cities will often compete with each other in their possession of handsome cars.

Teen-agers evaluate the status of boys partly by whether they have a car. Four-wheel mobility is highly prized by young people.

Increasing affluence is equated with the possession of not one but two cars. So much of suburban living is dependent upon transportation by car that many families have two or more cars.

Family Spending for Transportation

Changes in the use of transportation since the turn of the century are reflected in family spending. With higher real earnings and greater leisure, families of all income levels have elected to spend a large proportion of their income on travel and transportation. One dollar in every eight that families spent in 1960 was used for transportation. Over 90 per cent of this money was for user-operated transportation, or automobiles. The 1960 expenditure of over 40 billion dollars for transportation is almost double that spent in 1950.[2]

Most people do not keep careful records of what it costs to operate a car. Perhaps they would be unhappy to learn that one estimate is that a car driven 10,000 miles a year costs nine cents a mile, or $900 for the year.[3] *Changing Times* estimated that a new standard eight cylinder sedan with automatic transmission driven 10,000 miles a year would cost $1,078, a compact $902, and a Volkswagen $596. They also estimated that a three-year-old used car with six cylinders and a manual transmission would cost $763, and a similar five-year-old car $731. (A lower rate of depreciation on the older car is partially offset by higher maintenance costs.)[4]

In addition to gas, oil, and tires, maintenance, depreciation, insurance, and license fees should be considered. Depreciation is the difference between the purchase price of a car and the selling price when you get rid of it. If a new car costs $2,400 and you sell it for $1,400 at the end of the first year, the depreciation is $1,000. A new standard-size sedan depreciates about $530 per year, a compact about $450, and a Volkswagen about $250. These are rough approximations; the depreciation is greatest the first year and decreases each year thereafter. Also, certain car models of particular years develop a reputation for standing up well and do not depreciate quite so fast; their rate of depreciation may be $40 or $50 less per year.

Since the greatest car depreciation is in the first year and decreases each

---

[2] *Statistical Abstract of the United States, 1962* (Washington, D.C.: Government Printing Office), p. 315.

[3] Wilfred Owen, *The Metropolitan Transportation Problem* (Washington, D.C.: The Brookings Institution, 1956), p. 143. Data supplied by American Automobile Association.

[4] "How to Be a Two-Car Family," *Changing Times* (October 1962), p. 34.

year thereafter, keeping a car for several years reduces the average annual depreciation. (See Figure 37 and Figure 38.) Some families find a second car helps to extend the useful life of the first. The first car receives less use and can be kept longer. If a station wagon is kept six years instead of four, the average depreciation drops from $525 to about $400 per year.

Insurance is a substantial cost, usually about $110 to $140 per year in urban areas. (This is discussed more fully, in a following section, "Shopping for Insurance.") Cars that are not driven to work more than ten miles each way have lower premiums than do those driven longer distances to work or used for business. Most companies give a 25 per cent discount for a second car, and a 10 per cent discount for a compact.

License fees are usually related to the weight and size of the car and generally run from $10 to $20 per year.

The Cost of Running a Car[5]

Here's a rough guide on how to figure the cost of operating a car. You can estimate the cost of the two-car combination you own or contemplate with some simple computations, plus a look at some points raised in the accompanying article. Three sedans listed below are new—a Big Three standard eight with automatic transmission, a low-priced compact with automatic shift, and a Volkswagen. Two are used-three-year-old and five-year-old standard sixes with manual transmission.

It's assumed you'd keep any of the first four cars four years before selling it, but the five-year-old auto only three years. Operating expenses are figured on a per-mile basis; multiply by the number of miles you drive each year to get the annual cost. Fixed expenses remain the same no matter how many miles you drive a year. Insurance and license fees are figured for a suburb of a large Midwestern city and assume that the car is driven to and from work more than 10 miles each way.

	New Cars			Used Cars	
	Standard	*Compact*	*Import*	*3-year-old*	*5-year-old*
Operating Expenses (per mile)					
gas and oil	2.45¢	1.86¢	1.09¢	2.58¢	2.88¢
tires and maintenance	1.02	.99	.86	1.32	1.60
Total	3.47¢	2.85¢	1.95c	3.90¢	4.48¢
Fixed Expenses (per year)					
Depreciation	$530	$450	$250	$210	$150
Insurance	182	154	142	144	124
License	19	13	9	19	19
	$731	$617	$401	$373	$283

[5] From "How to Be a Two-Car Family," *Changing Times* (October 1962). Reprinted by permission from *Changing Times*, the Kiplinger Magazine.

If used as a second car, not driven to work, insurance is this much cheaper.	67	59	56	61	56
Total as second car	$664	$558	$345	$312	$227

NOTE: For a station wagon, add about one-fourth of a cent per mile for operating expenses and $60 to $85 a year for depreciation and insurance.

Shopping for a Car

The first thing to decide is if you really need to buy a car. Many people who live in cities use their car only on weekends—and then not every weekend or both days of the weekend. With the high cost of insuring and garaging a car in the city, it might be cheaper to rent a car as needed. Rental services abound in most cities. Usually they will deliver the car to your door at the time desired and pick it up when you have finished using it.

Buying a New Car

Shopping for a new car ought to be fun, a happy experience. But for many people it is both confusing and frustrating. There is an overwhelming number of makes, models, and extra equipment. Advertisements with attractive prices usually do not tell the whole story. The car may not be a bargain at all, or it is not in stock at the time.

Confused by the many alternatives and the variety of automobiles immediately available from a dealer, with varying equipment already installed, many buyers make poor decisions. Or they may make them in haste either because of their desire for a particular make and model that is available or a dealer's persuasive sales pitch. Cars bought in this way can be more costly than necessary. Also, they may not be the right choice for your particular needs.

PRICE. These pitfalls can be avoided by careful planning. Determine what you can spend on a new or used car. If you are planning to finance the car decide how much you can afford to pay per month. Include insurance and financing charges in your estimate. Limit your shopping to cars in the price range you can afford. Bear in mind that the price classes of cars overlap; a new compact, fully equipped, may cost more than a standard-sized car with no extras.

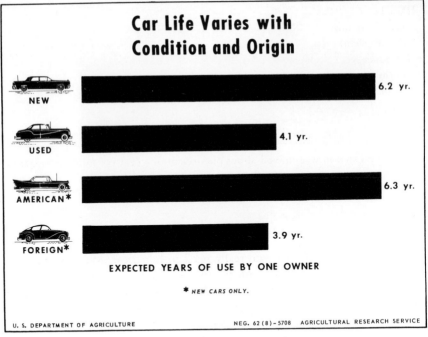

FIGURE 37. *(Courtesy of USDA.)*

SIZE. What size car do you want? If the car is to be used for a large family, then a large car or a station wagon might be useful. However, if the car is to be used as a second car just to go a short distance to and from work, a low-priced compact or small imported car makes sense. These cost less to buy and run than do full-sized automobiles.

MODEL. Within the line of cars offered by a manufacturer, there is a considerable price difference between the cheapest standard-size model and the more expensive ones. As you go up in price category, you get a little extra room, more attractive interiors, extra power you do not need, and a little more comfort—plus higher operating costs. Generally, the higher the price for more expensive models, the less the return for each additional dollar spent.

If you travel a lot and need space for baggage, then one of the standard-size cars with a big trunk is useful. Station wagons are ideal for hauling baggage and equipment. Hardtop models cost more—about $60 to $70. But you will get some of this back when the car is traded in.

MAKE. Although cars within a particular price range are quite similar, their styling differs. Some people buy a particular make because they have had good experience with it; others may like the styling of that year's model. From a dollars and cents point of view, it pays to pick the car within a certain price range that tends to depreciate slowly.

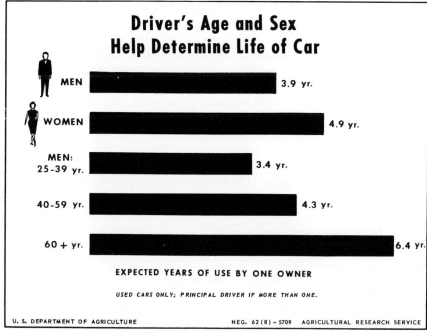

FIGURE 38. *(Courtesy of USDA.)*

CYLINDERS. Many makes and models offer a choice of six or eight cylinders. Eight-cylinder cars have more power; they accelerate more quickly, particularly when equipped with automatic transmission. But they cost about $100 more and are more expensive to operate. Gas consumption and maintenance costs are higher.

EXTRAS. Buying extras is where some people go wild. Extra optional features can add considerably to the total car cost. Some, like safety belts, give added safety and convenience; on others, such as a radio you can recover part of the cost when you trade the car in. Most optional extras do not bring a return representing much of their original cost when the car is traded in.

An automatic transmission is a great convenience in city traffic, but it will cost about $200 more. When the car is traded in, it is possible to get about a third of this back. However, an automatic transmission becomes a necessity if there are drivers in the family who do not know how to use a gear shift and would not like to learn.

Power steering, once just a frill, is a great help in steering and parking full-size cars. It is not necessary on compact cars or the small imports because these are very easy to handle. The extra cost is about $75, of which $30 might be returned on the trade-in.

Power brakes will stop a car with less effort, but not in less distance. They are a very popular extra that costs about $40, none of which is returned when the car is sold.

Seat belts, windshield washers, padded dashboards, and outside mirrors contribute to safety in driving. The cost of these, however, is not returned on the trade-in.

Whitewall tires, additional horsepower, power seats, and electric windows are extras that cost more and add very little to the usefulness of the car. Their cost is not returned when the car is traded.

Consider a Used Car

It may be more fun to buy a new car, but in most cases it is more expensive. New cars generally depreciate about half their initial cost in the first two years, and at a slower rate thereafter. Buying a two-year-old car that has already depreciated considerably saves this large amount of money. But it also may mean that the car is out of commission for servicing more frequently. (The notable exception is the Volkswagen, which only depreciates about one sixth of its purchase price each year.)

"Nearly every used car is on the market because its owner has, for one reason or another, become dissatisfied with it, or with its future prospects as they will affect his wallet."[6] Cars traded because the owner is tired of them, but that are in excellent condition, with low mileage, are hard to find. However, a carefully selected used car, middle-aged and fairly inexpensive, can give fairly low-cost transportation. Most annual repairs, except the replacement of a badly rusted body, will probably cost less than the annual depreciation of a new car.

Each person has to decide how to weigh economy versus the inconvenience of more frequent repairs. A one- or two-year-old compact or low-priced standard-sized car in good condition is a good choice if it fits your budget requirements. It will probably need a minimum of repairs. The smaller cars not only use less fuel, but they cost less to repair. Generally, it is best to buy used cars without an automatic transmission, power steering, power brakes, and power windows, because these things are most likely to need repairs.

If you find a used car that looks good to you, take it out on a road test. Many problems that are not evident on a car will show up when the car is driven.

Bargaining for the Best Price

List prices of cars are not firm prices. Dealers expect you to bargain. Start by knowing the list price. The law requires that this be posted on a ticket in the window of new cars. When buying a used car, consult the dealer's "blue book" for the average price of the particular make, model, and year of the car that you are considering.

6 "Shopping for a Used Car," *Consumer Reports* (September 1962), p. 424.

It definitely pays to shop around. Some dealers of new cars give concessions if you have a car to trade in. (They can make a profit on the sale of the used car if they have a used car lot.) Others will try to beat the price offered by different dealers. Then some car showrooms may be overstocked on a particular make or model.

If you are buying a new car without a trade-in, the dealer may offer a discount from the list price. If you are trading in a car, the dealer will usually list the full posted price for the car but may offer a discount as an overallowance on your old car. The simplest way to compare deals is by the actual dollars that must be paid.

Selecting the Time to Buy

By choosing the right time to buy, it is often possible to save money. Discounts on cars are usually largest in the fall just before the next year's models come out. However, when the new models are out, your car is already one year old. Even though it is brand new, it depreciates as if it were one year old. This is a good way to buy if you expect to keep the car for four or five years.

Buy in the winter. Dealers are often willing to cut prices during the traditionally slow winter season. *Changing Times* suggests that buying in a blizzard, when business is even slower than usual, would be ideal.

Car prices are usually cut during "contest" months. Manufacturers of

---

A B C's OF AUTOMOBILE BUYING

Accumulate knowledge about:
1. Rate of depreciation and best buying times.
2. Dealer reputation, reliability and service.
3. The advantages, disadvantages and costs of engines, transmission and power equipment, extra-cost equipment, big and little cars.
4. On the lot, on the road, and "shop" tests for used cars.
5. Automobile insurance - coverage, costs, legal requirements, agencies.
6. Kinds, costs, and terms of credit.
7. Federal and State regulations of contracts and credit purchases.

Bear in mind:
1. For whom and how the car will be used.
2. The price you can afford to own and operate a car.
3. Whether you want prestige or economy in a car.

Compare the costs:
1. The base price and the trade-in allowance for your present car, the cost of each item of extra equipment.
2. The dollar costs of credit.
3. The cost and coverage of automobile insurance.

FIGURE 39. *(Courtesy of June L. Smith.)*

cars offer rebates to dealers during these special contests, which some dealers pass on to the customer.

Toward the end of the month prices may be better. Salesmen are anxious to meet their quotas, and dealers want to look good to the manufacturers on their monthly statistics.

Considering the Servicing Facilities

While price is a very important consideration in selecting the place to buy a car, service is also important. The guarantee with a new or used car may be worthless if the dealer does not provide good service or refuses to honor warranty claims.

Also, the quality of service on your car during the original guarantee period may determine the durability of the car. You may have to take the car to the dealer often for minor adjustments in this initial period, so select one that does good servicing.

Financing the Car

The cheapest way to buy a car is to pay cash, particularly for a used car. Financing rates for used cars are higher than for new cars. If you can't scrape together the full price, pay as much down as you can—at least one-third. Then plan to repay the balance in as short a period as you can. The shorter the interest period, the less the interest costs.

Shop for the loan as carefully as for the car. In most cases, bank loans are the cheapest, then credit unions, and lastly dealer financing. However, dealer financing offers the convenience of one-stop shopping; you can buy the car and finance it at the one place.

Table 10 shows a comparison of the total outlays and monthly payments on a car loan of $2,000 for different repayment periods.

If you are financing a car, read all the fine print. Do not sign anything until all items are filled in. Get and keep a signed copy of the contract.

TABLE 10
Comparison of Total Outlays and Monthly Payments
on a $2,000 Car Loan*

| | 4½% | | 6% | |
	Total Repayment	Monthly Payments	Total Repayment	Monthly Payments
18 months	$2,135	$118.60	$2,180	$121.10
24 months	2,180	91.80	2,240	93.30
36 months	2,270	63.10	2,360	65.60

* From "Smart Way to Buy a Car," *Changing Times* (December 1962), p. 23.

Insuring the Car

The dealer has the right to require that you purchase comprehensive fire, theft and collision insurance when you finance a car. (Collision insurance pays for the damage to your car in the event of an accident.) But before you buy it from the automobile dealer, check rates elsewhere. If you have a good driving record, you can usually get cheaper insurance elsewhere. If you do buy your insurance from the dealer, be sure it is not added to the amount you are financing, or you will pay interest on the insurance premium too. On a loan of two or three years, this is a substantial and unnecessary charge.

Types of Coverage

The four most important types of coverage to carry for your own protection are: Liability, Medical, Collision, and Comprehensive. Uninsured Motorist coverage is considered desirable by many people.

Liability insurance, which includes bodily injury and property damage, pays the amount that you would be liable for if you injured a person or damaged property. It is compulsory in New York, Massachusetts, and North Carolina. In the other states, there are financial responsibility laws that make it highly advisable to carry liability insurance, although they do not require that one do so. Often it is difficult and very costly for a person without liability insurance to defend himself in court in case of a suit. If one is covered by insurance, the insurance company handles much of this. Some states require that drivers who do not carry at least a minimal amount of liability insurance pay an extra fee for a driver's license, which goes into a fund to reimburse people who are injured or for property damaged by uninsured drivers.

How much to carry is a difficult question. Court awards are getting higher, so many insurance agents suggest carrying large amounts. Liability limits are commonly described in thousands of dollars this way—10/20/5 or 100/300/10. The first number refers to the limits for bodily injury to one person, the second to the maximum coverage for bodily injury to more than one person in the accident, and the third to the maximum limit for property damaged. Many drivers carry only a minimum amount of coverage, 5/10/5. However, larger amounts of coverage do not cost much more. If 10/20/5 costs $100, then 100/300/10 will cost about $129.

Medical payments pay medical and hospital bills if you are injured and funeral expenses if you die in an automobile accident. This coverage also pays medical expenses if passengers in your car are injured.

Collision coverage pays you if your car is damaged in an accident, even if it is your fault. If your car is damaged in an accident that is someone else's fault, the insurance company can collect from them, but you would usually get paid fairly promptly for the damage (less the deductible amount, if any) by your own insurance company.

Collision insurance is generally sold with a deductible clause; you pay the first $50 or $100 of the loss and the insurance company pays you the balance. Although the deductible arrangement cuts the cost collision insurance is quite expensive; a $50 deductible policy might cost about $50, and a $100 deductible policy about $35, depending on the value of the car.

Some people claim that collision insurance is not worthwhile because you can collect from the other person if he is responsible for the accident, and can write the loss off on your income tax if you cannot collect. However, in the event of a major loss you will still have to come up with enough money from your own pocket to replace or repair the car. Also, it sometimes takes a very long time to sue and collect damages.

Comprehensive Coverage pays you if your car is stolen, or damaged by causes other than collision. The commonest claims are for replacing windshields and broken windows. Comprehensive coverage is also available with deductible clauses at reduced rates. The cost of comprehensive coverage varies with the car and your place of residence.

Uninsured Motorist Coverage protects you if you are injured by an uninsured motorist or a hit-and-run driver. The medical payments coverage provide you with the same kind of bodily injury liability that you carry for others, which is more than is included in most medical coverage clauses.

Shopping for Insurance

Drivers with good records, no chargeable accidents, liability or collision claims, and no moving traffic violations in the last few years can usually get low cost insurance if they compare prices and shop around. Generally, drivers under 25 and over 65 have difficulty getting bargain prices.

Draw up a list of specifications: so much liability insurance, medical insurance, and so on, and ask for an estimate of rates from various companies. Certain companies take only preferred risks at low rates; other companies charge according to your record.

Cutting Operating Costs

Good driving habits and regular maintenance can cut operating costs. Acquire habits that help you get the most for your money.

1. Let the engine warm up before driving. Drive slowly until the temperature is up to normal.
2. Accelerate smoothly and slowly to save gas.
3. Brake gradually to prevent excessive brake wear.
4. Watch for signs of wear and repair promptly.
5. Obey traffic rules and avoid accidents.
6. Adjust your driving speed to road conditions and the traffic.

7. Service your car promptly at a reliable service station. Have it lubricated regularly and checked completely at periodic intervals.

8. Keep your tires inflated at the recommended air pressure. Rotate them at regular intervals, usually every 5,000 miles. If they show uneven wear, have the wheels balanced.

9. Use low-priced gasoline if it works well in your car. Some independent stations sell gasoline at 2 or 3 cents a gallon less than do stations that are part of a chain. Private brands may be cheaper. An independent or private brand may have a lower octane rating.

Small cars, compacts, or foreign cars usually can operate with no loss of efficiency with the lower octane gasolines. It is helpful to have your engine tuned and the ignition timing reset before trying these lower-priced gasolines. If the engine doesn't knock or lose its pickup, then it is fine.

Automobile Safety

More people in the United States are injured or killed in automobiles than in any other type of conveyance. Motor vehicle accidents account for more than one third of all fatal accidents in the United States. Most of these occur in private automobiles while moving in traffic.[7]

Safety in passenger cars has been a national concern for a number of years. Efforts to reduce the accident toll have been centered about the following areas: improving the design of automobiles, the building of highways that reduce accidents, improving the maintenance of automobiles, and the education of drivers.

Among other things, automobile designers and manufacturers have developed better brakes, tires that blow out less easily, and stronger headlights. They now use safety glass and make padded dashboards and safety belts available at an extra charge.

Highway designers have tried to eliminate dangerous curves, to separate high speed traffic lanes traveling in opposite directions, to make entrances and exits of high speed highways safer, and to employ paving materials that reduce accidents.

Government agencies try to mark lanes of traffic clearly, to indicate safe passing areas, and to regulate traffic.

Some states now require motor vehicles to be inspected periodically. They usually check brakes, headlights, windshield wipers, and the functioning of the steering mechanism. Cars that do not pass inspection must be repaired within a specified time period.

A number of groups are trying to educate drivers in safe driving habits.

[7] *Statistical Abstract of the United States, 1962* (Washington, D.C.: Government Printing Office), p. 69.

Many high schools include driver education courses. The automobile associations and the National Safety Council have very active programs of safety education. So do some insurance companies and governmental agencies.

These constructive efforts seem to be having good results. Although the number of cars on the road increased 50 per cent from 1950 to 1960, the number of fatal accidents only increased 9 per cent.[8] Undoubtedly many more accidents could be prevented and injury to passengers reduced.

The Social Consequences of the Change in the Means of Transportation

Mobility is a fact of modern life. More people own cars and are going places. This has made for fun and happiness; families can take vacations away from home more easily, visit friends and relatives, or se .k recreation and change. But it has also resulted in jammed highways into our cities, particularly at "rush hours," and increased pollution of the air we breathe.

In spite of massive highway building programs in many metropolitan areas, we do not have enough roads for the increased number of cars at peak periods. New local highways are sometimes crowded as soon as they are opened. Interstate road building has kept ahead a little better, perhaps because the traffic has not increased quite as rapidly.

The use of public transportation has not kept pace with the growth in use of private transportation. As a result, many companies have not modernized their equipment and facilities, which in turn has made public transportation less attractive.

The dilemma of public transportation companies in urban areas has been particularly acute. Most people in metropolitan areas use public transportation only during the "rush hours." But it is difficult to operate these facilities economically on this basis. Public resistance and the regulatory agencies usually prevent the raising of fares to the point where operation of transportation facilities is profitable for the company. As a result, transportation lines have reduced service and would like to curtail it further.

Public interest demands the maintenance of certain public transportation facilities. As a result, some cities subsidize public transit companies or own their own. In spite of this there is still little public transportation to many suburban communities, and there are inadequate facilities for parking near public transportation in many others. Interest has been expressed by people in different parts of the country in the establishment of new kinds of public transportation facilities such as a monorail.

[8] *Statistical Abstract of the United States, 1962* (Washington, D.C.: Government Printing Office), pp. 69 and 563. This comparison is only approximate because data for fatal accidents is not presented for 1960.

Looking ahead, we need to plan for the handling of people and goods into and within our metropolitan areas. Population is expected to increase in the metropolitan clusters of cities and suburbs. More people mean that more goods and more cars will be on the roads.

SELECTED REFERENCES

"CU's Auto Insurance Project," *Consumer Reports* (March 1962), pp. 113-118; (April 1962), pp. 204-210; (May 1962), pp. 247-252; (June 1962), pp. 302-307; (July 1962), pp. 352-356.

"How to Be a Two-Car Family," *Changing Times* (October 1962), pp. 33-35.

KEATS, JOHN. *The Insolent Chariots*. Philadelphia: Lippincott, 1958.

MONEY MANAGEMENT INSTITUTE OF HOUSEHOLD FINANCE CORPORATION. *Your Automobile Dollar*. Chicago: Household Finance Corporation, 1963.

OWEN, WILFRED. *The Metropolitan Transportation Problem*. Washington, D.C.: The Brookings Institution, 1956.

PHILLIPS, E. BRYANT, and SYLVIA LANE. *Personal Finance*. Chap. 11, "Expenditures for Transportation," New York: Wiley, 1963.

"Shopping for a Used Car," *Consumer Reports* (September 1962), pp. 424-430.

"Smart Way to Buy a Car," *Changing Times* (December 1962), pp. 19-28.

U.S. DEPARTMENT OF LABOR. "The Revolution in Transportation," Chap. VIII, *How American Buying Habits Change*. (Washington, D.C.: Government Printing Office [n.d.]).

9

LEISURE AND

THE AMERICAN FAMILY

> Time is the raw material of life. Every day unwraps
> itself like a gift, bringing us the opportunity to
> spin a fabric of health, pleasure, and content.[1]

IN MODERN America men no longer toil sixteen hours a day, seven days a week. Their working day has grown shorter and the weekend longer. Most people have far more leisure than their forefathers did, time in which they can do what they please.

Historically, the concept of leisure for the masses is fairly new; in fact, the whole notion of leisure is part of the development of civilization. "Leisure as contrasted with work is largely foreign to primitive societies."[2] In ancient civilizations leisure belonged only to the ruling classes or, as in Rome, to citizen-scholars.

Until almost a century ago the masses were expected to work endlessly to support themselves and the aristocrats who were idle. Industrialization has reduced hours of labor for both farm and factory. One hundred years ago the average farm work week was seventy hours; this has been lowered to forty-five today. The factory work week has dropped from sixty-five hours to forty, and may go to thirty-five.

The average working day in industry is now eight hours and in offices, seven. During the working day there are many rest periods: the coffee break, the longer lunch hour, and sometimes even time off for shopping on Friday afternoon and before a holiday.

There are paid holidays throughout the year and summer vacations of two to four weeks. The United States Department of Labor noted in a 1961 study that 92 per cent of all major labor contracts provided for two or more weeks of paid vacation.[3]

[1] The Royal Bank of Canada, "Monthly Letter," Vol. 42, No. 9, p. 1.

[2] Ida Craven, "Leisure," *The Encyclopedia of Social Sciences*, Vol. V (New York: Macmillan, 1933), p. 402.

[3] U.S. Dept. of Labor, "Paid Vacation Provisions in Major Union Contracts, 1961," *Monthly Labor Review* (August 1962).

Women's work in the home has also been lightened. Today the average woman has fewer years of full-time child care. Most women have their last child before they are 30, and their youngest child is in school by the time they are 35. Many families have no children living at home by the time the mother is 45.

How Leisure Time Is Divided
Among the Population

Leisure is unequally divided among our population. At certain ages, and in some occupations, people have a great deal of leisure; in others, very little. Most adolescents do not enter the full-time work force until about age eighteen, although some work on a part-time basis before that. Students usually have a great deal of free time, from three to eight hours on school days, plus the weekend and holidays. Their home responsibilities are usually very limited. Most of their out-of-school hours are their own to use as they choose.

While the homemaker with several small children has one of the longest work weeks of any group, fifteen hours a day, seven days a week, the homemaker with children in school usually has some free time which she can use in leisure activities. The amount of time available to her increases as the children advance through high school. Housewives with older children have many leisure hours.

Working women, at least those who combine household responsibilities with paid employment have little leisure. They approach the work load of homemakers with young children, about fifteen hours a day, seven days a week.

Senior citizens, most of whom are not employed outside the home, have all day every day to devote to recreational pursuits. A person who retires at age 65 can expect to live six or more years in retirement. At present we have almost 17 million citizens aged 65 or older, and by 1970 we should have 20 million. This is a lot of people with "time on their hands."

People in certain occupations have much less leisure time than the average factory worker. Proprietors, executives, and managers generally work a fifty-three-hour week at their jobs. Industrial machinery has freed workers of much drudgery and backbreaking labor, but the managers of modern production have to spend more hours in planning and organizing to keep the wheels of production turning. Reuel Denney states that "the business man [manager or executive] may know a great deal about the sources of modern leisure, and yet all too little about the consequences of it."[4]

Spending for Leisure

Today's young American family is in a unique position. Unlike their parents, who may have attained maturity during the depression of the nineteen

[4] Reuel Denney, "The Leisure Society," *Harvard Business Review* (May-June, 1959), p. 46.

thirties, they have money to spend. Unlike their grandparents, who worked long hours six days a week, they are on a five-day thirty-five- to forty-hour week. The result has been the booming growth of whole industries catering to leisure pursuits.

Spending for leisure activities is often considered to be "discretionary spending" that is not required for daily necessities, but rather to give pleasure and satisfaction. Although recreational and other leisure pursuits may be considered discretionary in an overall view of family expenditures, to the individual and his family they often become part of the accepted mode of living, and very hard to give up or change. In times of curtailed income many people are loath to give up these expenditures.

Leisure-Time Activities

An understanding of the way people use their leisure requires recognition of the way in which life and work have changed in modern America. Where men once worked primarily for themselves as small farmers or merchants, today most men are employees of medium or large organizations. Their work is less taxing than in pioneer days, and the hours of toil are shorter, but their jobs are often routine and dull. For many people, work is a way of earning money, but little more. Satisfaction, excitement, and pleasure can only be found elsewhere. Consequently, more people are looking to their families for incentives and satisfactions of needs which once were formerly found in work. "The home in which one was once allowed a limited amount of recuperation and recreation in reward for working hard has now become the reason for existence, which in turn justifies working at all."[5]

People are marrying younger with the feeling that marriage is the admission card to the good life. These young couples are having children sooner, and more children than their parents had. "Parenthood becomes a major source of enjoyment for both parents. . . . The parents are promised that having children will keep them together, keep them young, and give them fun and happiness."[6]

New patterns for the use of leisure have developed. Activities centered around the home have become big business. Expenditures for television, hi-fi music, radios and record players, and musical instruments have soared. Backyard socializing has become a popular pastime. The cult of barbecue cooking has increased the sale of lounge chairs, picnic supplies, and charcoal briquettes. Backyard pools come in all sizes and shapes with a choice of filters, water fresheners, and ladders.

[5] Margaret Mead, "The Pattern of Leisure in Contemporary American Culture," *The Annals of the American Academy of Political and Social Science*, Vol. 313 (September 1957), p. 14.
[6] Martha Wolfenstein, "The Emergence of Fun Morality," *Journal of Social Issues*, Vol. 7, No. 4 (1951), pp. 15–25.

FIGURE 40. Fishing is a leisure activity that many age groups enjoy. (*Courtesy of Consumer Reports.*)

"Do it yourself" has become both a hobby and a necessity. The shortage of skilled repair people at prices homeowners can afford has stimulated many people to do their own repairs. Moreover, it has become fashionable to work around the house. Elaborate home workshops are features of many suburban homes.

New sports have developed popularity. Skiing, once the love of only a few people, has now become big business. Numbers of new multimillion-dollar ski resorts are opened each year. Ski shops, ski clothes manufacturers, ski resort operators, and travel agencies have shared in the prosperity engendered by the growth of just one sport.

Bowling and boating have shared this boom. In urban areas one can see many new bowling alleys. Furthermore, many of these are large and lavish. Some provide baby-sitting for mother, restaurants, cocktail lounges, and other comforts. Bowling has become a popular sport for the whole family. Colleges include bowling as one of their sports, junior high school students spend Saturday mornings bowling, and there are leagues for all age groups.

In many sports, specialized clothing and equipment are considered the mark of the person who "knows" the sport; in the case of bowling, the personal

FIGURE 41. This family is camped in the clean, crisp air of the high mountain country amidst superb scenery. *(Courtesy of U.S. Forest Service.)*

ball, case and bowling shoes are popular. This all adds up to a sizeable investment in the sport.

Boating has grown "like Topsy." In the last ten years major small craft harbors have doubled and tripled their facilities and still are overcrowded. The biggest growth has been in small power boats and outboard motors that can be attached to a rowboat. While its growth in popularity has not been as spectacular, sailing has also shared in the increase in the number of craft.

Another water sport that has shared the boating boom is water skiing. This has changed from a rare activity limited to resort areas, such as Florida, to a summer pastime all over the country.

Part of the growth in popularity of water sports can be attributed to the development of new water areas available for recreation. Water and dam projects have created vast inland lakes where none existed before. The Hoover Dam on the Colorado River created Lake Mead, 115 miles long, which is used for fishing, boating, and swimming, and the area around it for camping. This is in the midst of the semiarid New Mexico Arizona desert.

Another possible reason for the growth of water sports is the social status that has held over like a legend from the days of millionaires' luxurious yachts. Now many middle-income families can afford a small boat. One can see boats being carried on trailers on the highway, parked beside the car in the garage, and dotting rivers and lakes across the country.

Less active hobbies have also grown. Photography is very popular and fashionable. It can also be a large drain on the family budget. In addition to a camera, film, and the cost of developing, many amateur photographers also feel it desirable to have a second camera, flash attachments, light bars, a light meter, a tripod, and telephoto lenses. Most department stores, discount stores and many drugstores now have large photography departments, in addition to the specialized photography stores.

Reading is on the upgrade. Paperbound books have accounted for a substantial part of this growth: old classics are now published in paperback form, new books are often put out in paperback editions shortly after the original publication, and many books are written specially for the paperback market. A feature of many large cities is the proliferation of paperback bookstores.

Various other nonathletic activities are popular, such as listening to hi-fidelity music, acting in local theater groups, collecting stamps, and building railroad cars. Almost every imaginable type of activity is being engaged in as a hobby.

Travel has become a major leisure activity, ranging all the way from the Sunday afternoon drive to trips abroad. Just a glance at the highways of America will convince one that Americans are on the move. Park, picnic, and camping facilities have become overcrowded. Reservations for a camp in many major camping areas must be made months ahead. In 1960, 259 million visits were made to state parks. This represents a sharp increase in the use of public park facilities. In 1950 less than half this number visited the national parks and monuments, and only about one fourth used the national forests.[7]

Attendance at nongovernmental recreational facilities has also increased. Nineteen million people attended major league baseball games in 1961; in 1950 attendance was only 17.6 million.

In 1960, 11 million people purchased hunting licenses, and 19 million bought fishing licenses. The Fish and Wildlife Service of the Department of the Interior estimates that 131 million days were spent at fishing or hunting in 1960 as compared to 118 million in 1950.

A large part of our automobile expenditures are recreational. Many trips are made for purposes other than business.

Certain types of activity are hard to classify; some people consider them leisure activities, others as a chore. Gardening is one of them. In the Jackson-Meyersohn study of leisure, 16 per cent of the people who were asked if they enjoyed gardening replied "No."[8]

As some activities have developed new or increased popularity, others have declined. Since World War II attendance at movies has dropped sharply. This

[7] *Statistical Abstract of the United States, 1962* (Washington, D.C.: Government Printing Office), p. 202.

[8] Robin Jackson and Rolf Meyersohn, "The Social Patterning of Leisure" (Chicago: Center for the Study of Leisure, 1958).

is probably due to the fact that many families now own television sets. Americans have changed the kind of liquor they drink: consumption of hard liquor has declined, and beer drinking has increased.

Who Shapes the Leisure Market ?

The rulers of the leisure market are families in the middle-income group, the large segment of our population with a family income of $4,000 to $9,000 per year. This group has constantly expanded in the last twenty years. Even allowing for inflation, the majority of American families have attained middle-income status and have money to spend on leisure activities.

The Club Spirit

Many of our leisure activities are carried on in groups. Since the early 1800's, when De Tocqueville called us "the greatest joiners in the world," we have been known for our clubs, lodges, associations, and other voluntary groups. The proliferation of organizations in any one community attests to the fact that Americans have not changed much on this count.

In one community one can easily find charities such as the Red Cross, the Community Chest, Cerebral Palsy, the National Foundation, and others; social groups such as lodges, fraternities, and private clubs; youth groups such as the Scouts, the Campfire girls, PAL groups; as well as PTA's, church auxiliaries, garden clubs, book clubs, college alumni associations; and less formal groups such as bridge clubs, canasta groups, and others.

Time on Our Hands Is Troublesome

The newly increased leisure of American families has created prosperity for leisure industries and also a new pattern of living for many families. Recreation and leisure pursuits are often activities involving only one member of the family. Mother may have her bridge club, Dad his bowling league, Junior the basketball team and his gang, and Sister "the girls."

Expenditures for recreation have become very large. This often creates pressures on the family. If a member wishes to participate in the activities of his friends, it usually involves spending some money to do so. The combined pressure of all of the family members for spending money is often a source of family disagreements.

Some age groups have caused serious community concern about the way in which they use their leisure time. Young people with few home demands on their time may have both money to spend and the time in which to spend it. Some of the results have been disastrous. Juvenile delinquency, once thought to be a product of poverty and neglect, has pervaded more comfortable communities. Drinking and automobile accidents are too frequent to be ignored.

Senior citizens generally have more time than they can fill productively or with satisfaction. One can see the parks of urban areas filled with older people just sitting. Most of us know several older people who just don't seem to know what to do with themselves. One of the problems is that as people get older, both their physical health and their independent mobility deteriorates. They are less able to do the vigorous or active things they once enjoyed. Many lack a means of transportation if their physical limitations prevent their using subways or buses. Others lack sufficient income to be able to visit their family and friends freely if they are located at any distance. Even when their children are nearby, they are often engrossed with their own young children.

Community and religious organizations are very cognizant of these problems and many have organized golden age clubs and social activities to meet the needs of the senior-citizen group. At best, however, they reach only a small group.

A large number of married women who are not employed are unhappy about the "time on their hands." Although many women fill their lives with satisfying and useful community work or jobs when their children are grown, others have nothing but overfastidious housekeeping or endless socializing with which to fill their time. Riesman makes the point that the woman who is not caring for a large family may face the problem of using her leisure time in a way to justify her existence; "care for the house and children is frequently her self-justification and escape.[9]

Cutting Recreation Costs

Without careful records, one is apt to underestimate the cost of recreational activities. An obvious place to save money, if you feel impelled to do so, is by substituting less costly recreational activities for those that require considerable sums of money. It is unwise to budget recreation out of family activities because it offers most people a chance to unwind, a change of pace from their ordinary routine.

If you enjoy taking trips by car, you might plan to camp out and make your own meals. Fifty per cent of the cost of recreational trips is consumed by food and lodging. Inexpensive camping facitilies are available over much of the country. Or you might try picnic meals for much of the time; they are far less expensive than eating in restaurants.

There are many types of low-cost entertainment in most communities.

[9] David Riesman, Nathan Glazer, Reuel Denney, *The Lonely Crowd* (New York: Doubleday, 1950), p. 73.

FIGURE 42. Golf is a popular pastime for many people. *(Courtesy of Du Pont Company.)*

Public concerts in museums, parks, and schools are often excellent and free. Some, if not free, charge a very low admission rate.

Art exhibits sponsored by community groups charge very little. An afternoon of looking at a gallery that sells pictures usually costs nothing. Museum fees are nominal and many are free. Some museums have special days when there is no charge.

Local theater groups can provide a fine evening of fun at prices well below that of more professional groups. Sometimes local community organizations sponsor first-run shows at reduced prices.

Many sports are not costly. Swimming, fishing, hiking, and hunting can provide fun and pleasure at low cost. Of course, one can purchase elaborate equipment and spend considerable money, but many people enjoy these sports at little cost. Tennis and golf can be played expensively at private courses and clubs. Many people like to play at these places for their social value. However, in many communities these sports can also be enjoyed for less expense at public facilities.

Sports equipment can often be purchased at budget prices by careful shopping. Many standard items are now available in discount stores.

Community organizations provide many programs of activities for family members at nominal cost or free. Public school recreational programs, the activities of the "Y," or those provided at community centers are inexpensive. Many fraternal and social groups have interesting activities.

Lastly, consider activities that might be done at home. Reading, playing bridge, or gardening need not be costly. Plan social activities with friends on an exchange basis. A dinner party might be a potluck affair, with everyone bringing something.

The Challenge of Leisure

"All work and no play makes Jack a dull boy." The same can be said of Mary, Mike, and Grandma. We all need healthy outlets for our interests and energies, well-chosen recreation can contribute much to our happy living.

Many people are unaware that they have time for recreation. These people may fill their leisure hours with activities that are socially acceptable, but not satisfying to them. They may be on a treadmill of accumulating possessions or pursuing social obligations designed to fit them into the role demanded by their station in life or their hoped-for station.

Other people arrive at their later years without having learned to play. They have no hobbies or recreational outlets that are satisfying to them, no way of spending time that is pleasant and fun. This is particularly true of men who have worked hard most of their lives. During their active years, their work was both a hobby and a pleasure. Faced with retirement, or reduced working hours, they do not know how to fill them happily.

It is important to learn to play early in life, to develop rewarding activities to carry on throughout one's lifetime. Some of these things could be learned during the school years, when new things are easily grasped. Courses in music, art, home economics, athletics, and industrial arts might focus more attention on the joy and pleasure people may get from them. As part of general education, these courses might expand their function by also becoming education for leisure.

SELECTED REFERENCES

BRIGHTBILL, CHARLES K. *Man and Leisure: A Philosophy of Recreation.* Englewood Cliffs, N.J.: Prentice-Hall, 1961.

DENNEY, REUEL. "The Leisure Society," *Harvard Business Review* (May-June, 1959), pp. 46-60.

FISK, GEORGE. *Leisure Spending-Behavior.* Philadelphia: University of Pennsylvania Press. 1963.

KAPLAN, MAX. *Leisure in America.* New York: Wiley, 1960.

LARRABEE, ERIC, and ROLF MEYERSOHN (eds.). *Mass Leisure.* New York: Free Press, 1958.

Sales Management. "What's Happening in the Family Fun Market?" (May 19, 1961), pp. 63-64, 66, 93-98.

10

SAVINGS
AND FAMILY FUNDS

> Some persons believe that all families should have
> a regular savings plan since such a plan helps
> people to accumulate a reserve and also enforces
> economy. Others believe that money should be
> profitably used, rather than hoarded.[1]

EARLY pastoral societies counted wealth in cattle or oxen. This presented many problems. If something was worth a quarter of a cow, did you butcher the cow? Obviously, the cow was more valuable alive and whole. Wheat, other grains, and tobacco also had disadvantages as currency. If kept too long they spoiled. Eventually, most commodities were dropped as currency and the precious metals, particularly gold, became the common form of money. Gold had the advantage of being quite scarce and not easily destroyed. It is still the base for the value of our paper currency.

Since the days of ancient Babylon men have engaged in the business of holding money for other people. Priests in the temples handled this and laws regulated the way in which it was done. During the Roman Empire large banks handled business affairs with far-flung parts of the empire. The National Currency Act of 1863, signed by President Lincoln, established a single national currency for the United States and a system of national banks supervised by the federal government.

Why Families Save

Most people save to have money for the things they want. (See Figure 43.) Perhaps it is a college education for their children or a home of their own. Or maybe they want to have enough money for their old age.

The needs and wants of people differ. Therefore, so do patterns of saving.

[1] Frances Lomas Feldman, *The Family in a Money World* (New York: Family Service Association of America, 1957), p. 125.

FIGURE 43. People save for many different purposes. *(Courtesy of Joint Council on Economic Education.)*

Some people spend everything they earn and save nothing. Others try to put away so much that they feel pinched in their everyday living. Developing a savings plan should be part of the total family plan for living. Long- and short-term goals and needs should be considered: the unexpected illness that will eat the family funds or the plan to go to Europe or to send the children to college.

Places to Save

There are many ways to save. Each has its own characteristics. The choice of a manner of savings should depend on what you want to do with your savings and when you plan to use the money.

Short-term savings to cover monthly expenses should be available quickly and easily. A savings or checking account in a bank is convenient. Savings for emergency use might be placed either in a bank or invested in government bonds that can be cashed in at any time without delay. Money that is accumulated for long-term goals might be invested in stocks, bonds, real estate, or life insurance, including annuities.

Banks

A bank is a financial institution chartered by the federal or state government to do certain things. One of the most important of these from the point of view of the average family is to receive deposits of money that can be withdrawn either on demand or after notice is given. (In practice no notice is required.) The bank invests a portion of these funds. The type of investments and proportion of their total funds that may be invested in each of several types of ways is carefully controlled to safeguard the depositors.

In addition, many banks are insured to safeguard the depositors. Insurance may be with the Federal Deposit Insurance Corporation, which insures deposits up to $10,000 for each depositor, and $20,000 for a joint account, or with private insurance companies. Most large banks are members of the Federal Deposit Insurance Corporation.

Commercial banks are the common ones that most people use regularly. They are owned and operated by stockholders. In the United States they offer both checking and savings accounts. However, in some states, savings and checking accounts are offered in different types of commercial banks. Commercial banks also offer services such as the renting of safety-deposit boxes, personal and mortgage loans, trust facilities for managing funds, cashier's checks (checks issued by the bank), certified checks (the funds are set aside by the bank so that the check is guaranteed good). Many also sell traveler's checks, and sell and redeem government bonds.

Mutual savings banks differ from commercial banks in that they are owned by the depositors. These operate largely in the Northeast. They offer facilities for savings accounts and mortgage lending. Dividends are paid on savings accounts which is similar to interest in commercial banks. Other services of mutual savings banks are limited.

Chartered banks in Canada are similar to commercial banks in the United States, except that they do not have trust facilities. Separate trust companies provide trust facilities. These companies also offer savings accounts and checking accounts in some situations.

Most banks have mail deposit and withdrawal service. A fairly new service is one offered by some employers; at your request your employer will deposit a portion of your wages or salary directly to your account.

When considering a bank to use, inquire if the deposits are insured, and by whom. The most dependable insurance in the United States is that guaranteed by the federal government (FDIC). Banks that belong often post this notice in their window or advertise it prominently. Canadian banks are not insured but are carefully regulated by the government to protect depositors.

The rate of interest paid on savings accounts should also be considered. Bank rates in the United States vary from time to time and in different parts of the country. Sometimes they even differ in neighboring cities. The interest rate, at any one time, of all Canadian chartered banks is the same; trust companies usually pay a little higher rate.

Are the services of the bank convenient for you? Sometimes you can arrange to have your savings and checking account at the same bank. Many banks are open evenings. Others have drive-in banking facilities; you can drive right up to an outside teller's window.

THE CHECKING ACCOUNT. A checking account is a method of having money available for payment of expenses by check. The check is a form

FIGURE 44. School savings plans encourage youngsters to develop the savings habit early. (*Courtesy of American Bankers Association.*)

furnished to the depositor by the bank which directs the bank to pay a stated amount to a particular person. It is also a record that can be used as proof of payment.

Checking accounts do not earn interest or dividends. There is usually a monthly charge for the use of the account or a charge for each check written by the depositor. Checking accounts that do not charge for service usually require that a minimum balance (a certain amount of money) be maintained in the account at all times.

An account can be opened quite simply. The customer furnishes on an application information about himself such as his place of birth, address and telephone number, his occupation and employer, and the names of his parents. Also the customer fills out a signature card in the same form as his signature will appear on checks. Then the customer is given a receipt for his initial deposit and a checkbook. Information about the bank and the method of writing checks, if desired, is usually given when an account is opened.

Deposits to checking accounts are made by going to the bank and filling out a deposit slip, or in many cases, by a mail deposit procedure. Most banks furnish self-addressed stamped forms for banking by mail. Some banks have provision for deposits after hours. Often this is a drop to which the depositor has a key.

Deposits can be in the form of cash and checks. They may also be in the form of promissory notes (a document stating that someone promises to pay a certain sum), postal money orders, and coupons from bonds.

Most banks give monthly statements; once a month they send the customer a statement of all transactions and the cancelled checks for the month. This statement also shows the balance remaining in the account at the end of the period. This balance should agree with the checkbook stubs if all the checks written have been cashed. Sometimes a check may be "outstanding"—that is, a check that was written has not as yet been deducted from the account.

Checks are cleared—that is, money is exchanged between banks to enable a depositor to receive credit at his bank for a check drawn on another bank. Banks exchange checks through a Clearing House. The Clearing House credits each bank with the checks it delivers and charges the bank for the checks it receives.

Banks in small communities maintain balances with banks in other cities and other parts of the world to facilitate the collection of checks and transfer of funds. The Federal Reserve Bank, through its 12 banks and 24 branches, serves as a central bank for other banks. Checks are cleared through it and money is transferred from one Reserve Bank to another. The busiest check-clearing operation in the United States is at the main office of the Federal Reserve Bank of New York.

If a check is lost or stolen, the bank should be asked to stop payment. It is possible to call the bank and request that this be done, but usually banks also like the request to be made in writing. There is often a small charge for this. However, although banks will try to stop payment, they are not responsible for the loss if the check has been paid. Sometimes checks are stopped when merchandise or services performed are not satisfactory.

All checks should be clearly written in ink. The date should be the date on which the check is drawn. A check which is dated on a Sunday is as good as one drawn on another day, but many people do not like to accept a check made out on a Sunday. The check number is for your convenience in keeping track of which checks are outstanding. The person or firm to whom the check is to be paid should be filled in after "Pay to the Order of." It is best to make the check out to someone or a business firm, rather than to "Bearer" or "Cash," because anyone can cash the check if "Bearer" or "Cash" is used. Also, a check made out to a person or firm serves as a receipt for payment when it has been cashed.

The amount of the check in numbers should be put in close to the dollar sign so that no other figures can be inserted. Cents should be stated as a fraction—that is, $18 20/100. On the following line the amount should be written out in words. Start as far left as possible to prevent the insertion of a word. Both the number and written words of the amount should agree. If they

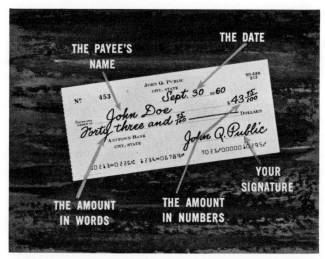

FIGURE 45. The correct way to make out a check. (*Courtesy of Joint Council on Economic Education.*)

do not, the law generally gives preference to the amount which is stated in words. Your signature should appear exactly as you wrote it on the signature card when you opened the account.

Before a check can be cashed or deposited, it must be endorsed—that is, it must be signed on the back, preferably at the extreme left end. A check can be endorsed in several ways. The most usual method is to sign your name on the back. This is known as a blank endorsement. It makes the check negotiable to the bearer. This should be done only when you are cashing the check or turning it over to someone else as payment. If you are depositing the check by mail to your bank, it is better to use a restrictive endorsement, such as "For deposit only, John Jones." When you receive a check on which your name is spelled incorrectly, the correct procedure is to endorse it exactly as it has been written on the check and then to write your correct signature under this.

It is always wise to cash a check promptly. The person who gave it may not keep the funds in the bank very long or may die. Also, although theoretically checks are good up to the Statute of Limitation, which is usually six years, many banks refuse to honor checks older than six months.

There are many reasons why a bank may refuse to honor a check. The most usual reason is that there are insufficient funds in the depositor's account to cover the amount of the check. Another reason may be that the check has been altered. If you make a mistake in writing a check, it is wisest to tear it up and write another one. Banks will not honor postdated checks, and most banks will not accept checks if the figures and the words do not agree. If the check has a stop order on it (that is, the person who originally wrote the check has requested that it not be paid), or if the person who wrote the check has died, the bank will not cash it. Also, most banks will not cash checks unless the person requesting payment is properly identified.

There are some cases when a person will not accept an ordinary check. Real estate transactions usually require that payment be made by "certified check." To certify a check the bank sets aside the money for the amount of the check so that it cannot be used for any other purpose and stamps the check to indicate that it certifies the funds are being held.

A SAVINGS ACCOUNT. A savings account earns interest that is usually computed quarterly on a compound basis. Compound interest computed quarterly is figured in the following manner. Let us assume that a person has deposited $100 in a bank that gives 4% interest compounded quarterly starting on January 1st. On April 1 he would receive $1.00 in interest (1/4 of 4%). On June 1 the interest would be figured on a balance of $101, and be $1.01. On October 1 the interest would be computed on $102.01 and be $1.02; on January 1 it would be computed on $103.03 and be $1.03.

Actually, interest compounded quarterly earns a little more than interest at the same rate computed once annually. In the example given above, the compound interest at 4% on a $100 deposit held for one year was $4.06. If it were computed only once annually at 4%, it would be $4.00.

Quarterly computation of interest also has another advantage to the depositor over an annual computation. Interest is usually computed on the minimum balance maintained during a quarterly period. If the amount in the account is high for only one quarter, it will earn interest on this amount for this one quarter. Some banks have a policy of allowing deposits to be made 15 days after the quarterly period begins and still be counted for interest computation as if the deposit had been made at the beginning of the period.

Deposits may be made at any time. Withdrawals usually can be made at any time, although banks can legally require 30 to 90 days' notice. Depositors are given a passbook, which is a duplicate of the bank's record of their account. Deposits, withdrawals, and interest are recorded in the passbook, which must accompany any transaction. Interest is generally based on the average minimum balance maintained during the period.

Several kinds of accounts may be opened at a savings bank. Some of these are:

(a) The individual account. This is where one person, either an adult or a minor, is the sole owner and the account is payable only to this person. This type of account can be opened with as little as $1.00 at most banks. The maximum that may be deposited is not usually limited, but since only $10,000 per person or $20,000 for a joint account is insured in this type of account by FDIC and most bank insurers, this is the maximum amount that prudent people usually would keep in one bank.

(b) Joint and survivorship accounts. Two people may want to use the same savings account. Joint or survivorship accounts are usually held by a husband

FIGURE 46. Checking and savings accounts may be established in one name only or as joint accounts. (*Courtesy of Joint Council on Economic Education.*)

and wife. Each must fill out an application, and each has the right to withdraw funds during the lifetime of both parties. (Checking accounts may also be joint accounts.)

If either one dies, most states forbid the bank to honor checks or withdrawals until the tax claims of the state and federal government are paid and all other claims against the estate are settled.

(c)   The voluntary trust account. These can be opened by an individual in trust for another person. Often this is done with funds intended for a child. The person who holds the trust account has full control of the funds during his lifetime; upon his death, however, it is payable to the person for whom it is in trust. The person who opens the account has the right to change the beneficiary at any time that he wishes to do so.

(d)   The organization account. This is an account in the name of a nonprofit group such as a professional society, church, or fraternal organization.

(e)   The fiduciary account. This account is a means of handling entrusted funds for a minor or an incompetent person. Usually the executor or administrator of an estate, and the guardian of an individual would use this type of account.

(f)   Christmas Club accounts. These are accounts that do not pay interest. Regular amounts are deposited that are returned by withdrawal or check shortly before Christmas.

(g)   Other types of special accounts. School savings bank accounts are owned by students who make deposits in schools who have cooperating arrangements with banks. The purpose of these accounts is to promote thrift in young people.

Vacation club accounts are similar to Christmas Clubs, except that the funds are saved for a vacation.

Payroll deduction accounts are special accounts in which business firms deposit to an employee's account each pay day authorized deductions from his salary or wages.

Savings and Loan Associations

Most savings and loan associations are mutual associations—that is, they are owned by their members. In many ways they are similar to mutual savings banks. Everyone who has an account is a member of the association. Dividends are paid on the money deposited in the account, as interest is paid on an account in a savings bank. However, the interest rate of savings and loan associations is usually higher than that of banks.

All deposits in federally chartered savings and loan associations are insured with the Federal Savings and Loan Insurance Corporation up to $10,000 per account. Savings and loan associations who are members of this federal insuring association usually display in FSLIC insignia. State chartered associations may be insured under the FSLIC program, but are not required to be.

Two types of accounts are available: savings accounts and investment accounts. A savings account is similar to a savings account in a bank. Accounts earn dividends which are usually computed on a compound basis twice a year.

Investment accounts are opened with a deposit of $100 or even multiples of $100. Deposits must be made in multiples of $100. Semiannual dividends are paid to the investor by check.

Sometimes a maximum limit is placed on the amount that can be deposited in one account. Generally, money is available on demand, but legally, associations may require written notice. The proportion of liquid assets held as reserves is a measure of how well the association can meet the withdrawals of its members on demand or if borrowers should be unable to repay their loans.

When a federally insured savings and loan association is declared a failure, there may be a long lapse of time before the depositors are paid. First, the Federal Savings and Loan Insurance Corporation tries to have the association taken over by a stronger one. If this is not possible, the shareholders are paid what is owed to them up to the insured limits. By contrast, when a federally insured bank fails, the Federal Deposit Insurance Corporation pays depositors what is due them in about ten or eleven days.

Credit Unions

Credit unions are associations of people who have some common bond; they may work for the same company or belong to the same union or trade association. The purpose of a credit union is to promote thrift. A person joins by purchasing one or more shares which usually sell for five dollars each. Any amount may be deposited after joining.

The current rate of interest for money deposited in a credit union is slightly higher than that of banks, most savings and loan associations, or government bonds. (Part of the reason for this higher rate is that credit unions are exempt from federal taxes and they do not seek to make a profit.) In addition, members of credit unions can borrow money at 12 per cent, which is a lower rate than that charged by most department stores and finance companies. Also, many credit unions provide for their depositors, without extra charge, life insurance that is worth an additional one-half of 1 per cent for young people, and even more to people past age 45. This is group insurance which remains in effect only as long as one remains a member of the credit union.

Credit unions are chartered by either the federal government or a state. In Canada they are chartered by a province. An auditor from the chartering group usually examines the records and books of each credit union once a year.

The members manage credit unions. In some cases, a credit union is managed by volunteers; in others, a person may be employed as manager. If there is a paid executive, it is usually the treasurer. Many business firms are willing to give office space to a credit union and some time off to the officers so that the firm will not be bothered with requests for pay advances to meet emergencies of the employees.

Credit unions have an excellent record of collections. The borrowers in most cases are employees of the same company as the officers. Since everyone in a firm knows when people are paid, it is hard for a borrower to evade his obligations to the credit union.

The liquid reserves of a credit union may vary and thus their ability to meet withdrawals on demand. Federally chartered credit unions must add 20 per cent of their annual net earnings to the reserve each year until they equal 10 per cent of the shares outstanding, plus an additional amount for overdue loans.

Government Savings Bonds

Government savings bonds, unlike other types of bonds, have fixed redemption value and are available in varying amounts. There are two types of government savings bonds designed for small investors: Series E and H. Series E bonds are appreciation bonds; they are purchased at 75 per cent of their value at maturity (that is, cost $75 for a bond worth $100 at maturity). The Series H bond is a current income bond; full payment of the face value is made at the time of purchase (that is, a $100 bond costs $100) and interest is paid to the bondholder by check every six months.

The most popular type at present is the Series E type. These can be purchased and redeemed at most banks without charge. In addition, many firms will deduct part of your salary (at your request) and purchase these savings bonds for you.

If held over the full term—7 years, 9 months—E bonds earn 3¾ per cent interest. However, the interest is computed on a sliding scale, depending on how long the bonds have been held. Government savings bonds are not a

FIGURE 47. Most banks sell U.S. Government Savings Bonds. *(Courtesy of American Bankers Association.)*

good investment unless they plan to keep them for at least one and a half years, because if held for less time the rate of interest they pay is below that of many banks. Bonds may be held for ten years beyond maturity at the maximum rate of interest.

E Bonds are an excellent way to hedge against the possibility of unemployment or to save for retirement because you can postpone paying tax on the interest until the bonds are cashed in. In the event of unemployment or retirement, one's income is likely to be curtailed, and the amount of tax due on the interest earned by the bonds would therefore be reduced.

H bonds earn the same amount of interest as E bonds. Since the interest is paid by check every six months this makes them a very useful type of investment for people who want the interest as a regular income.

It is possible to exchange E bonds, upon maturity or before, for Government H bonds and defer paying income tax on the accumulated interest of the E bonds until the H bonds are cashed in. This would be very useful for people approaching retirement. Couples who have a very modest retirement income might avoid paying any tax on the interest earned by their original E bonds.

If savings bonds are lost, stolen, or destroyed they can be replaced. Write to the Bureau of the Public Debt, Division of Loans and Currency, 536 South Clark Street, Chicago 5, Illinois. List the serial numbers of the bonds, the date of issue, and your name and address. You will receive a form to complete, and new bonds will be issued. If you change your name because of marriage or divorce or wish to add another person as co-owner, contact the Bureau of the Public Debt.

A new series of savings bonds has been issued by Canada each year. Information about these can be obtained at any chartered bank.

Postal Savings

The U.S. postal savings program was established in 1910 by an Act of Congress. Its purpose was to provide immigrants with a safe place to deposit savings. The federal government promises to pay all money deposited in postal savings.

Postal savings were heavily used during the depression of the 1930's when many people wanted the reassurance of having their deposits guaranteed by the government. Since 1947 there has been a steady decrease in the use of postal savings because bank interest rates have generally risen above the 2 per cent paid by the postal savings system. Money deposited during a month begins to earn interest on the first day of the next month. However, it must be on deposit for three months to earn interest. Interest is compounded annually.

Deposits are shown by certificates issued in amounts of $1.00, $2.00, $10, $20, $50, $100, $200, and $500. Deposits must be made in combinations of these amounts. Certificates of deposit are issued in the depositor's name that serve as a receipt of the deposits similar to the passbook issued by a bank. These certificates are not negotiable; they cannot be transferred to another person, but can be cashed in at any time without a waiting period.

Postal savings stamps may be purchased in denominations of 10 cents, 25 cents, $1.00, and $5.00. Stamps do not earn interest, but they can be used to purchase postal savings certificates or U.S. savings bonds.

Postal certificates are registered in one's name and will be replaced if lost or destroyed upon proper identification. Postal savings stamps, however, are not individually registered and therefore cannot be replaced if lost.

Accounts may be opened by persons ten years of age or older. The amount on deposit may not exceed $2500 exclusive of accumulated interest, and the account can only be in the name of one individual. Joint accounts or trust accounts are not permitted.

Other Methods of Transferring Funds

Sometimes you may wish to send funds to someone in another part of the country or out of the country who will not accept your personal check. A certified check is one way of doing this. Another way would be to ask the bank to send its check and you give the bank the money. This is called a "bank," or "cashier's check." You can also purchase a bank money order or buy American Express Company money orders. Postal money orders, both national and international, would also serve this purpose. They can be bought at the post office.

Traveler's checks are very useful if you are going on a trip; it is much safer to carry funds this way rather than in cash. They are not negotiable until signed, and will be replaced if lost. They can be purchased at most banks. At the time of purchase the buyer signs each check with his usual signature in the upper left-hand corner. When he wishes to cash one, he signs it again in the presence of the person who will cash it.

Other Forms of Savings

There are many ways to save. Life insurance and social security are means of saving. The cash values of life insurance may be borrowed against or the policy cashed in after it has been in force for a period of time. Although assets in one's social security account cannot be borrowed against or taken out, these funds do furnish income at certain points in one's life. These are discussed more fully in Chapter 12, "The Social Security System," and Chapter 13, "Life Insurance."

A real estate investment is another form of saving. Carefully chosen real estate can produce income and/or increase in value. Most individual home purchases are not made with an eye to their investment value, but rather to whether they will provide comfortable living conditions.

Stocks and bonds are also an important type of investment. These are discussed more fully in Chapter 11.

Safeguarding Family Documents

Records of family savings, and investments, and insurance need to be kept in a safe place. One of the best places is a safe deposit box. This is a small metal drawer kept in a section of the bank's vault for use by customers. Each box has its own separate lock with a key. However, most boxes cannot be opened unless both the customer's key and the bank's key are used. The rental charge for a small box is nominal, about $7.00 per year. A safe-deposit box is the best place to keep valuable documents such as stock certificates, insurance policies, real estate deeds, wills, and other family valuables. Bank books which are used frequently may be inconvenient to keep in a safe deposit box.

SELECTED REFERENCES

CLENDENIN, JOHN C. *Introduction to Investments*. New York: McGraw-Hill, 1955.

CREDIT UNION NATIONAL ASSOCIATION. *Credit Union Yearbook* (published annually). Madison, Wisc.

Facts You Should Know About Saving Money (latest ed.). National Better Business Bureau, Chrysler Building, New York 17, N.Y.

Savings and Home Financing Source Book (latest ed.). Federal Home Loan Bank Board, Washington, D.C.: Government Printing Office.

Savings and Loan Fact Book (latest ed.). United States Savings and Loan League, Chicago, Ill.

THE AMERICAN BANKERS ASSOCIATION. *The Commercial Banking Industry*. Englewood Cliffs, N.J.: Prentice-Hall, 1962.

11

INVESTING IN STOCKS

The stock you'd like to buy, of course, is the one that just doesn't exist. You'd like a stock that is completely safe, one that pays a liberal dividend, and one that is bound to go up.[1]

MILLIONS of people want their savings to earn more than is possible through government savings bonds or deposits in a savings bank. Many of these people look to the stock market as a place to earn higher rates of return.

Investing in the stock market takes careful consideration, just as does any other important use of money. First, one needs to be sure that he has sufficient cash or easily obtainable reserves for monthly expenses and small emergencies that may arise. Stock market investments should be made with funds planned for long-range purposes. Since the stock market fluctuates, it is not wise to invest funds that will be needed in the near future because if funds are needed when the market is low, selling may entail a considerable loss.

Second, consider the purpose of investing. Is it merely to keep ahead of inflation or is the aim to make a lot of money? How you invest will depend on this. Generally, the less risk the smaller the rate of return but the more secure the investment—that is, the chance of losing what you invest is less.

How a Stock Company Operates

Stock market investments are usually in the form of common stock, preferred stock, and bonds. What is common stock? To answer that, let us look at an example of how a company is formed.

Suppose you have invented a new type of vacuum cleaner. You have had it patented and you are sure there is a market for it. You would like to begin producing, but you do not have enough money to rent a factory, buy machinery and hire employees. Assume that you need $40,000 to start this business. Therefore, you decide to form a company and sell shares in it to raise money. Thus the ABC Vacuum Cleaner Company is formed.

[1] Louis Engel, *How to Buy Stocks* (New York: Bantam Books, 1957).

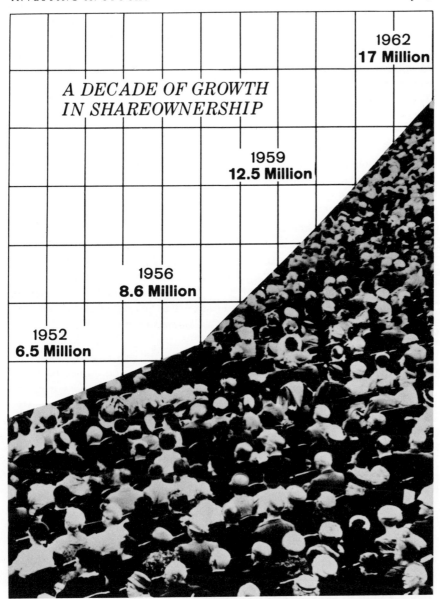

A DECADE OF GROWTH IN SHAREOWNERSHIP

1962
17 Million

1959
12.5 Million

1956
8.6 Million

1952
6.5 Million

FIGURE 48. *(Courtesy of New York Stock Exchange.)*

You might consider selling forty shares at $1,000 each, 80 shares at $500 each, or 400 shares at $100 each. Suppose you sell 400 shares at $100 each. Then every person who bought a share would own 1/400 of the company and be a shareholder. The 400 shares are the common stock of the company. The original selling price of $100 is the *par value* of the *common stock*.

The stockholders elect a board of directors to supervise the operation of the business. Each person who owns one share is entitled to one vote. If he owns two shares, he is entitled to two votes, and so on. The board members usually give only part-time to supervising the company, so they elect a president and officers who will be the full-time managing officers. The officers report to the board of directors periodically, and once a year the board holds a meeting for the stockholders.

At the end of the first year, say, the ABC Vacuum Cleaner Company found it had a profit of $5,000. The board of directors decided to put $3,000 towards more machinery and distribute the remaining $2,000 as dividends. Since there were 400 shares outstanding each stockholder would receive $5, or a 5 per cent return on his original $100.

When the ABC Vacuum Cleaner Company found it needed money to buy additional machinery, the board of directors suggested to the stockholders that they issue 400 more shares of stock. The stockholders approved this plan, and the company offered *rights* to the stockholders. These rights entitle existing stockholders to buy the new stock in proportion to the amount of stock in the company they presently own. When the time in which to exercise these rights expired, the new issue was offered to people who did not own any of the original stock. (Often rights are offered to stockholders at a price below the prevailing market.)

Some years later the ABC Vacuum Cleaner Company wanted to buy a vacuum bag manufacturing company, but they did not have enough money to do so. The owner of the bag company wanted to retire and use the money from the sale of his business to give him a safe and regular income. Since the ABC Vacuum Cleaner Company seemed to be sound and well managed, the manufacturer arranged to sell his vacuum bag company to them in return for 500 shares of *preferred stock* at a value of $100 each, in the ABC Vacuum Cleaner Company. This preferred stock was offered to purchasers with a yearly dividend of $5 per share, which was to be paid before dividends could be paid to holders of the common stock. In the event that the ABC Vacuum Cleaner Company should become bankrupt, the holders of the preferred stock would be paid before the holders of the common stock.

Suppose that the ABC Vacuum Cleaner Company wanted to consolidate its bag making plant and its vacuum making plant in one building. It would need $250,000 to build a new modern factory. They might finance this with bonds. Bonds are issued to give a company long-term credit of a large amount. Bonds have a fixed rate of return and stand ahead of both preferred and common stock when distribution of company profits is made and if the company is liquidated. In the event that the ABC Vacuum Cleaner Company failed, the bondholders would be paid first. Bonds of large successful companies are considered the most secure and conservative type of investment in the stock market. They generally pay a lower rate of return than common or preferred stock, but are least likely to become worthless.

Types of Securities

Although there are many good stocks, none can promise to be completely safe, pay liberal dividends, and go up in value. As compared with other stocks, one might consider a relatively safe stock to be one in a solid, stable company that has weathered many economic storms. Many public utilities are in this category. If you want a growth stock—that is, one which might increase greatly in value, then you need to take more risk. The stock of a company in a new industry, such as space communications, might be an example of a growth stock.

Stocks and bonds are issued by corporations. A stockholder owns part of a corporation. In the eyes of the law a corporation is a legal entity separate from the owners. This separate entity has the right to own property, incur debts, sue and be sued. The stockholders of a corporation have what is commonly referred to as "limited liability." If the corporation in which they possess shares is unable to pay its debts, they are in no way obligated. (This is unlike many types of partnerships where the partners have a personal obligation for the firm's debts.)

Common Stocks

One of the most frequent reasons why people buy common stocks is that they serve as a hedge against inflation. Over a long period, as the prices of consumer goods have risen, stock prices have also risen. This type of investment tends to keep pace with the rising cost of living. (This does not mean, however, that every stock has kept pace with inflation, but only that the broad trend of stock prices has kept pace.) Another way of stating this would be to say that stock prices have risen in a way to compensate for the decreasing value of the dollar. For instance, some stocks purchased in 1910 might have been sold for three times as many dollars in the 1960's. However, because of the rise in prices, it would have taken three times as many dollars to buy the same type of goods as in 1910.

Two other reasons that many people buy common stocks are: (1) They offer the possibility of higher returns than do other classes of securities. The average yield of common stock for the last ten years has been higher than either bonds or savings banks. (2) If they are sold at a profit, and have been held for more than six months, they are taxed as capital gains. The tax on capital gains is no more than half the rate one would usually pay and in any case no more than 25 per cent. For people with a substantial income, the possibility of a tax saving may be important.

Although there are many sound reasons for buying common stock, there are also reasons not to buy. First, the past performance of common stocks is not any prediction of their future activity. Conceivably a widespread depression could greatly reduce their value for a prolonged period. Also, it is difficult to determine which stocks will increase in value during a period of inflation. Although the general trend may be upward, this does not insure that every stock will move, or even move at an equal rate.

Common stocks vary greatly in quality. Some are highly speculative; others have a long and consistent record of paying dividends. So while common stocks in general may be considered less secure than either bonds or preferred stock, some common stocks are considered very secure investments. This type of stock is sometimes called a "defensive" stock—that is, in a period of deteriorating business it is likely to do better than average from an earnings point of view. Utilities fall in this category; people need services even when business conditions are poor. Gold mining stocks are also considered defensive. In periods of depression the cost of mining drops, while the government continues to buy the whole output. Companies that make habit-forming products such as gum, tobacco, soft drinks, and candy bars, also tend to maintain their value in depressed periods.

The opposite of the defensive stocks are those that fluctuate with the business cycles. These are often called "cyclical" stocks. These stocks pay good dividends and rise in periods of inflation, but are hit hardest when business conditions deteriorate. Some of the cyclical industries are the railroad, automobile and steel industries, and building materials.

At one time it was felt that savings banks, insurance companies, trust funds, and individuals who were wholly dependent on stock market investments should buy primarily bonds and preferred stock to conserve the principal of the funds. However, in recent years these investors have turned more and more to good quality common stocks to hedge against inflation and increase their earnings.

Preferred Stock

Preferred stock resembles bonds more than it does common stock because there is a fixed return on the investment if dividends are paid. If the return is good and the company has a record of paying it regularly, preferred stock may be a good conservative investment. It has the advantage of standing ahead of common stock if the company is forced to liquidate.

Although the return on preferred stock is usually fixed, there is a type of preferred stock known as "participating preferred," in which the stock shares in the earnings of the company if the earnings are sufficient. This stock would receive its regular dividend, and then if there was some income left after the common stock received a similar dividend, the balance would be divided between the common and the preferred stock.

Some preferred stock is issued as convertible preferred stock—that is, the purchaser has the right to convert it to common stock at a fixed ratio. This gives preferred stockholders a hedge against inflation. If the price of the common stock rises, then the preferred can be exchanged for common stock. The conversion feature has made this a popular type of preferred stock in recent years.

The dividends on preferred stock may be of the cumulative types—that is, if they are not paid quarterly as they should be, they accumulate to the credit of the preferred stockholder and must be paid when the earnings of the company permit, and before dividends can be paid on common stock.

There is also preferred stock that is callable; the issuing company can call in the stock to retire it. Preferred stock is often issued as callable stock. Usually the company must pay a premium to the preferred stockholders when calling the stock in.

Since many institutions now buy preferred stock, there is generally not a great spread in price between good quality bonds and preferred stocks. As a result these are often not attractive investments for individual investors.

Bonds

Bonds are really notes indicating that money has been loaned to a person or a corporation. They differ from stocks in that they are evidence of a debt, rather than ownership in a corporation.

Most bonds are held by institutional investors. There are several reasons for this. Bonds are sold in large denominations, usually $1,000. It takes a great deal of time, energy, and study to make good bond investments, and the difference in return between good bonds and U.S. savings bonds is very small.

Bonds are a particularly attractive investment in periods of depression because even if dividends on stock are withheld, interest on high quality bonds may continue. Also, bondholders have first call on the assets of a company if the company becomes bankrupt. As a result, the prices of high-grade bonds usually rise in depression periods. The income from state and municipal bonds are exempt from federal income tax, which makes them an attractive investment for people in high income brackets.

The value of a bond depends on the rating of the bond, its yield, how the bond is to be retired (if it is to be retired), and the financial status of the company issuing the bond. There are a number of services which rate bonds— that is, they assign a classification to the bond which gives an idea of the approximate quality of the bond. Some of the best-known rating services are Standard and Poors, Moody's, and Fitch.

Bond yield is determined by dividing the coupon rate (this is similar to interest except that bonds have coupons which are turned in to receive payment) by the price the bond is selling at. For example, a $1,000 bond might be selling at $1,500 and have a coupon rate of $30 per year, payable quarterly. This would be a yield of 2 per cent.

The value of the bond is also influenced by whether it is callable—that is, whether the company can choose to retire it. If it is callable, the price at which the company can buy it back is an important factor in determining the value of the bond.

Bonds are of two types: secured and unsecured. A secured bond is not only backed up by the company's promise to pay, but also by the pledge of

188]   THE FAMILY AS CONSUMERS

certain property if the company is unable to pay. For example, a mortgage bond pledges the property if the person who borrowed the money is unable to pay. Corporations may issue bonds with property or machinery as collateral. While the security behind the bond is important in determining bond value, the reputation and financial status of the company issuing the bonds is even more important.

The usual procedure is for bonds to be issued for a specific period, after which they are retired (that is, the debt is repaid). Good financial practices require companies to set aside regularly reserves to be used to retire the bonds. This procedure known as a sinking-fund is to the advantage of the bondholder because it means that there is a definite cash reserve towards redemption of the bonds.

Buying and Selling Securities

Buying and selling securities is a business venture, and it should be based on careful analysis and deliberation. Unfortunately, many small investors view the stock market as a place to get rich quick and assume that they can make sound investments with little knowledge and study. It rarely works this way.

If you are planning to buy securities, it is wise to buy from a reputable broker in a reliable brokerage house. Get advice from knowledgeable sources —your bank, your broker, and investment advisory services. Do not follow the lead of tipsters and well-meaning friends; often they do not know much about the securities market.

Knowing when to buy securities is most difficult. Ideally, one would like to buy when stocks and bonds are cheap and sell when they are dear. But this is not easy to do. Fluctuations in business trends are often difficult to analyze and predict. Also, not all industries react the same way to business conditions. Even within an industry, businesses often do not react in exactly the same way.

To reduce your need to sell at disadvantageous times, it is wise to: (a) buy stocks and bonds that have a good yield—that is, their income in relation to price is sufficient so that you are not forced to sell to realize something on your investment; and (b) plan to buy only with funds you do not expect to need in the immediate future.

It is always a good idea to diversify one's investments wherever possible, so that if one investment does not do well there is a chance that the others will not be in the same position. This means investing in several companies in different types of businesses. Also, it may mean buying different types of investments, stocks, bonds, and preferred stock according to your personal needs and plans. A young man with expectations of an increasing income might want more common stocks and fewer bonds or preferred stocks to achieve maximum increase in his assets. A man or woman past retirement

FIGURE 49. The stock of many industries is traded in the stock market. *(Courtesy of New York Stock Exchange.)*

who wants to conserve the principal might buy more bonds than common stock.

Mutual Funds and Investment Plans

The rapid growth of a middle-class population with modest sums of money to invest has led to the development of investment companies tailored to meet the needs of small investors. An investment company is an organization which manages the savings of a number of people by investing them in a variety of stocks and/or bonds. The securities in which the company holds stocks or bonds is called their *portfolio*. (The term *portfolio* is also used to refer to the group of stocks held by an individual or institution.)

One of the most popular investment plans for the small investor has been mutual funds. Rather than buy shares of stock, the investor purchases shares in a company which in turn invests these funds in stocks and bonds. How much one's investment earns will vary with the management of the fund. Broadly speaking, mutual funds belong in three categories: growth funds, balanced funds, and income funds.

The purpose of a growth fund is to invest in assets that will appreciate in value. Usually the investments of these companies are about 90 per cent common stocks.

A balanced fund tries to hedge more against losses in a falling market; about 60 per cent of its investments are in common stocks and 40 per cent in bonds and preferred stock. In a rising market, balanced funds do not increase in value as rapidly as most growth funds, but in a falling one they tend to maintain their value better.

Income funds invest primarily in securities yielding a high income. Some funds will take more risks than do others to give a high rate of return. Generally, income funds invest in preferred stocks, bonds, and high-yield common stocks. The value of the shares in this type of fund is less likely to depreciate in a falling market than that of investments in either a growth fund or a balanced fund.

Investment funds have two types of income. They earn interest and dividends on their investments. Also, they make money by selling securities at a profit. All profits on securities held over six months qualify as capital gains, for investors in the higher income brackets. In reporting income to their investors investment companies indicate whether or not it is a long-term gain so that the investors can use this information in computing their personal income taxes. However, the investor may receive both types of profits in one combined check.

It is often difficult for a potential investor to determine whether an investment company or mutual fund is a good one in which to invest. Often a salesman will paint a glowing picture of the funds' profits. However, although many funds have done much better than an average investor could hope to do by direct personal investing, others have not; or if they have, their management expenses have been so high that it offsets the profits. (Investment companies, including mutual funds, charge a percentage for management, usually about 8 per cent.) Closed-end companies (that is those which issue only a limited amount of stock which is traded on an exchange) tend to have lower management fees.

One of the ways in which one could check on a company in which he was considering investing would be through a broker or bank or by reading some of the comparative studies of these funds in business journals. A usual comparison is whether the investment fund has done better than the average prices of a group of leading stocks, such as the Dow-Jones industrial average.

The Monthly Investment Plan offered by member firms of the New York Stock Exchange is another plan for the small investor. Monthly, the investor deposits a certain amount of money in his account that is used to buy the stock or stocks which he has selected. If the amount of money invested is not exactly the same as the selling price of even shares of stock, a fraction of the share is credited to the investor's account. In this plan, stock is owned outright by the investor, whereas in mutual funds it is owned by the fund. The Monthly Investment Plan has not been as successful as its sponsors originally hoped probably because brokerage fees run high in buying and selling small lots of stock.

Investment clubs managed by a group of people not in the investment business have also become popular for the small investor. The members pool their money and buy shares in the name of the club. Generally, the stocks are selected by majority vote. Some clubs study the stock seriously before investing; others give it only a casual perusal. Many stock club members have learned that not all stocks go up, and good investments are hard to locate.

Government Regulation of the Security Market

Since 1932 regulations have been established to assure honesty in the stock market. Federal laws and the Securities and Exchange Commission (SEC) serve to regulate some aspects of the securities market. New issues of stock must disclose accurate information about the company's earnings, assets, and volume of business. This is set forth in a brochure called the "prospectus."

It is illegal to manipulate stocks by spreading rumors or misleading record keeping. The SEC watches carefully to see that market manipulations do not take place. It is also necessary for all securities listed in an exchange to be registered with the SEC.

Placing an Order

Cash or Credit

Securities may be bought for cash or for credit. Credit transactions are usually margin purchases where the purchaser puts up some of his own money and borrows the rest from his broker. The Federal Reserve Board specifies how much of the purchase price must be cash and how much may be borrowed. This ratio is changed from time to time, depending on the general financial market. If the margin is set at 50 per cent, this means that the borrower must put up 50 per cent of the purchase price. A rate of 75 per cent means that the purchaser must put up 75 per cent of the purchase price. If the market price of the stock purchased on margin drops, the purchaser must put up more cash to keep the margin ratio within the legal limits. For example, if a stock is purchased at $100 a share on a 50 per cent margin, the purchaser need only put up $50. However, if the market price drops to $50 after he purchased it, he must put up an additional $25 per share. (When a stock price drops, it is considered that this drop comes out of the portion the purchaser has paid.)

How an Order Is Handled

When a prospective purchaser asks his broker to buy a certain stock, the broker sends this order to the floor representative of the firm (the person who is actually on the floor of the stock exchange), who in turn negotiates the purchase. (See Figure 50.) However, although orders are executed quickly on the floor of the exchange, buying and selling is not as simple as this. A purchaser can request his broker to buy a particular stock at no more than a particular price or at market (whatever the stock is selling for). Similarly a seller can put in an order to sell at market or at a specific price. The stock market is really an auction market. Prospective purchasers bid on a stock at a price, and prospective sellers offer it at a price.

In addition to the above, several other types of orders can be placed to buy stock. A *stop* order is one designed to limit losses. You can put in an order to sell a stock if it hits a certain low price on the market. If the stock declines to this level, your broker will sell it.

Stocks are generally sold in lots of 100 shares (round lots). However they may also be purchased in smaller quantities (odd lots). Odd lots are handled on the floor of the exchange by special odd lot dealers. The brokerage cost to buy odd lots is a little higher than that for round lots, which is usually about 1 per cent of the selling price. The purchase and sale of both round lots and odd lots can be arranged by your local stockbroker.

Stock prices are usually quoted in eighths of a point ($22\frac{1}{8}$, $29\frac{3}{8}$). Bond prices are quoted similarly, except that they have an "and interest" figure added to the price. The purchaser of a bond pays the interest accrued since the last date the bond paid interest. For instance, if a specific bond pays $25 in interest on both January 1 and June 1, the person who purchases this bond on April 1 would have to pay $12.50 above the price of the bond which would be the accrued interest.

It is possible to buy and sell securities one does not own. However, this is a very risky procedure; if the market goes the opposite way from what is expected, financial losses can be very great. If a person sells stock he owns, it is called a *long* sale. If he sells stock he expects to buy but does not presently own, it is called a *short* sale. Within a certain period the person who has sold stock short must actually buy stock to deliver.

FIGURE 50. *(Facing page)* How an order is executed. TOP: The order is phoned in. MIDDLE: The order is relayed to the floor of the exchange. BOTTOM LEFT: The floor man arranges for the purchase. BOTTOM RIGHT: The transaction is recorded on your account. *(Courtesy of New York Stock Exchange.)*

Stock Market Terminology

The stock market is sometimes referred to as a *bull* or *bear* market. If there is a general buying trend in the stock market, it is called a bull market; if there is a general falling trend, it is called a bear market. Sometimes the market may be referred to as *bullish* or *bearish*, indicating evidence of one of these trends.

Trust Services

Banks, trust companies, and certain types of investment companies have departments that will manage securities and investments for a fee. These are professional services that generally invest in a conservative manner. Their aim is usually to provide income and conserve the principal. These companies can manage a portfolio more effectively than can most individuals who have little time to devote to this and no training in this area.

Most trust companies deal only with large portfolios of stocks, over $50,000. However, sometimes the trust departments of banks or brokerage concerns will handle smaller portfolios.

This management service is available to handle both funds for individuals and for their heirs. It can be arranged to leave assets to be managed as a trust fund. A trust arrangement can be quite flexible, with arrangements to use principal as well as income for such purposes as providing a college education for a youngster.

Wills and Estate Planning

Anyone with any assets or dependents should write a will. This should be drawn up by a competent attorney in line with the laws of the state or province. Through a will, it is possible to arrange guardianship of minor children in the event that anything happens to the parents. Also, financial assets can be given for the benefit of dependents.

If there is no will, funds will be distributed according to the law of the state in which the deceased resided. Also there may be a costly legal procedure before the assets can be turned over to the family. When the estate is small and there is no will attorneys' fees and court expenses can consume a major portion of the legacy.

Also, a will helps to carry out the purpose for which the funds have been saved. In many states the law provides that if there is no will, the remaining funds must be divided between the wife and children. Children under the age of 21 must be protected by certain custodial arrangements for the handling of money, which is costly. Often a small estate is made even smaller and less useful to the remaining family under this procedure.

SELECTED REFERENCES

BADGER, RALPH E. *Investment Principles and Practices.* Englewood Cliffs, N.J.: Prentice-Hall, 1961.

BOARD OF GOVERNORS OF THE FEDERAL RESERVE SYSTEM. *The Federal Reserve System—Purposes and Functions.* Washington, D.C.: Government Printing Office, 1961.

CASEY, WILLIAM J. *Mutual Funds and How to Use Them.* New York: New York Institute of Business Planning, 1959.

COHEN, JEROME B., and ARTHUR W. HANSON. *Personal Finance, Principles and Case Problems.* Homewood, Ill.: Richard D. Irwin 1964.

DOANE, C. RUSSELL, and E. C. HARWOOD. *How to Invest Wisely.* Great Barrington, Mass.: American Institute for Economic Research, 1957.

ENGEL, LOUIS. *How to Buy Stocks.* New York: Bantam Books, 1962.

FEDERAL RESERVE BANK OF NEW YORK. *Money: Master or Servant?* Washington, D.C.: Government Printing Office, 1955.

NEW YORK STOCK EXCHANGE. *Fact Book 1962.* New York: New York Stock Exchange.

12

THE SOCIAL
SECURITY SYSTEM

As the real wage of the worker increases and
also as employment becomes more certain, unemployment and the absence of income acquires
its contrasting horror. With increasing income
it also becomes possible to think of old age: the
individual expects to survive.[1]

SECURING food, clothing, and shelter—the necessities of
life—has always been one of man's basic problems. Industrialized societies use money as the medium of exchange
and the means of purchasing the necessities. The need to provide money for
family living expenses when the wage earner was not earning because of unemployment or due to old age led to the enactment of the Social Security Laws.

The Social Security Act was bipartisan legislation enacted in 1935. Its purpose was to provide financial help and support for people on a nationwide
basis. Responsibility to provide financial protection against life's hazards is
fairly recent in the history of the world. Bismarck instituted the first national
program of compulsory insurance against accidents, sickness, widowhood,
and old age in Germany in the 1880's. Great Britain followed with a program
of old-age pensions, unemployment insurance, and, later, old-age insurance.

Social Forces that Brought About
Social Security Legislation

Recognition of the need for these laws grew out of the changing nature of
the American economy. When the United States was largely an agrarian society, people were not dependent on cash wages in industry and older people
did not automatically stop working at a specific age. However, as a result of
the growth of industrialization and the shift from rural to urban living, when
the wage earner was unemployed or retired, families often found themselves
without either the facilities or funds to care for themselves.

The changing nature of family patterns also contributed to the problem

[1] John Kenneth Galbraith, *The Affluent Society* (Houghton Mifflin, 1958), pp. 109–10.

of providing family security. Most households are small. The average household contains only parents and their dependent children. Most older persons and single people live alone. Each independent household needs a certain minimum income. Even in prosperous years, contributions by adult children to their parents have been shown to be insufficient to provide security for parents older than 65. The Committee on Economic Security (1935) showed how few could save enough by the age of 65 to care for themselves. A national study in 1957 (a prosperous period) disclosed that in only 5 to 10 per cent of the cases where children or relatives contributed to the support of older people were the contributions large enough to be meaningful. The median yearly contribution from children or relatives to those older people who did receive them was $300 for a couple and $240 for unmarried individuals.[2]

Another reason why public provision for family security seemed desirable was that the number of retired unemployed persons has increased tremendously. People are living longer and retiring earlier. As late as 1900, average life expectancy was only 47 years;[3] today it is almost 20 years longer. Since most industries and jobs have fixed ages for retirement, more people have many years between the end of an income-producing occupation and death. During this period they need an income on which to live.

The United States did not seriously consider social security until the impact of the depression of the 1930's was nationwide. The widespread depression of the 1930's was a shattering and terrifying experience for many people. Families who had frugally saved for the day when they might need it found their savings wiped out. Hard work and ability did not seem to provide people with an income that would give enough money for even the necessities of life. Families and friends could not help each other when whole communities were without money.

Two new principles of American life gained acceptance during the depression of the 1930's.

> One principle is that the fortunes of individual Americans are inextricably interlocked; that we are "all in the same boat"; and that if any of us fall into deep trouble it is the job of the rest of us—not simply family and friends and neighbors, or even the local community, but the federal government itself if need be—to help them.
>
> The other principle is that it is the job of the federal government, through whatever means, to see that there shall not be another Great Depression.[4]

[2] U.S. Dept. of Health, Education and Welfare, Social Security Administration, *Income of Old Age and Survivors Insurance Beneficiaries,* Bureau of Old Age and Survivors Insurance, Highlights from Preliminary Data, 1957 Survey (Washington, D.C.: Government Printing Office, 1958).

[3] U.S. Dept. of Health, Education and Welfare, Social Security Administration, *Filial Responsibility in the Modern American Family* (Washington, D.C.: Government Printing Office [n.d.]), p. 3.

[4] Frederick Lewis Allen, "Economic Security: A Look Back and a Look Ahead," *Social Security, Programs, Problems, and Policies* (Homewood, Ill.: Richard D. Irwin, 1960), p. 35.

Since the 1930's, it has been accepted by the people that the federal govern-ment has a responsibility to prevent economic depressions and to provide at least a minimum level of financial security for families of workers.

Prior to 1935, the general American attitude had been that compulsory insurance plans were somewhat socialistic and unnecessary. Federal pensions for veterans had been established since the Civil War, but these were con-sidered a way of expressing the nation's appreciation to former servicemen rather than a means of providing for economic security.

At present the national philosophy seems to be that each worker or self-employed person must contribute in his own behalf. This is in contrast to the earlier frontier attitude of "laissez-faire," whereby each person was ex-pected to provide for himself.

The Social Security Program

Social security is a form of social insurance that shares the cost and spreads the risk among many workers. The theory is that most families need financial assistance at various points, but not all families need them at the same time. For example, providing for old age is a common problem. Everyone who lives long enough will become old, but at any one time only a segment of our population is retired and in need of a retirement income.

Social security "substitutes hope for fears."[5] Before the advent of social security legislation, it had not seemed possible for most individuals to spread their earnings over a lifetime. Very few people were able to save enough money to care adequately for family financial emergencies, such as illness and disability, or to provide for their years beyond retirement.

Most people use the term "social security" to refer to only one part of the social security system, the Old-age, Survivors, and Disability Insurance plan. However, the Social Security Act covers nine different types of programs which may be grouped in the following categories:

A. Social Insurance
1. Old-age, Survivors, and Disability Insurance
2. Unemployment insurance
B. Public Assistance to the Needy
1. Old-age assistance
2. Aid to the blind
3. Aid to dependent children
4. Aid to the permanently and totally disabled
C. Children's Services
1. Maternal and child health services

[5] Arthur J. Altmeyer, "Some Assumptions and Objectives in Social Security, *Survey Graphic*, September 1945. Reprinted in *Social Security, Programs, Problems, and Policies*, eds., William Haber and Wilbur J. Cohen (Homewood, Ill.; Richard D. Irwin, 1960), p. 2.

2. Services for crippled children
3. Child Welfare services[6]

Federal funds help to finance all of these programs, but the federal government administers only one, the Old-age, Survivors, and Disability Insurance
Program. This program provides protection for a worker and his family when
the worker's earnings are cut off by retirement, disability, or death. The
other eight programs are administered by the individual states with federal
cooperation. Benefits and regulations of the programs administered by the
states vary considerably from one state to another.

Old-Age, Survivors, and Disability Insurance

The Old-age, Survivors, and Disability Insurance benefits under social
security now cover almost all people in gainfully employed occupations, as
well as most of those who are self-employed. The aged and many disabled
people receive benefits. Since these benefits are popularly referred to as "social security," we shall use this term in the following discussion: although
OASDI is only one of the nine social security programs.

Old-age, Survivors, and Disability Insurance benefits are paid out of trust
funds built from the taxes paid by employers, employees, and self-employed
individuals. Benefit payments to workers and their families are based on the
record of contributions made by each insured individual. The federal Old-
age, Survivors, and Disability Insurance Program is really an insurance plan
purchased by employees and employers.

DEDUCTIONS FOR OASDI. A percentage of the wages or salary of
employees is deducted from every pay check for Old-age, Survivors, and Disability Insurance. The employer sends both his own and his employees' contributions to the Internal Revenue Office in his district. These are accompanied
by a report which is forwarded to the Social Security Administration, where
the record of each worker's contribution is kept. (Table 11 shows the present
tax rate and scheduled increases to 1968 and after.)

TABLE 11
The Present Tax Rates and Scheduled Increases*

Calendar Year	Employee Per Cent	Employer Per Cent	Self-Employed Per Cent
1963–65	3⅝	3⅝	5.4
1966–67	4⅛	4⅛	6.2
1968 and after	4⅝	4⅝	6.9

* U.S. Dept. of Health, Education and Welfare, Social Security Administration,
Your Social Security (Washington, D.C.: Government Printing Office, 1963), p. 17.

[6] U.S. Dept. of Health, Education and Welfare, Social Security Administration, *Social
Security Handbook* (Washington, D.C.: Government Printing Office [n.d.]), p. 2.

FIGURE 51. The Social Security Administration relies on modern equipment to handle what's called "the biggest bookkeeping job in the world." Giant electronic computers keep the earnings records current and supply the data for figuring the benefits payable when a worker retires, dies, or becomes disabled. *(Courtesy of Social Security Administration.)*

WHO IS COVERED? Social security covers most working people. People employed in covered occupations are subject to social security taxes and entitled to social security benefits. Almost all employees and wage earners in private industries are covered as well as many employees of state and local governments. (The state must enter into an agreement with the federal government, and the majority of eligible employees must elect to join the social security plan.) Employees of the federal government come under social security if they are not part of the federal retirement system. The armed forces are also covered by social security.

Most of the self-employed groups, except physicians, are part of the social security system. Farm operators and ranchers (and farm landlords under certain conditions) must join as self-employed participants if their net earnings are $400 or more a year. A self-employed farmer must report his earnings. Clergymen may elect to participate within about two years after receiving ordination, commissioning, or licensing.

Domestic employees are taxed if they receive $50 or more in a calendar quarter for work. Employers of domestic help are required to report the wages and send in their part of the taxes if a domestic employee is eligible

TABLE 12
Amount of Work Needed To Be Fully Insured*

A Worker Who Reaches 65 (62 for Women) Or Dies	Will Need Credit for No More Than This Much Work
In 1957 or earlier	1½ years
1958	1¾
1959	2
1960	2¼
1961	2½
1962	2¾
1963	3
1964	3¼
1965	3½
1966	3¾
1967	4
1968	4¼
1969	4½
1970	4¾
1971	5
1975	6
1979	7
1983	8
1987	9
1991 or later	10

* U. S. Dept. of Health, Education and Welfare, Social Security Administration, *Your Social Security* (Washington, D. C.: Government Printing Office, 1963), p. 2.

under the above provisions. This means that the employer must deduct the social security tax from the employee's salary, match it with his own contribution, and turn both into the district office of the Internal Revenue Service.

Recently attention has been focused on the groups that are not part of the social security program. In addition to physicians, the following are not subject to compulsory contributions to join: children employed by parents, medical interns, and student nurses. The trend has been to include the groups not formerly covered. Teachers in some states, dentists, and, most recently, parents who work for children have been included.

The dependents of people covered by social security are entitled to certain benefits when the contributor retires, dies, or is disabled.

BECOMING INSURED. Eligibility for Old-age, Survivors, or Disability Insurance benefits at some time in the future depends on one's having worked long enough under social security to become insured. The length of time necessary to become insured depends on one's date of birth. Under the recent revisions of the law many older people can become insured more quickly. However, a minimum of a year and a half of employment under social security is required.

TABLE 13
Eligibility for Benefits*

Retirement Payments

Monthly payment to—	If you are—
You as a retired worker and your wife and child	Fully insured.
Your dependent husband 62 or over	Both fully and currently insured.

Survivors Payments

Monthly payment to your—	If at death you are—
Widow 62 or over	Fully insured.
Widow or dependent divorced wife, if caring for your child who is entitled to benefits	Either fully or currently insured.
Dependent child	Either fully or currently insured.
Dependent widower 62 or over	*Both* fully and currently insured.
Dependent parent at 62	Fully insured.
Lump sum death payment	Either fully or currently insured.

Disability Payments

| Monthly payment to— | Generally if you have— |
| You and your dependents if you are totally disabled for work | Social Security credit for at least 5 years in the 10-year period ending when you become disabled. |

---

* U.S. Dept. of Health, Education and Welfare, Social Security Administration, *Your Social Security* (Washington, D.C.: Government Printing Office, 1963), pp. 6, 10.

The social security program has two classifications of insured people: "fully insured" and "currently insured." These classifications are the basis for determining which benefits one is entitled to receive. The size of the benefit is determined by the previous wages earned. An individual is "fully insured" for life if he or she has worked in covered employment for forty calendar quarters, or ten full years, and has received $50 or more in each quarter in covered employment, or if he or she will be 65 (62 for women) before 1987 and has the amount of work specified in Table 12.

A fully insured worker and his dependents are eligible for disability, retirement, and survivors benefits even if he leaves insured employment after becoming fully insured.

However, although an individual is not fully insured, he may be "currently insured." One is "currently insured" if at the time of death he has received $50 or more in six of the preceding thirteen quarters ending with his death, disability, or retirement. That is a worker must have been employed for at least half of the three years preceding death, disability, or retirement to be "currently insured." A worker who is only "currently insured" is not entitled to retirement or disability benefits, but his dependents can receive death benefits. (See Table 13.)

Although the eligibility for all benefit rights is based on the number of calendar quarters of insured employment, the size of the benefits depends on the average monthly earnings before applying for benefits. Benefits to an individual and his family are usually greater if the wage earner is both "fully insured" as well as "currently insured."

Special Provisions for Disabled Workers

The Disability Insurance Trust Fund was established in 1956 to provide benefits to disabled workers up to age 65 and their families. Part of the social security tax (one-half of 1 per cent of the first $4,800 of the wages of an employed person, matched by the employer's contribution) goes into the Disability Insurance Trust Fund. (Three-eighths of 1 per cent of the first $4,800 of net income of self-employed persons goes to this fund.)

Monthly benefits may be paid to disabled workers under 65 years and their dependents. The wife of a disabled worker is eligible for benefits at age 62. However, if the wife of a disabled worker has in her care a child eligible for benefits (under age 18 or over 18 and disabled from childhood), she may get benefit payments regardless of her age. The disabled children of retired, disabled, or deceased workers are eligible for benefits if they are over age 18, but disabled before they reached 18.

Under the provisions of the 1960 law, beneficiaries of disability payments who return to work will receive benefits for twelve months, whether they obtain work independently or under a vocational rehabilitation plan. After nine months of employment, a decision will be made by the social security board as to whether the beneficiary has regained the ability to work. If he is able to work, he will receive benefits for only three more months; if not he will continue to receive benefits.

Beneficiaries who regain the ability to work but become disabled for a second time within five years are eligible for disability benefits without the usual six-month waiting period to establish evidence of disability. These provisions for disabled workers are designed to help disabled people try to regain a functioning position in society.

Benefits for the families of disabled workers are also available. Monthly payments to a wife, child, or dependent husband are one half of the worker's benefits.

RETIREMENT BENEFITS. Retirement benefits are available for the folowing groups if they have accumulated sufficient credit to be fully insured:

1. Workers in paid employment at the age of 62. Benefits are permanently reduced if a person elects to retire before 65.

It is possible to earn some money after retirement and still collect social security benefits. If a beneficiary earns $1,200 or less, he will receive full benefit payments for twelve months. If he earns between $1,200 and $1,700 in covered employment, one dollar of benefits will be withheld for every two dollars from $1,200 to $1,700. For every dollar earned beyond $1,700, one dollar of benefits will be withheld.

No matter how much a beneficiary earns he is entitled to a benefit check for any month in which he earns less than one hundred dollars in covered employment. At present, income from pensions, stocks, bonds, real estate, and certain other investments are not included in computing eligibility for benefits.

After reaching age 72 a beneficiary can earn any amount and still be eligible for payments, beginning with the month in which he reaches 72.

2. The dependents of a retired worker.

(a) A wife when she is 62. (However, if the wife elects to receive benefits before age 65, she will receive permanently reduced benefits.)

(b) A husband at age 62 who has received at least one half of his support from his wife when she was eligible for benefits.

(c) Children under 18 if they are not married, and children of any age who were severely disabled before 18 years old.

(d) A wife at any age if she is caring for the child of a worker entitled to benefits.

SURVIVORS BENEFITS. Survivors benefits are payable to:

1. Children under 18 who are unmarried and dependent, and children over 18 who were totally disabled before 18.

2. The widow of a worker who has the care of children eligible for benefits. Benefits continue until the youngest child is 18 and then resume to the widow when she is 62 if she has not remarried.

3. The widow of a worker at age 62 if she has not remarried.

4. A divorced wife if she has the care of children eligible for benefits, and if her support was from the insured worker at the time of his death pursuant to a court order.

5. A dependent widower at age 62, if he has not remarried before applying for survivors benefits, and if his wife had been fully and currently insured.

6. Dependent parents at 62.

Dependent widowers and parents must file proof of support within two years of the death of the worker to be able to claim death and survivors benefits.

Benefits to a dependent spouse if there are no childreen are payable only if the marriage had existed for one year, unless the dependent spouse was entitled to a dependent's benefits on the account of another worker in the month preceding the marriage.

In addition, lump sum death benefits are payable to survivors of either currently or fully insured workers. The size of the payment may go up to $255 according to the amount of the previously earned wages of the insured worker. If there is no surviving spouse, payment may be made to the funeral home for unpaid expenses. Reimbursement may be made to the persons who paid the burial expenses or the funeral home.

In establishing eligibility for benefits, military services and wages earned in employment covered by the Railroad Retirement Act may be included in certain cases. The Social Security Administration computes benefits all possible ways and pays the highest benefit.

ESTIMATING BENEFITS. There are a number of ways to compute social security benefits. When an application for benefits is made to the Social Security Administration, benefits are figured in all possible ways and the highest amount paid. The size of the benefit depends on the previous average monthly earnings of the insured worker in covered employment.

Benefits under the Old-Age and Survivors Insurance Program are based on the premise that people in similar economic situations have the right to equal benefits. All people who have the same wage earnings history should receive the same benefits. People in Arizona are treated on the same basis as those in Vermont or Oregon or other areas. A man who has worked for thirty years at the salary of $4,800 per year under covered employment in a factory in Oregon gets the same benefit as a man who has had a job at the same salary for the same length of time in an office in Mississippi.

To estimate your own benefits, figure your average monthly earnings, then look in Table 14 for the average earnings figure closest to this amount. The average monthly earnings figure is the total dollar income for the insured period divided by the number of months of work. However, there are some special rules that may raise benefit levels.

Most people may figure their average yearly earnings by:

1. Counting the number of years after 1955 and up to, but not including, the year they reach 65 (62 for women). (If the result is less than 5, increase it to 5.)
2. Selecting an equal number of years after 1950 in which their earnings were highest. (Do not count more than: $3,600 a year for 1951-54; $4,200 a year for 1955-58; $4,800 a year for 1959 and after.)
3. Averaging their earnings in the selected years.[7]

One may omit up to five calendar years after 1950 with the lowest earnings. After excluding the dropout years, and any period in which your record was frozen for disability, divide the income in the remaining period by the

[7] U.S. Dept. of Health, Education and Welfare, Social Security Administration, *Your Social Security* (Washington, D.C.: Government Printing Office, 1963), p. 4.

TABLE 14
Examples of Monthly Payments
Beginning After 1958*

Average Yearly Earnings After 1950	$800 or Less	$1,200	$1,800	$2,400	$3,000	$3,600	$4,200	$4,800†
Retirement at 65 or later Disability benefits	$ 40.00	$ 59.00	$ 73.00	$ 84.00	$ 95.00	$105.00	$116.00	$127.00
Retirement at 64	37.40	55.10	68.20	78.40	88.70	98.00	108.30	118.60
Retirement at 63	34.70	51.20	63.30	72.80	82.40	91.00	100.60	110.10
Retirement at 62	32.00	47.20	58.40	67.20	76.00	84.00	92.80	101.60
Wife's benefit at 65 or with child in her care	20.00	29.50	36.50	42.00	47.50	52.50	58.00	63.50
Wife's benefit at 64	18.40	27.10	33.50	38.50	43.00	48.20	53.20	58.30
Wife's benefit at 63	15.00	24.60	30.50	35.00	39.00	43.00	48.40	53.00
Wife's benefit at 62	15.00	22.20	27.40	31.50	35.70	39.40	43.50	47.70
Widow 62 or over	40.00	48.70	60.30	69.30	78.40	86.70	95.70	104.80
Widow under 62 and one child	60.00	88.50	109.60	126.00	142.60	157.60	174.00	190.60
Widow under 62 and 2 children	60.00	88.50	120.00	161.60	202.40	236.40	254.00	254.00
One surviving child	40.00	44.30	54.80	63.00	71.30	78.80	87.00	95.30
Two surviving child.	60.00	88.50	109.60	126.00	142.60	157.60	174.00	190.60
Max. family payment	60.00	88.50	120.00	161.60	202.40	240.00	254.00	254.00
Lump sum death pay.	120.00	177.00	219.00	252.00	255.00	255.00	255.00	255.00

* U. S. Dept. of Health, Education and Welfare, Social Security Administration, *Your Social Security* (Washington, D. C.: Government Printing Office, 1963), p. 10.
† Because earnings of $4,800 cannot be credited for any year before 1959, benefits in this column will not generally be payable for a few years to come.

number of months in the remaining period. (If there are fewer than 18 months left, you must divide by 18.)

The present minimum benefit to a retired individual is $32 per month, and the maximum is $127. (However, most people do not get the maximum amount at this time. In a few years, when average earnings are computed only on income earned after 1958, more people will be able to get the maximum amount.) The maximum family payment is $254 and the minimum is $60. If there is only one survivor, the minimum is $40.

Dependents and survivors benefits are a part of the insured worker's benefits. The following are the proportions of an insured worker's benefits for dependents and survivors.

1. If the wage earner is retired,
    (a) The wife's benefit is one half of the worker's benefit. However, if the wife applies for benefits between the ages of 62 and 65 she will have a permanently reduced benefit.
    (b) The child's benefit is one half.
2. If the wage earner is deceased, the survivors benefits are a proportion of what he would have received if he had lived and received retirement benefits.
    (a) The widow's benefit is 82.5 per cent.
    (b) The benefit for each child is three-fourths.
    (c) A dependent widower, a widow under age 62, and a divorced wife with a dependent child in her care receives three-fourths.
    (d) A single dependent parent's benefit is 82.5 per cent; two dependent parents receive three-fourths each.

At the present time most benefits are weighted to aid low income wage earners. That is, regardless of how low the previous earnings of a worker have been, he is entitled to a certain minimum level of benefits. This provision has aroused much controversy.

THE RIGHT OF APPEAL. An applicant for benefits has the right to ask for an appeal or a review of action regarding his benefits if he is not satisfied with the decision made by the social security board. The local social security office can assist in arranging for reconsideration, a hearing, or an appeal.

RAILROAD EMPLOYMENT. Retired railroad workers who have ten years of railroad work and also enough work to qualify for social security insurance are eligible to receive retirement benefits under both programs. If a railroad worker has less than ten years (120 months), he may credit his railroad employment to his social security account.

Survivors of railroad workers are entitled to benefits under only one program, even if the worker would have been eligible under both the railroad retirement program and social security insurance. The local social security office or the Railroad Retirement Board, 844 Rush Street, Chicago 11, Illinois, can furnish specific information.

MILITARY SERVICE. Active military service after 1956 is treated as any other covered employment for social security purposes; deductions are made from base pay for old-age and survivors insurance, and credit given on the individual's social security account. The Government acts as an employer and pays the matching amount.

Credit is given for active duty during World War II (September 16, 1940, through July 24, 1947) and the post-World War period (July 25, 1947, through December 31, 1956). The wage credits are $160 for each month of active duty if the discharge or release was other than dishonorable. Unless the discharge or release was for disability or injury in the line of duty, ninety days of active service are required.

American citizens who served in the military forces of foreign countries during World War II and entered this service before December 9, 1941, may receive the same $160 per month wage credits, if the foreign country was at war on September 16, 1940, with a nation that was an enemy of the United States in the Second World War.

While the credits for military service between September 1940 and January 1957 count in the same way as wages in insured civilian occupations, they are not listed on one's social security record. It is not necessary to take any action to have military service credited on one's account for retirement benefits. At the time of retirement, proof of military service is needed.

APPLYING FOR SOCIAL SECURITY BENEFITS. When one first accepts a job in an occupation covered by social security, a form called Application for Social Security Number must be completed. Following the completion of this application, the Social Security Administration issues a social security card with an account number to the individual. Every person has a separate account kept by the federal government against which are credited all payments made by his employers. In the case of self-employed individuals who have net earnings over $400 per year, payments are made directly by the individuals when income tax returns are filed. This record is kept over the working lifetime of an individual and is the basis for his social security benefits.

It is possible that in the course of keeping this record, some mistakes may be made. Therefore, it is very important to check on one's social security account every few years. A statute of limitations prohibits the correction of errors older than five years. There are special cards to use in checking on an account. These cards can be obtained from either the post office or the local social security office. It is a simple matter to keep a record yourself and check your account every four years with the social security office.

Social security benefits are not paid automatically; one must apply for them. Therefore, it is wise to check with the local social security office at those times when one is likely to be eligible for benefits. Similarly, it is important to apply promptly because there is a time limit on retroactive benefits; no more than twelve months of benefits can be received retroactively.

REQUEST FOR STATEMENT OF EARNINGS

	ACCOUNT NUMBER			
	DATE OF BIRTH	MONTH	DAY	YEAR

Please send me a statement of the amount of earnings recorded in my social security account.

NAME { MISS / MRS. / MR. _____

) Print Name and Address In Ink Or Use Type-writer

STREET & NUMBER _____

CITY, STATE AND ZIP CODE _____

SIGN YOUR NAME AS YOU USUALLY WRITE IT _____

Sign your own name only. Under the law, information in your social security record is confidential and anyone who signs someone else's name can be prosecuted.
If your name has been changed from that shown on your social security account number card, please copy your name below exactly as it appears on that card.

FIGURE 52. Check on your status by mailing this card or a request for information to the Social Security Administration, Baltimore 35, Maryland. *(Courtesy of Social Security Administration.)*

The location of the nearest social security office is in the local telephone directory.

All applications for benefits are reviewed by the Social Security Administration and if one is eligible, payments begin. Several types of documents are usually necessary to establish eligibility. Some of these are a birth certificate, a marriage certificate, and children's birth certificates. If one is applying for a widow's benefit or a death benefit, a certificate of death is also needed. If there has been a second marriage, some proof of how the previous marriage ended is necessary. This might be a death certificate for the former spouse or divorce papers.

WHEN TO CHECK ON ELIGIBILITY FOR BENEFITS.

1. Before retirement it is important to get in touch with the social security office to determine what benefits you may be eligible for. This is age 65 for men and 62 for women.

2. At age 72 one should contact the social security office because benefits after age 72 are based on age, regardless of what one may earn.

3. If the wage earner becomes disabled, the family should contact the social security office to determine if the wage earner or the family is entitled to benefits and if the account of the disabled worker needs changing. There are special provisions of the social security regulations for handling the account of a disabled worker. These generally increase the benefits available to disabled workers and their families.

4. When there is a death in the family, the family members should check with the social security office to determine if there is accrued credit for death benefits. There may also be benefits for dependents and children under 18 years old.

PROBLEMS OF EVALUATING WHO SHOULD GET BENEFITS. Evaluating eligibility for benefits is a problem that has received considerable newspaper publicity recently. Many people feel that social security benefits should be based only on objective evidence and should not involve inquiries into personal family situations. Often it is difficult for the Social Security Administration to decide on an individual's eligibility for benefits without some personal information about the family situation. For example, were the parents of a deceased man wholly dependent on his income, or are his children who reside with a divorced wife his dependents?

Where to Obtain Information About Social Security Benefits in the United States

Facilities for most of the programs described in this section are available to at least a minimal extent in every state. For information or help with any of these services, benefits, or insurance, the following agencies in your local area or state capital should be consulted:

Employment Security
    Local Public Employment Office
    State Unemployment Compensation Agency
        (in some states called Employment Security Agency)
    U.S. Department of Labor

Old-Age, Survivors, and Disability Insurance
    Social Security Administration Office
        (consult your local telephone book)
    Bureau of Old-Age, and Survivors Insurance, Social Security Administration,
        U.S. Department of Health, Education and Welfare

Public Assistance—To the needy, aged, needy blind, dependent children, and the
        permanently and totally disabled
    Local Public Welfare Office
    State Public Welfare Office
    Bureau of Family Services, Welfare Administration, U.S. Department of Health,
        Education and Welfare

Child Welfare
    Local Child Welfare Office
    State Public Welfare Agency
    Children's Bureau, Welfare Administration, U.S. Department of Health, Education and Welfare

Services for Crippled Children and for Maternal and Child Health
    State or Local Public Health Office (Maternal and Child Health)
    State Crippled Children's Agency
    Children's Bureau, Welfare Administration, U.S. Department of Health, Education and Welfare

ecial features of the text—

rganized around the family as members
f a consumer group and as an economic
rce in the national economy

mphasizes family decision-making in
egard to time and money, discussing the
lternatives available to the family as a
onsumer unit

onsiders the adolescent as a consumer,
s well as the senior citizen and the
ecial problems of old age.

scusses sources of help and protection
r families from private groups as well
from federal, state, and local agencies

cuses on the important role of women
planning and managing family spend-
g, recognizing that they currently form
e third of the nation's work force

out the Author

e Oppenheim (Ph.D., New York Uni-
ity) is Assistant Professor of Home
nomics, New York University, Presi-
t of the Council on Consumer Informa-
, 1964-65, and Vice-President of the
Jersey Home Economics Association,
4-66.

THE FAMILY AS CONSUMERS

Irene Oppenheim

The Family as Consumers acquaints today's college students with the effective use of personal and family financial resources. It offers a realistic, up-to-date approach to the problems and potentials of family spending and consumption in the modern world.

A comprehensive and concise source of information, this unusual text presents an overview of the choices available to families in an affluent society, discusses the relationship of these choices to home and family living, and considers the potentiality for strengthening family and community life through the effective use of time and money.

Directed to undergraduate courses in consumer economics and family finance, *The Family as Consumers* is equally valuable in the home economics and business fields. It is designed to help individuals of all ages—from adolescence to retirement—to cope with the problems of family living and spending, managing personal finances, and becoming intelligent consumers.

Unemployment Insurance

Unemployment insurance was established in the Social Security Act of 1935 as a Federal-State system. The federal government levies a 3 per cent excise tax on the payrolls of firms in industry and commerce with four or more workers during twenty or more weeks per year. The original act stated that if a state passed an unemployment insurance law that met basic provisions of the federal law, the firm's state tax for unemployment insurance could be credited against 90 per cent of the federal tax. This arrangement known as the tax-offset provision resulted in the rapid passage of unemployment insurance in all states as well as the District of Columbia, and Hawaii (at that time a territory). Wisconsin was the only state with an unemployment insurance program before the passage of the Social Security Act of 1935.

An employer with a low rate of unemployment is excused from paying part of the tax. Alaska is the only state that does not provide for an experience rating—that is, a lower tax for employers with a low rate of unemployment. In three states, employees as well as employers are taxed for unemployment insurance. Some states also include employers in the unemployment insurance program who do not qualify under the federal act.

Each state deposits its unemployment insurance collections in the Unemployment Trust Fund of the United States Treasury. A separate account is kept for the state, which may be drawn upon only to pay unemployment benefits.

The size of the unemployment insurance benefits and eligibility for them are established by state law. The individual states decide who may receive benefits, how one qualifies for benefits, the amount of the benefit, and the duration of the benefit period. While the unemployment insurance laws of the states differ, they have some general things in common in establishing eligibility for benefits.

1. An individual must register for work at a public employment office and file a claim for benefits.

2. The claimant must have previously worked at a job covered by unemployment insurance under the state law. Most state laws cover almost all factory and commercial occupations in large firms. In some states only jobs in firms that employ four or more people are covered. There are special federal programs for federal civilian workers, ex-servicemen, and veterans. (See the section, below, titled "Special Federal Programs.")

3. The claimant must have had at least a minimum level of earnings during a stated period prior to claiming benefits.

4. The individual applying for benefits must be able to work. Most states do not pay unemployment benefits to workers who are ill or unable to work.

5. The claimant must be available for work and willing to take a suitable job.

6. The claimant is not disqualified. (This is described more thoroughly, below, under the section "Disqualification.")

THE AMOUNT OF BENEFITS. The weekly benefits of an unemployed worker vary according to the benefit formula in the laws of each state. Benefits are usually about one half of the full-time weekly pay of the worker within top and bottom limits. Maximum benefit payments range from $26 to $45 per week for an unemployed worker with dependents. In some states workers with particular types of dependents are eligible for an extra allowance. The minimum amount of benefits vary from $3 to $17 per week. Thirty states have a minimum of $10 or more as the lowest benefit. Every state provides partial benefits for partial unemployment.

The duration of the benefits if a worker remains unemployed depends on the claimant's previous employment and earnings. The period varies from five to twenty-six weeks. All eligible claimants in thirteen states receive weekly benefits for a fixed time if they remain eligible and unemployed. The uniform duration period in these thirteen states varies from twenty to thirty weeks.

CLAIMING BENEFITS. A claim for benefits must be filed by the unemployed worker at the office maintained by the state for this purpose. He must also register for employment at the state unemployment office. Usually the unemployment service and unemployment insurance offices are located together. The claim may be filed in any state, even if the worker was previously employed in another state. The benefits, however, are paid directly by the state in which the claimant has previously been employed.

If the claimant has not found a job within the stated "waiting period," usually one week after filing a claim, the benefit payments begin. However, if the worker has obtained a regular full-time job, he will not be entitled to benefits.

DISQUALIFICATION. Unemployed workers may be disqualified from eligibility for benefits for a variety of reasons, even if they have accumulated wage credits. The laws of the various states differ on policies pertaining to disqualification. Some of the reasons for which a worker may be disqualified are:

1. If he quits his job voluntarily without good cause. (In some states the law says "without good cause attributable to the employer" or "connected with the work.")
2. If he was discharged for misconduct in connection with his work.
3. If he refused or failed, without good cause, to apply for or accept an offer of suitable work. (What is "suitable" work is generally decided by the State: however, under Federal law no worker may be denied benefits because he refused to accept a job under conditions where labor disputes or labor standards are involved.)
4. If he is unemployed because of a stoppage of work as the result of a labor dispute.[8]

[8] U.S. Dept. of Health, Education and Welfare, Social Security Administration, *A Brief Explanation of the Social Security Act*, (Washington, D.C.: Government Printing Office [n.d.]), pp. 11–12.

Some states have additional bases for disqualification. Disqualification means that benefits are either postponed for a few weeks or in some states reduced as well as postponed. A few states cancel all benefit rights for disqualification. This means a worker cannot receive any benefits until he has again earned enough wage credits to be eligible.

A worker has the right to appeal any decision on a claim for benefits. Usually it is necessary to file the appeal within five to ten days after receiving notification of the decision on a claim. The appeal is filed at the same unemployment insurance office that the claim has been made. Employers also have the right of appeal if they to not agree with the decision on a worker's benefits.

SPECIAL FEDERAL PROGAMS. There are two special federal programs which are administered by the states: unemployment compensation for federal civilian employees and unemployment compensation for ex-servicemen. Unemployed civilian employees who were formerly employed by the federal government and ex-servicemen are entitled to the unemployment benefits established by the laws of the particular state in which they reside. The size of their benefits is figured as if their federal pay had been covered under the state law. Benefits for ex-servicemen are figured on a basis which assigns a cash value to allowances and base pay. The cost of these special federal programs is paid by the federal government.

When workers claim unemployment benefits at the unemployment insurance office, the personal situation can be very involved. For instance, a widow with four small children may be laid off a factory assembly job. She is offered another job on a night shift. The woman claims that she is unable to take a night job because there are small children at home. Should she receive the benefits to which her wage record entitles her or has she refused suitable employment and therefore become ineligible for benefits? What if she is offered a laundress job or that of a cleaning woman? She may claim that the work is too heavy and the wage too low to justify her taking it. Again is she refusing suitable employment?

Public Assistance

The American way of life has included local and church responsibility for needy people ever since the founding of the first colony. As communities grew, care of the needy became a town or county responsibility. Later the states assumed the job of assisting local communities care for the needy. With the passage of the Social Security Act of 1935, the federal government assumed the responsibility of helping states provide monthly cash payments for certain groups who were in need and who were not eligible for assistance under the other phases of the social security program. In 1950 the federal responsibility was broadened to help states pay medical care costs for these same groups. These groups were old people without a means of support, blind people who needed help, children who lacked parental care and support, and more recently, permanently and totally disabled needy individuals.

The public assistance programs enable needy people to remain with their family and friends by providing minimum cash income. This income also helps some people back on the road to self-sufficiency by giving them a small measure of economic security while they lack other means.

Public assistance is a partnership of the federal and state governments; the states operate the programs under a plan approved by the federal government, but both federal and state governments share the costs. The federal government shares the cost of payments to individuals, payments to suppliers of medical care, and costs of administering these programs. The formula for this sharing of cost is based on each state's average monthly payment times the number of people receiving aid. There are stated maximums on payments eligible for federal sharing. A state, however, may make larger payments by using state and local funds.

In all states an individual must be in need to be eligible for public assistance. The determination of need is made by the states, but they are required by federal law to consider all income and resources of the individual, except they must disregard stated amounts of earned income of a blind person. There are different limits in the various states regarding the property or assets one may have and still be eligible for public assistance. In most states ownership of a modest home does not disqualify an individual. The amount of assistance varies widely from state to state for individuals in similar situations because of several factors: the individual's resources and the levels of the program of the state.

Federal law requires that all payments for public assistance that have any federal funds in them be made in cash, except for medical care. Social services are provided for people on public assistance and they must be done in such a manner as to help beneficiaries "attain the degree of self-care, self-support, and strong family life appropriate to his own situation."[9]

Public assistance payments are available to the aged, the blind, and the permanently and totally disabled who are living either in their own homes, in private institutions, or in public medical institutions, except for patients hospitalized for tuberculosis or mental illness. If a state makes payments to people in institutions, the state must have one or more state authorities that establish and maintain standards for such institutions.

Applications for public assistance are filed at the local public welfare office. An individual may apply for aid under any of the existing programs, and the state determines whether the individual is eligible for aid and how

[9] U.S. Dept. of Health, Education and Welfare, Social Security Administration, *A Brief Explanation of the Social Security Act*, (Washington, D.C.: Government Printing Office [n.d.]), p. 39.

much he should receive. A person has the right to request a hearing with the state agency if his request for aid is denied, reduced, or delayed by the local agency.

Old-Age Assistance

Old-age assistance provides financial help and help with medical care costs for needy persons 65 years or older. All states provide some old-age assistance. Assistance payments may be made to individuals to supplement the income received from old-age insurance. All states' old-age assistance programs also pay some medical costs for the needy aged. Hospital care and nursing home care are the services most common among the states. All but nine states pay for some medical care for persons who receive aid to the blind or aid to the permanently and totally disabled. All but twelve states pay for some medical care for needy families receiving aid to dependent children.[10]

Assistance is available only to citizens of the United States in some states. Many states also require a period of residency in the state prior to eligibility for old-age assistance. The most common requirement is that the person have lived in the state for at least a year.

Aid to the Blind

All of the states have aid programs for the needy blind where federal funds supplement the states' contributions. Payments are made to needy people who have so little vision that they meet the state's definition of blindness. Each state has its own definition but all require an eye examination of the applicants. However, the individual applying for aid may decide whether he wishes his eyes to be examined by an optometrist or a physician who specializes in eye diseases. The most common definition of blindness is vision with glasses of $20/100$ or less in the better eye. Blindness in one eye does not qualify if the other eye has vision with glasses better than $20/100$. "Legal blindness" $20/200$ or less in the better eye is the requirement for federal tax exemption privileges and in some states for aid.

Some only give aid to blind adults, although the federal law does not set any age limit. In these states blind dependent children, and needy blind people over 65 may be able to secure aid from other assistance programs.

Very few states require citizenship, but most do require a period of residence in the state, usually five years, not necessarily consecutive. In some states, if a blind person refuses recommended eye treatment, he may not be continued as a beneficiary.

On any earnings by blind individuals up to $85, a month and one half of the earnings must be disregarded in computing eligibility for assistance. The purpose of this is to encourage blind people to work, if possible.

[10] U.S. Dept. of Health, Education and Welfare, Social Security Administration, *Social Security Bulletin*, Table 9, March 1964.

Aid to Dependent Children

Aid to dependent children is available in all states for needy children whose parents are dead, incapacitated, continuously absent from home, or unemployed if the children are living with a parent or other relative. In some states help for children between 16 and 18 is granted only if they are in school, although federal funds are available to states that help any needy child under 18 years of age.

Most states have a residence requirement; a needy child must have lived in the state for a year prior to applying for assistance. If the child is less than one year of age, the parent or relatives with whom the child is living must have lived in the state for a year.

Aid to the Permanently and Totally Disabled

Since 1950 a program of federal grants to states for aid to permanently and totally disabled individuals who are over eighteen and needy has been in existence. Most of the state eligibility provisions for other programs of assistance, such as residence, also apply to this public assistance program.

A state establishes its own definition of permanent and total disability within the federal interpretation. To be eligible for benefits the person must be "unable to engage in any substantial gainful activity."[11] In evaluating an individual's disability, a doctor and a social worker consider medical findings and the individual's capabilities and impairment as a guide to how disabled the person is as a wage earner or homemaker. Many states aid partially disabled people from state funds; no federal funds are available for this purpose.

Thirty-one states have programs of Medical Assistance to the Aged. This pays some or all medical costs for low-income people who are 65 years or older. This program helps the aged who have enough income for their maintenance needs, but not enough for all their medical costs.

Services for Children

The federal government helps states provide services for children through the programs of maternal and child health services for crippled children, and child welfare services. The federal government helps state agencies to provide services, not income. Each state develops its own plan for each type of service that must be approved before federal funds are assigned. The states share in paying for the cost of the programs.

Maternal and Child Health Services

A program of maternal and child health is in operation in every state. However, these services have not been available in many counties, particularly

[11] U.S. Dept. of Health, Education and Welfare, Social Security Administration, *If You Become Disabled* (Washington, D.C.: Government Printing Office, 1963), p. 6.

in the rural areas. A new amendment to the law provides that federal grants be used to improve the services for mothers and children in rural districts.

The sizes of the federal grants are related to the number of births in the state, the number of rural births, and the state's ability to provide help for mothers and children. Most of the federal grant funds are used to pay the salaries of personnel, doctors, nurses, medical social workers, child welfare workers, and other professional people. However, they may also be used to pay for the hospital and convalescent care of crippled children and the care of children in foster homes.

Services for Crippled Children

Every state has an agency to work with crippled children. Part of their job is to locate crippled children and to arrange for diagnosis and treatment. They may also provide medical and surgical care, hospitalization, and any other services needed. In some cases the agency helps parents locate means for proper care, but does not provide it.

Child Welfare Services

The Social Security Act makes provisions for services to children in difficult situations: the homeless, the dependent, the neglected, and children who may tend to become delinquent. Programs are in operation in every state under the plan developed by the state public welfare agency in cooperation with representatives of the Children's Bureau. The law specifies that each case must be evaluated and the facilities of voluntary and community agencies used if available.

Social Security in Canada

Monthly benefits are provided under the Old-Age Security Act for all Canadian residents 70 years or older who have resided in Canada for at least ten years. There is no test of need and it is not necessary to retire in order to be eligible. Applications should be made for benefits as soon as one is 69½, to the Regional Director of Old-Age Security, Department of National Health and Welfare, in the capital of the province.

These benefits are financed by three taxes: a sales tax, a tax on personal income, and a corporation tax.

The *Old-Age Assistance Act* provides payments for needy people between 65 and 69. The federal and provincial government share the cost.

Trends in United States Social Security Legislation

Clearly, the present trend in social security legislation has been to increase social security benefits, to broaden the eligible groups under the state

218]   THE FAMILY AS CONSUMERS

public assistance programs, and to extend the programs to more and more people.

Recent changes in the social security legislation seem to indicate a trend to increase the benefits provided by the federally administered program, OASDI. Such increases tend to decrease the number of aged or disabled who will have to depend on state public assistance programs for the needy.

These projected changes to increase benefits cost money. As each new addition is made to the social security benefits and as larger numbers of people qualify for retirement or disability insurance under the program, more funds are needed. Thus it is probable that increases in contributions through social security taxes beyond those now scheduled will be needed.

Some areas of public need have not received as much active legislative consideration as those mentioned above, but may well be included in future social security legislation. The most critical problem is that of a large number of children in families who are living on very meager levels. This is particularly the case for the many children in large families who lack bare essentials. Approximately half of the nation's children are members of families with three or more children. It is in this group that the need for aid is greatest. Allowances to these families for each child have been proposed as a solution. The basis for public assistance to needy children may be revised. While it is true that the cost of maintaining a child is less than the cost of maintaining an adult, it is often considerably more than many state programs now give under their program of aid to families with dependent children.

The policy of variable grants to states on the basis of their per capita income will probably increase still further. Some of the poorest states in the nation have the largest proportion of needy children and adults. Moreover, many of these states cannot, with the present federal assistance, provide an adequate minimal level of medical services and financial aid. Perhaps in the future some funds may come exclusively from federal sources.

Medical care is a new and growing area of need in which state and federal resources will probably be helping more. Modern medicine requires more costly diagnosis, more expensive drugs, and for many people, prolonged treatment and hospitalization. Moreover, the demand for high quality of medical services has grown enormously. As a nation, we are beginning to accept the fact that everyone has the right to good health. The cost of adequate medical care is a tremendous burden on the poorer segments of our population: large families, the aged, and the disabled.

Many people hope that future planning for family security will include increasing provisions for such things as public housing, physical and vocational rehabilitation, employment counseling, and developing better means of helping people from geographic areas with limited opportunities. As a nation we seem to be moving in the direction of helping all people achieve an adequate level of living.

SELECTED REFERENCES

ACKERMAN, LAWRENCE J., and DAVID IVRY. *Fundamentals of the Federal Old-Age, Survivors, and Disability Insurance System.* Bryn Mawr, Penna.: American College of Life Underwriters, 1962.

HABER, WILLIAM, and WILBUR J. COHEN. *Social Security: Programs, Problems, and Policies.* Homewood, Ill.: Richard D. Irwin, 1960.

U.S. DEPARTMENT OF HEALTH, EDUCATION AND WELFARE, Office of Program Analysis. *Handbook on Programs of the U.S. Department of Health, Education and Welfare.* Annual. Washington, D.C.: Government Printing Office (n.d.).

————. *Health, Education and Welfare Trends.* Annual. Washington, D.C.: Government Printing Office.

————, Social Security Administration. *Your Social Security.* Washington, D.C.: Government Printing Office, 1963.

————, Social Security Administration, Bureau of Family Services. *Aid to the Blind.* Washington, D.C.: Government Printing Office, 1962.

————, Social Security Administration, Bureau of Public Assistance. *If You Become Disabled.* Washington, D.C.: Government Printing Office, 1963.

————, Social Security Administration. *If You Become Disabled.* Washington, D.C.: Government Printing Office, 1963.

————, Social Security Administration, Bureau of Family Services. *Old-Age Assistance.* Washington, D.C.: Government Printing Office, 1962.

————, Welfare Administration, Bureau of Family Services. *Aid to Families with Dependent Children.* Washington, D.C.: Government Printing Office, 1963.

————, Welfare Administration, Bureau of Family Services. *Medical Aid for Older Persons Through Public Assistance.* Washington, D.C.: Government Printing Office, 1963.

————, Welfare Administration, Bureau of Family Services. *Old-Age Assistance: The People it Helps and How They Live.* Washington, D.C.: Government Printing Office, reprinted 1963.

13

LIFE INSURANCE

About 134 million Americans of all incomes, all educational levels, and all geographic regions owned some form of life insurance protection at the end of 1962.[1]

THE AVERAGE family's most valuable assets are their home and their life insurance. As with any other important purchase, planning for life insurance requires careful selection among the available alternatives. It means considering things such as: Do you need life insurance? If so, how much do you need? Is this the time to purchase it? What type would be best? Where should it be purchased?

Life insurance protects families against the financial disaster resulting from the death of the wage earner. All insurance is based on the principle that while events cannot be predicted with certainty for an individual, they can be predicted for a large group of people. A statistician cannot accurately forecast the length of your life, but he can say that for a large number of people of your age group and present health so many will die each year. Insurance is really a way of having a large number of people join a fund to provide assistance for whichever ones need help. Life insurance benefits help the families or beneficiaries of the insured. Alternatively, if the policyholder lives, he may use the savings represented by the cash values of his policy if it is a type that accumulates a cash value.

Why Should You Buy Life Insurance?

The following are some of the most common reasons for purchasing life insurance. As you read the list you might consider whether any of these reasons apply to you. Is this one of your needs, and is insurance the wisest way to care for it?

1. To provide funds for the last expenses of the wage earner—a final illness, funeral costs, estate, and inheritance taxes. Other items that might be included are the attorney's fees, moving costs, and expenses in liquidating an estate.

[1] Institute of Life Insurance, *Life Insurance Fact Book, 1963* (New York: Institute of Life Insurance), p. 5.

2. To provide income for a dependent family. Life insurance can provide (a) a lump sum which can be invested for an income, or (b) a regular monthly income for the life of a dependent or for a specific number of years.

3. To provide for the repayment of debts or for other purposes. For example, a mortgage policy would help pay off the mortgage on your home; an endowment policy would finance the college education of your child.

4. To provide a regular means of saving. Life insurance policies, other than term policies, provide for a cash value accumulation. This means that if you wish to cash the policy in, or to borrow against it, there is a certain amount of money that is available to you. Often people feel that this kind of "forced savings" helps them save when they would not otherwise put aside these funds.

5. To serve special purposes. A business firm may insure each of its partners so that the others could buy his share if he died. Parents may buy insurance policies for children to start them on a savings program at an age when premiums are low.

6. To accumulate emergency funds. Loans may be made against permanent life insurance policies after two or three years. A table in the policy gives the loan value at each interval. Insurance loans have two advantages: (a) the company cannot refuse to make it, and (b) the interest rate is fixed at the rate stated in the policy. Moreover, the rate for small loans is no higher than that for large loans, usually about 5 per cent.

Unpaid loans, of course, reduce the face value of the policy at time of claim. This means that if the insured person dies before the loan is paid, the benefits will be reduced by the amount of the loan outstanding. However, life insurance loan privileges can be of great help in many family emergencies.

How Much Insurance Do You Need?

There is no one answer to this question. Most young people cannot afford to carry enough insurance to provide their dependents with an adequate lifetime income if the wage earner dies. A good way to find out what your family might need is to make an estimate following these steps.

1. Make a list of your assets, your savings, the cash value of your equity in your home, the wife and children's benefits from social security, and what the wife could earn if she had to work. From this list make an estimate of the monthly income your dependents would receive at the various stages of family life: preschool, high school, and college.

2. Outline the minimum amount of money that will be needed by your dependents at the various stages of family life, and by the wife when the children are grown. Then add to this amount any debts which you have because these would be deducted from your estate before your family would receive funds. Also include an amount for a final illness and burial expenses.

3. Estimate the difference between the amount that your family will need and what would be provided by social security benefits, existing pension plans, and other assets. Many life insurance agents will do this for you if you furnish them with the pertinent information.

4. Discuss with several insurance agents the types of policies available to fit your family needs, and the costs. Give yourself plenty of time to consider the various alternatives and the relationship of insurance costs to your family budget. Consider both term insurance and permanent policies. If your need is only for protection, term insurance would cost less if you are under fifty. Savings could then be made by deposits in a bank. On the other hand, many people find that the forced savings of a permanent type of policy helps them to save.

The Right Time to Buy Insurance

The Single Person

Unless you are supporting someone else, there is no real need for insurance for protection except to cover your debts and final expenses. However, many young people buy insurance at this stage because the rates are low and they are usually easily insurable. With each year of age, a small proportion of the population develops ailments that impair their health and disqualify them from obtaining individual life insurance at standard rates or perhaps from obtaining individual life insurance at all.

The Newlyweds

This is the point at which most young people first think about life insurance. As long as the wife is able to work and there are no sizeable debts, there is little need for insurance except to cover final expenses. However, this is a period when young couples start to plan for living as a family, and therefore may be a good time to start on a modest life insurance program. If the couple has borrowed money for household furnishings, to equip an office, or to start a business, life insurance is a way of insuring that the wife would be able to keep these things if anything happens to the wage earner.

The New Parents

As children come into the family circle, insurance should be added to provide protection for their future. Estimates of how much insurance is useful at each stage of family life needs revision as the family size and situation changes.

Although wage earners are covered by social security, these benefits do not provide enough income for most growing families. Often it is difficult for a mother with small children to join the labor force full time or to earn a large enough income to maintain the family unless she has special training and skill. Life insurance can be used to supplement social security income.

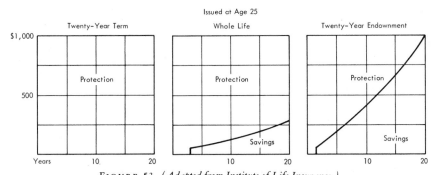

FIGURE 53. *(Adapted from Institute of Life Insurance.)*

Life insurance can also be used to insure outstanding debts so that if anything happens to the wage earner, the wife will not be left with these to pay.
A common type of insurance is a decreasing term policy which covers the a-
mount of the outstanding mortgage on the family home. (Term insurance is
explained more fully, below, under the section "The Types of Life Insurance
Policies.") Unpaid debts, installments on cars and home furnishings, and mortgages are serious liabilities to a widow with children to raise.

The Family with Grown Children

Most parents in their late forties no longer have dependent children under
age 18. However, many have their children's college education to provide for.
Social security will not help because payments for the care of a child cease when
the child becomes 18. Funds provided by life insurance could be used to pay
for a child's college education if anything happened to the principal wage
earner.

A widow may also need to be provided for. If her youngest child reaches
age 18 when she is 42, she would not be eligible for social security benefits
until she is age 62—a period of twenty years. Unless she has some skill with
which she could support herself, she would need an income, which
could be provided by life insurance. Even if she is able to return to employment, many women find their skills are outmoded and do not earn adequate incomes. Insurance income could supplement whatever a widow
might earn.

The Types of Life Insurance Policies

Basically there are three types of life insurance policies: (a) term insurance which provides insurance protection for a limited period of time
with no savings features, (b) whole or ordinary life, which has savings

features as well as insurance incorporated into the policy, and (c) endowment which is mostly a savings policy with insurance protection features.
All other types of policies are a variation or combination of these three
types of life insurance.

In purchasing life insurance, one makes a contract with the company.
This is known as a *policy*. The charge for this policy, which is paid at
regular intervals, is called the *premium*. The person who would receive
the money from the insurance policy when the insured person dies is the
beneficiary. The amount that will be paid to the beneficiary is the *face
value* of the policy. Policies other than term policies accumulate a cash
reserve or *cash value*. One can borrow against this cash reserve for a loan,
or cash the policy in and receive this money.

Term Insurance

Term insurance can be compared to insurance on a car. It is pure insurance
protection, nothing more. When one buys an automobile insurance policy, he
insures the car and its driver for the duration of the policy. At the expiration
of the period covered by the policy, the policy has no further value. Term insurance operates in this same way.

Since it has no savings features, term insurance costs less for a policy of a
stated face value, for example, $10,000, than a straight life insurance policy
which does have savings features incorporated. The low cost of term insurance
makes it very useful to growing young families who need a lot of protection
and have small incomes. It is a way of providing a lot of insurance protection
for a family at minimal cost.

The cost of term insurance below age 45 to 50 is the lowest per thousand
dollars of insurance. Although the premium for term insurance below age 50
is much less than for other types of policies, it increases with each renewal
until by age 50, when the cost ratio begins to reverse. For example, the premium on a $1,000 term insurance policy for five years is only $6.10 per year
at age 25, but $7.44 at age 35, and $12.11 at age 45.

A term policy may be renewable or nonrenewable. With a renewable policy
the company agrees that at the end of the insured period it will renew the insurance on the individual for the same face value without a medical examination. However, the renewed policy will be at a higher rate. There is usually
an upper age limit of 55 to 65 for these renewable privileges.

Term policies may also be convertible. A convertible policy can be exchanged
for a permanent type (one that incorporates savings features) without a new
medical examination, but at a rate based upon the age of the policyholder
at the time of conversion.

Term insurance may also be purchased as a decreasing policy. For instance,
a twenty-year decreasing term policy could guarantee dependent children a
fixed income for the remaining period of their dependency. If a twenty-year
policy was taken out when the children were born, they would be assured of an

income until they were age 20. For example, if the insured father dies when the child is 5 the insurance payments would be made for fifteen years. If the insured father dies when the child is 15, payments would be made for only five years. Decreasing term insurance can also be used to cover decreasing debts such as a mortgage on a house or the balance due on a car.

Whole Life

Whole life insurance policies provide insurance protection and accumulate cash values which are nonforfeitable. There are several types of whole life insurance. Straight life, which is also known as ordinary life insurance, is the oldest. Premiums of the same amount are paid for each insured year.

Many people purchase this type of insurance with a combined purpose: for insurance protection during the period when they have dependent children and to accumulate savings. When their dependents are on their own, they may discontinue payments and use the cash value to provide a retirement income.

A limited-payment policy is a modification of the straight life policy. Insurance protection continues for the lifetime of the insured, but is concentrated in a shorter period of time, usually twenty to thirty payments. Since the insurance is paid for in less time, each annual premium is higher.

The Endowment, or Retirement Income Policy

An endowment policy is a life insurance policy with very large savings features. It enables one to accumulate a sum of money for whatever purpose he desires. Most endowment policies build up cash value very quickly because there is a very large amount of savings in the premium. At the end of the specified period the cash value of the endowment policy is equal to the face value of the policy. Consequently, the premiums for endowment policies are much higher than those for straight life policies.

If the policyholder dies before the endowment matures, his beneficiary will receive the face value of the policy. Thus insurance protection and cash accumulation are involved in endowment policies. Two of the most common uses for endowment policies are to provide for college education and retirement income.

Combination Policies

Combination policies combine the features of more than one of the above types of life insurance policies. A common type is the family policy which contains whole life insurance for the husband and smaller amounts of whole or term insurance for the wife and children. This is an insurance package that is difficult to purchase separately. (See Figure 54.)

Premiums are based largely on the father's age and are not generally affected by the number of children in the family. All the children in the family, even those born after the policy is issued, are included in the coverage. The pre-

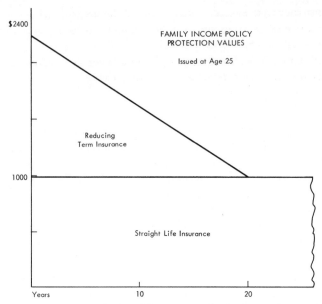

FAMILY INCOME POLICY
PROTECTION VALUES

Issued at Age 25

$2400

Reducing
Term Insurance

1000

Straight Life Insurance

Years   10   20

FIGURE 54. *(Adapted from Institute of Life Insurance.)*

miums on family policies, which are sold by several companies, are close to the total one would pay for the husband's insurance and the wife's insurance bought separately. Therefore, one gets for very little additional cost insurance coverage for the children and such features as having the rest of the family's insurance premiums paid up if the father dies.

A very common form of the family life policy is:

1. $5,000 of whole life coverage on the father with the premium based on his age.

2. $1,000 of term to 65 coverage on the wife if she is the same age as her husband. If she is younger than he, she is usually insured for a little more than $1,000; if she is older, for somewhat less. A new trend is for the wife's insurance to be permanent insurance.

3. $1,000 of term coverage on each child. The coverage continues to between ages 18 and 25. At the expiration date the child may convert to a permanent plan and get up to $5,000 of insurance, regardless of his health or occupation.

Riders to Policies

Additions can be made to basic whole life insurance policies at the time of purchase for an additional charge. These are called riders.

A rider may be dropped and the extra charge for it eliminated when one no longer needs this type of protection. Dropping a rider does not change the basic policy to which it is attached. A common rider that can be added to whole life policies is the family income rider.

This is a decreasing term insurance policy which is attached to a whole life policy as a rider. The rider usually runs for a definite number of years at the end of which payments stop. Often it is so arranged to pay a stipulated monthly income to the family from the time the breadwinner dies until the children are independent.

As with other forms of decreasing term insurance, monthly payments to the beneficiaries are only guaranteed for the balance of years listed when the policy was taken out. For example, with a twenty-year rider the twenty years start when you buy it. If the insured person dies at the start of the fifteenth year, payments will be made for five years. Family income riders can be purchased for periods of time ranging from ten years or more, until the insured is age 55. The most common periods are ten, fifteen, or twenty years.

Annuity Contracts

"The fundamental purpose of an annuity is to provide a vehicle for the scientific liquidation of capital. It is to assure a person an income he cannot outlive."[2] Annuities give a larger income than the same amount of capital could earn because annuity payments are a combination of both capital and interest. The purchase of an annuity gives the insured person an income starting at a fixed date and continuing for a specified period of time such as a number of years or for the rest of his life.

Generally, annuity payments begin when the insured reaches age 65, but the contract may be written to start at any age. Annuities may be purchased in installments over a period of years or by a single lump sum payment.

Two of the most popular types of annuity contracts are the life annuity: period certain and the refund annuity. In the period certain life annuity, the annuitant who is the recipient of the benefits is promised an income for life starting at a specific age, but also guaranteed at least a minimum number of payments. If the annuitant dies before he has received the guaranteed number of payments, the balance of the payments will be made to his beneficiary. In the refund annuity policy, the agreement is made that if the annuitant dies before he has received the cash value equal to his purchase price, the difference will be refunded to his beneficiaries. This refund may be as installment payments (installment refund annuity) or as a lump sum (cash refund annuity).

The usual annuity covers only one person. However, contracts may be written making payment upon several lives. The most common annuity covering more than one life is the joint and last survivorship annuity. A policy of

[2] Robert I. Mehr, "Contracts-Annuities," in Davis W. Gregg, ed., *Insurance Handbook* (Homewood, Ill.: Richard D. Irwin, 1959), p. 66.

this type which covered both a husband and wife could provide income throughout the lifetime of the one who lived longer.

Shopping for Life Insurance

As was suggested earlier, the first step in shopping for life insurance is to determine your family's needs. (See Figure 55.) The next step is to shop the market. The following are a few general guidelines in buying insurance.

1. Take advantage of low-cost insurance plans such as group insurance and savings bank life insurance if you are eligible. Savings bank life insurance is available to people who live or work in Connecticut, Massachusetts, or New York. These are particularly good buys on small amounts, from $1,000 to $5,000. Larger policies are not always cheaper than those of insurance companies. There are many group insurance plans available through employers or social and professional organizations that are cheaper than individual policies. The cost is lower because there is less administrative and commission cost in insuring large groups. Moreover, some of these plans offer term insurance contracts not readily available to individuals. Some firms pay all or part of a group insurance plan for their employees.

When one leaves the group through which one is insured—that is, changes jobs or does not join the organization through which the insurance was purchased, there may be provision for converting the policy to one on an individual basis, usually at a higher cost. Sometimes, however, there is no provision for continuing a group insurance policy when one leaves the group.

A well-known plan for employees of federal, state, or municipal governments is the Government Employees Life Insurance Plan.[3] Another group plan for teachers is the Teachers Insurance and Annuity plan, which was founded in 1918 with help from the Carnegie Foundation for the Advancement of Teachers.[4]

2. Compare premium costs. The prime consideration is to buy a life insurance policy that meets your needs and that you can afford. Once you have evaluated what kind of protection you want, it is possible to discuss with agents of several companies the type of policies they offer and the premium cost.

Also, the various companies have plans to fit differing needs, and the cost of one company's package is different from the plans offered by another company. One company may offer $5,000 of whole life insurance for 25-year-old men, with low premiums for the first five years and higher ones in the later years. Another may have only even-size premiums for the duration of the policy. Shopping around is a means of finding the insurance policy that is most useful for you.

[3] For further information write Government Employees Life Insurance, Washington 5, D.C.

[4] Information is available from Teachers Insurance and Annuity Association, 730 Third Avenue, New York, N.Y.

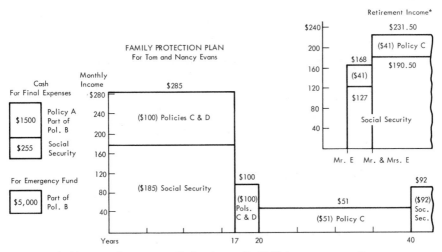

*Based upon the life insurance Tom owns at age 25. Tom plans to add to his life insurance program and to accumulate other resources over the years. In addition his company is putting in a pension plan.

FIGURE 55. *(Adapted from Institute of Life Insurance.)*

Comparison of premium costs is complicated by the fact that there are not only a variety of plans available, but there are also two types of insurance issued: participating and nonparticipating. Nonparticipating policies are issued principally by stock companies, and the premium is the actual cost to you of the policy. Participating policies are usually available from mutual companies. The premiums on participating policies are calculated on a more conservative basis and the excess charge refunded as dividends. (National Service Life Insurance, commonly called G.I. Insurance, operates like a mutual insurance company; excess charges are refunded as dividends.)

Although the long term premium cost (60 or more years) of competing companies is similar because they are all regulated by the state's insurance commission, there is a difference in dividend rates. The net cost of a participating policy is the premium minus the dividends. Comparative net costs of insurance companies, that is the premium minus the dividend and the increase in cash value, are listed in *Life Insurance and Annuities from the Buyer's Point of View*,[5] which is revised annually. (See Figure 56.)

3. Select the method of payment that suits your needs. It is least expensive to pay premiums annually. Biannual, quarterly, or weekly payments cost more. Some people who pay annually try to space big family expenses over the year. For example, if automobile insurance premiums are paid in September, it may be arranged to pay life insurance premiums in January. Other people prefer to pay the extra charge and make smaller, more frequent payments because it is easier for them to manage their funds that way. (See Figure 57.)

[5] Available from the American Institute for Economic Research, Great Barrington, Mass.

WHAT VARIOUS POLICIES COST

Approximate Annual Premiums for $10,000 of Insurance*

TYPE OF POLICY	AGE AT WHICH POLICY IS ISSUED					
	20	21	22	23	24	25
Five Year Term..............	$ 56.50	$ 57.00	$ 58.00	$ 59.00	$ 60.00	$ 61.00
(Renewable and convertible)						
Ten Year Term	68.00	69.00	70.00	71.00	72.00	73.00
(Renewable and convertible)						
Straight Life................	141.50	145.00	148.50	152.50	156.50	161.00
Life-Paid-Up-at-65	162.00	166.00	171.00	176.00	181.50	187.00
20 Payment Life............	258.50	263.00	267.50	272.50	277.50	283.00
Retirement Income at 65.....	255.00	263.00	271.50	280.50	290.50	301.50
20 Year Endownment........	469.50	470.00	470.50	471.00	471.50	472.00

> *Rates shown are approximate premium rates for $10,000 of life insurance protection for men. Rates of "participating" policies would be slightly higher but the cost would be lowered by annual dividends. "Non-participating" policy premium rates would be somewhat lower than those shown and no dividends would be paid. Policies under $10,000 will be a little higher in premium rates and lower for $25,000 and over. Policies for women are at lower rates in recognition of somewhat lower mortality rate.

FIGURE 56. (*Adapted from Institute of Life Insurance.*)

If the cost is no greater or only slightly higher for several small policies instead of one larger one, many people find it convenient to purchase smaller policies and space the payments for each over the year. Also, this offers the advantage of being able to drop a portion of one's life insurance program without touching the rest if one's need for insurance decreases or if one has a sharp drop in income and can no longer maintain as much insurance.

4. Consider the policy provisions regarding a lapse of payment. In the course of a lifetime many people have some emergency and cannot meet a premium payment. Some permanent policies provide that in the event that a premium is not paid the company will make an automatic loan from the cash value of the policy to pay the premium. However, like all loans against life

WHAT $100 A YEAR WILL BUY (Approximate Amounts)

(MALE AGE 22)

	Amount of Ins. $100 a Year Will Buy*	Cash Value at Age 65 Per $100 Annual Premium
1. Term (5 year renewable & convertible)	$19,500	None
2. Term (10 year convertible, non-renewable)	19,300	None
3. Straight Life...............................	7,000	4,200
4. Life-Paid-Up-at-65..........................	6,250	4,475
5. Modified Life (5 years)	6,000	3,510
6. Family Income (20 years).....................	5,600	3,360
7. Endowment at 65............................	5,400	5,400
8. 20 Payment Life	4,100	2,935
9. Retirement Income at 65	3,960	6,555
10. 20 Year Endownment	2,200	Matured (age 42)

> *(Most policies are issued in $1,000 units or in multiples of $500.)

FIGURE 57. (*Adapted from Institute of Life Insurance.*)

insurance policies, such a loan reduces the face value of the insurance until the loan is repaid.

Permanent policies that have been in effect for two or three years have cash surrender value. They may be cashed in or the cash value used to purchase paid-up insurance of a smaller amount, or the policy may be converted into extended term insurance equal to the face value of the policy.

Most companies will permit one to use the accumulated cash value of a permanent policy to purchase a smaller amount of paid-up insurance, or term insurance.

5. Buy insurance with the thought that some day you may want to revise your protection program. Some life insurance policies offer options such as paid up whole life that is convertible to an annuity, or term insurance that is convertible to permanent insurance. These should be considered when trying to plan a long-term program. It is very useful to select policies that have flexibility so that they can be changed to other plans at minimal cost as family needs change.

6. Select the settlement option that suits your needs. Some of the common settlement options are:

(a) A lump sum equal to the face amount of the policy. This is the usual method of settlement with small policies because most families need the money to meet final expenses. However, with larger policies there is a disadvantage in selecting this option, as many beneficiaries are not prepared by training or experience to handle large sums wisely.

(b) A guaranteed income for a fixed period of time. If the wife is the beneficiary, this would assure her of income for a certain length of time, perhaps until the youngest child enters school. If the wife does not live the full guarantee period, the balance of the cash value remaining in the policy would go to the children.

(c) A stated income for life to the beneficiary. This is a very useful option if the face value of the policy is large. But it may be too small an income on moderate or small policies to be really useful during the period when the dependents need the most help. For example, on a $10,000 policy a widow of 30 would get only about $35 per month.

Beneficiaries

One has the right to name a beneficiary to whom the policy is payable if the insured person dies. If no beneficiary is named, the proceeds of the policy will be paid to the estate of the insured person.

The federal estate tax does not apply to estates with a net value under $60,000. However, some states tax sums under this amount. Insurance benefits are usually exempt from creditors' claims and sometimes from inheritance and estate taxes up to certain amounts if a beneficiary is named.

It is often wise to name both a beneficiary and a contingent beneficiary. For instance, a husband may name his wife as the beneficiary and his children as the contingent beneficiaries.

Adapting a Life Insurance Program to Changing Family Needs

Life insurance is not something to buy and then forget about. A marriage, death, birth in the family, or a major change in income calls for a reevaluation of your plans. At least every five years you should go over your program to see if there are any additions or changes that would be advantageous. Your life insurance agent can be helpful in this analysis. A sound, flexible life insurance plan contributes to a family's sense of security and helps to meet changing family needs.

SELECTED REFERENCES

COHEN, JEROME B. *Decade of Decision*. New York: Institute of Life Insurance, 1964.

GREGG, DAVIS W. (ed.) *Life and Health Insurance Handbook*. Homewood, Ill.: Richard D. Irwin, 1959.

GUDMUNDSEN, JOHN. *The Great Provider: The Dramatic Story of Life Insurance*. South Norwalk, Conn.: Industrial Publications Company, 1959.

LINTON, ALBERT M. *How Life Insurance Can Serve You*. New York: Harper, 1958.

MACLEAN, JOSEPH B. *Life Insurance*. New York: McGraw-Hill, 1961.

14

PROTECTING FAMILY HEALTH

Optimum health is the state of the highest obtainable physical, mental and social well-being, not merely the absence of disease or infirmity.[1]

PONCE DE LEÓN once searched for the fabled "Fountain of Youth" on this continent, looking for the elixir that would enable him to stay eternally young. Modern medicine and technology, coupled with government measures, have given us some of what he sought. Today Americans not only live longer, but maintain good health and vigor for many more years than did earlier generations. An interesting illustration of this is that in the last few years whole new communities for retired people have been developed that include provisions for active sports such as golf, swimming, and boating.

At birth an American's life expectancy is 69.3 years. For white males it is 67.1 years; for white females, 73.5 years; for nonwhite males, 60.3 years; and for nonwhite females, 65.2 years. Projections indicate that by 1975–80, life expectancy at birth will be 73 years, and that by the year 2000 it will be over 74.[2] This contrasts sharply with life expectancy in 1900, which was about 49.6 for a white person.

The Miracle of Modern Medicine

Dramatic strides have been taken in understanding the prevention, cure, and control of many diseases in the last forty years. Our understanding of the relationship of nutrition and health has grown. Vitamins have been isolated and synthesized. Vaccines for many diseases have been developed and improved. New drugs with very potent effects have been developed.

Medical science has made it possible to conquer diseases that have ravaged

[1] Charter of the World Health Organization.

[2] U.S. Dept. of Health, Education and Welfare. *Health Statistics from the U.S. National Health Survey*, Series B, No. 28 (Washington, D.C.: Government Printing Office, 1961).

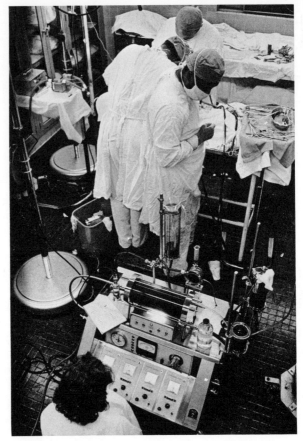

FIGURE 58. Modern medical care requires both skilled manpower and expensive equipment. (*Montefiore Hospital, N.Y. Publications.*)

mankind for centuries, such as typhus; and to control and limit others, such as tuberculosis and dysentery. In the United States, typhoid has been eradicated from cities and malaria has been eliminated from most of the southern states. It is possible to imagine that arteriosclerosis, arthritis, cancer, and many other deadly diseases might eventually be controlled and cured.

The Individual's Responsibility for Good Health

Given a good body and a fairly healthy environment, each of us can improve or injure our state of well-being. While good medical care is important, even the best medical care cannot give one good health. People also need wholesome food, good housing, healthful living habits, and freedom from emotional disturbances.

Many people are poorly fed either because they are ignorant of the rules of good nutrition or they satisfy their food urges without regard to their relationship between good eating habits and health. Although a physician may advise vitamin and mineral supplements during childhood, pregnancy, and for other situations, these are not necessary for a healthy adult who eats a good balanced diet.

A study of Americans' nutritional status[3] disclosed that between 10 and 15 per cent of the adults in the United States lacked essential nutrients in their diets, and a slightly higher percentage of teen-age boys and girls were short. Our best-fed group were children under twelve.

A well-balanced diet includes the following foods: leafy, green and yellow vegetables; other vegetables and fresh fruits; proteins in the form of meat, poultry, fish, or cheese; whole-grain breads and cereals; milk and milk products; and butter or fortified margarine. Generous amounts of these important food groups furnish us with the protein, energy, vitamins, and minerals necessary for growth and vigor.

After age twenty-one, a person's metabolism slows down; therefore, most people require less food to maintain their weight. But snacks are tempting, and our cultural patterns seem to encourage between-meal eating. Obesity is a major health problem in the United States. Life-insurance statistics show that overweight people have a sharply reduced life expectancy. People who are 50 per cent overweight have a 50 per cent increase in mortality.

Most adults decrease their physical activity as they get older. Few people get adequate exercise after they finish high school or college. Modern mobile America is also sedentary. However, a moderate degree of regular exercise at all ages is conducive to good health. It helps to maintain body tone and keeps one's weight down.

The use of tobacco and alcohol are part of our social pattern. Overuse of alcohol is often related to liver ailments and kidney disorders, as well as to automobile accidents. There seems to be a definite relationship between smoking and lung cancer. Once the habit of the use of tobacco or alcohol has been formed, it is difficult to change. Educational programs designed to deter young people from smoking are being offered in schools, often starting in the sixth grade.

Many people have become their own doctors, spending large sums of money for drug items they do not need. As a result, the patent medicine business has grown enormously in recent years. Often people use self-prescribed medications and fail to consult a doctor about serious problems until too late.

[3] Agnes Fay Morgan (ed.), *Nutritional Status U.S.A.*, Bulletin No. 769 (University of California, Division of Agricultural Sciences: California Agricultural Experiment Station, 1959).

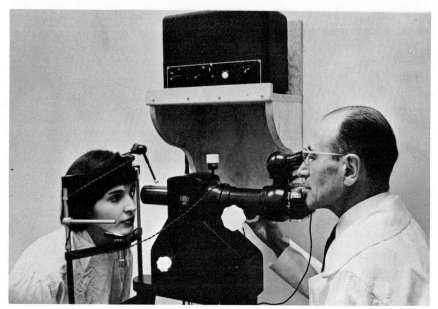

FIGURE 59. This camera takes a picture of the back of the eye. (*Montefiore Hospital, N.Y Publications.*)

Dr. George M. Fister, past president of the American Medical Association, lists nine factors for good mental and physical health.[4]

1. Good medical care. Regular checkups can prevent minor ailments from becoming major and catch others early enough for treatment. The family physician who is acquainted with the individual and his health problems is the best person to consult.

2. Proper nutrition. Learning how much to eat and what to eat at each age is vital to the maintenance of good health. Good health is not possible without good nutrition.

3. Exercise and rest. Good health requires regular exercise and adequate rest. Your family physician can advise what is desirable for you.

4. Immunization. Inoculation against serious and dreadful disease is becoming a more important part of our health protection program. Vaccination for smallpox has almost eliminated the disease in the United States. This type of procedure should probably be extended to polio, diphtheria, influenza, whooping cough, and typhoid.

5. Environmental sanitation. Disease can be eliminated or reduced in some parts of the country by cleaning up refuse, polluted water, and unsafe milk.

6. Efficient hospitals. Well-equipped, good hospitals, easily available, enable doctors to use the most effective methods of treatment.

[4] George M. Fister, M.D., "How to Keep Your Good Health," *Today's Health* (July 1962), p. 6.

7. Health insurance for medical care. Hospitalization is a costly procedure. Insurance plans through their prepayment features help families meet the high cost of illness.

8. Community and family programs for active recreation for senior citizens. Considerable study needs to be expended on the needs of senior citizens, to provide adequate and safe housing and recreation.

9. Provision should be made for the safety of elderly people in the home and outside. This is necessary because of their decreased mental and physical functions.

What Families Spend on Medical Care

"Medical-care costs for more than a decade have increased at a faster rate than any other kind of personal expense, according to the consumer price index."[5] From the base period 1947–49 to 1961, medical-care costs rose 61 per cent to six per cent of family income. This increase is due primarily to the rising cost of hospital care, which has been brought about by the use of expensive equipment and facilities and the need for more and more trained hospital personnel. One out of every eight Americans was admitted to a hospital in 1961 for an average stay of 7.6 days.[6]

The amount an individual family spends for medical care varies widely. The Health Information Foundation studies stated that sex and age have an important bearing on medical expenses. People over age 65 have the highest rate of expense and children under 6 the lowest.

Americans in 1962 paid 30 cents out of their medical-care dollar for hospital services; 29 cents went for physicians' fees; 25 cents for medicine and applicances; 10 cents for dental work and 6 cents for all other medical care.[7]

Prepaying Medical Expenses
Through Health Insurance

Although most Americans are optimistic about the future, few believe that trouble will never hit. Many people have decided that it is better to prepare for problems that can be anticipated. Consequently, health insurance plans have grown rapidly. In this way it is possible for families to prepare for the economic emergencies that accompany accidents and illness. (See Figure 60.)

Reaching its highest peak in history, health insurance in 1962 covered more than 141 million persons, representing 76% of the civilian population in the United

[5] Health Insurance Institute, *Source Book of Health Insurance Data, 1962* (New York: Health Insurance Institute), p. 52.

[6] American Hospital Association. *Hospital Guide Issue* (August 1961).

[7] Health Insurance Institute, *Source Book of Health Insurance Data, 1962* (New York: Health Insurance Institute), p. 62.

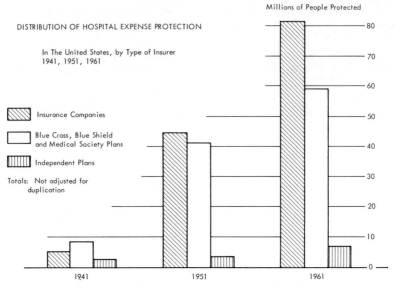

FIGURE 60. *(Adapted from Health Insurance Institute.)*

States. Last year's coverage figure represents an increase of three-and-one-half million persons over the previous record high of 136½ million Americans so protected in 1961.[8]

Although most people will have a major medical expense every eight or ten years, at any one time only a small percentage of families will be affected. By having health insurance coverage, families know that a moderate annual premium will guard them against an unduly large bill when the emergency occurs. In effect, they are sharing the risk for any one year with a large group.

Five types of health insurance plans are on the market. Four of these—hospital expense, surgical expense, ordinary medical expense, and major medical expense—cover the cost of medical and hospital care. The fifth type, loss of income protection, provides income when the disability of the wage earner cuts it off.

Hospital Payments

This type of insurance pays for hospital expenses for a limited period of time. Hospitalization insurance is the most common type of health insurance. Almost everyone who carries a form of health insurance is insured for hospital expenses. Most hospital insurance plans help pay for hospital expense in a semiprivate room for a period of from 21 to 120 days, or even 365 days. If

[8] Health Insurance Institute. Data taken from material compiled for *Source Book of Health Insurance Data*, 1963.

one wishes a private room, the amount that would have been paid for a semi-private room can usually be applied toward the cost. Generally, these plans include hospital room and board charges, and such routine services as general nursing care, use of operating room, anesthesia, X-ray and laboratory examinations, drugs and medicines and surgical dressings. Hospital admission for diagnosis and private-duty nursing care are excluded. Maternity benefits covering the delivery and subsequent hospitalization of the mother and child are available under a separate benefit clause in most plans. Usually this must be in effect for 240 days prior to the birth of the baby for the family to be eligible for insurance payments.

Blue Cross is the best-known plan for hospital payments. Although the name "Blue Cross" is widely used, each state has its own program and is organized separately. Benefits and costs are based on the plan of the particular state.

A trend toward reducing the cost of hospital care is "progressive patient care," a plan whereby the patient performs more functions for himself as his convalescence progresses. Services to patients in a hospital under this plan are provided by grouping patients in sections of the hospital according to how much care they need. As patients become more able to manage themselves, they may even go to a cafeteria for meals.[9] (See Figure 61.)

Surgical Costs

A surgical-expense policy covers the physician's fee for surgery. When one is hospitalized, there are usually two large bills: the hospital bill and the doctor's bill. This type of policy pays the doctor for surgical care.

Emergency care given in a doctor's office when a hospital is not nearby is usually covered under this type of policy. For example, an accident at a ski resort might be handled in a doctor's office as emergency care if the hospital is a considerable distance away.

Maternity benefits to cover the doctor's fee are available for a slightly higher higher premium. Usually the mother must be insured under a family plan for ten months prior to the birth of the baby to be eligible for benefits.

Blue Shield is the surgical-cost plan organized similarly to Blue Cross. The Blue Shield plan has an income qualification feature under which the participating doctors agree to accept fixed rates of payment as full payment if the subscriber has an income in certain ranges. Under this agreement, a family with a larger income can be charged a higher rate. In this case Blue Shield would pay the portion of the medical bills which would be equal to the amount a subscriber within the prescribed income limits would receive, and the excess cost would be paid directly by the subscriber.

[9] Howard Earle, "How Progressive Care Cuts Hospital Costs," *Today's Health* (May 1961), p. 56.

General Medical

General medical insurance policies cover routine medical expenses for non-surgical treatments, including care rendered at home, in the hospital, or in a doctor's office. They frequently include diagnostic, X-ray, and laboratory fees not covered under hospital expense insurance. The benefits and coverage vary with the policies; each policy specifies the amount payable and the number of calls covered for each sickness or injury.

Major Medical Expenses

This type of insurance is designed to cover prolonged and costly illnesses in which expenses are larger than those covered by "basic policies" such as Blue Cross and Blue Shield or insurance company plans. Most major medical policies include a deductible clause of from $100 to $500 or more, and coinsurance provisions. Deductible policies are those that do not pay the deductible amount; they only pay expenses beyond that level. Coinsurance means that the insured person or his family pays a portion of the expenses beyond the deductible amount. For instance, if a policy is a $500 deductible one with 80 per cent coinsurance, the following situation would prevail in the case of an illness where the hospital charges were $1,000. The first $500 would be paid by the sick person or his basic hospital insurance plan. The next $500 would be paid jointly by the major medical policy and the sick person; the major medical policy would pay 80 per cent of this $500, which would be $400. Most major medical plans pay 75 per cent or 80 per cent of charges up to $5,000, $7,500, or $10,000 after the deductible clause has been satisfied.

"Comprehensive major medical insurance" is a combination program with a low deductible amount ($25-$50), which includes both basic hospital, medical and surgical insurance, and major medical coverage. Such plans pay up to 80 per cent of prescribed care up to $10,000, $20,000, or more.

Income Protection

This type of policy is called loss of income or disability insurance. It replaces loss of earned income with cash payments if one is ill or disabled.

Policies vary in (a) the duration of the "waiting period" before payments begin—ranging from one week to thirty, sixty, ninety days or more; (b) the size of the cash benefit; and (c) the duration of payments. Many jobs and industries provide for sick-leave benefits for their employees, and this should be taken into consideration in selecting a plan. (Some firms have benefits of only a few days, which in the case of serious illness deprives the wage earner of income for his family.) A new form of protection is Group Long-Term Disability, which provides high levels of income protection. For example, some of these group plans pay up to $1,000 or more (depending on salary) per month until age 65, in the event of illness, or during lifetime for accident.

FIGURE 61. The patient, usually in the later stages of convalescence, is expected to wait on himself to some extent. (Today's Health, *published by the American Medical Association.*)

All-Inclusive Medical Care Programs

Some plans of comprehensive prepaid medical care have been developed in recent years, most notably the Health Insurance Plan of New York and the Kaiser Permanente Plan of California. In the New York Plan the premium includes all medical care, doctors' visits for routine and minor illness as well as medical and surgical insurance, but not dental or psychiatric care. The premium is usually deducted from the wage earner's salary, based on the number of dependents and the type of coverage desired—that is, with or without maternity benefits.

One of the cheapest ways to cover all medical and hospital costs is enrollment in one of these comprehensive plans. For an annual fee, almost all medical costs are covered. These plans are usually available on a group basis; only a limited number of individual subscribers are accepted.

Some people object to these comprehensive plans because they limit the choice of doctors, and the relationship between the doctor and patient may not be as personal as with a private physician. It should be noted, however, that the doctors in these plans are selected and supervised by the central organization of the insuring group which helps to guarantee good quality medical care. Comprehensive group plans have been very successful in recruiting able specialists, but there has been considerable turnover among general practitioners.

Shopping for Health Insurance

Shopping for health insurance is like shopping for any other commodity. There are various types of policies and variations in the degree of coverage and cost. Few families will disagree that all five types of health insurance coverage are desirable, but most will feel that they cannot afford everything. Therefore, the problem is to select the types of coverage that fit the family pocketbook and are most likely to be needed by the family.

Regular medical expenses, doctors' visits, inoculations, and minor illnesses can usually be budgeted for by families. More serious illnesses that require hospitalization can bankrupt a family. Therefore, most families should carry at least basic hospital and surgical insurance, if possible. Major medical insurance is desirable if the family can afford it because it helps the family protect itself against the financial burden of a really serious and prolonged illness or injury.

Lastly, the family needs to consider the total income available to them in the event that a wage earner becomes disabled (that is, Workmen's Compensation, formal sick-leave provisions, social security disability provisions, and so on) in determining the amount and duration of benefits needed under a loss of income policy. The longer the waiting period in the policy, the lower the premium.

Paying for Health Insurance

Health insurance premium costs can be substantially reduced if the individual or family purchases coverage as a member of a group, since group insurance is one of the cheapest ways to purchase basic medical and hospital coverage. In most plans lower rates are available to business firms, schools, or professional organizations, who bring in a considerable number of subscribers.

Some employers pay all or part of these policies for the employee; some even pay for coverage for the family. Usually an employee may elect to pay for his family's coverage at group rates if only he is insured by his firm. The present trend is to include major medical coverage as well as basic surgical and hospital-costs insurance as part of the fringe benefits provided by employers.

If the group rate coverage is not available, the best procedure is to shop a number of insurance companies, including the nonprofit plans such as Blue Cross and Blue Shield. Since there is considerable variation in the extent of coverage and the rates, be sure to read the policy. In one state Blue Cross may be the cheapest coverage available, but in another it may be higher priced than a policy offered by a private insurance company.

Budgeting for medical care through insurance is one of the best ways to spread the cost of medical care evenly over the years. As proof of this, it is interesting to note that many medical societies now offer health and hospital insurance for doctors.

Dental Insurance

Dental care has not been included in health insurance plans. A separate dental insurance plan, believed to be the first of its type, was introduced by the Continental Casualty Company of Chicago in New Jersey, with the cooperation of the Essex County and New Jersey Dental Societies.[10] In this plan, there is coverage for "all types of dental care service, including fillings, cleanings, bridge work, dentures, oral surgery, X-rays, gum disease and orthodontics."

The plan operates similarly to most health insurance plans, with each family selecting its own dentist. The insurance company pays 80 per cent of thee dental bill and the patient 20 per cent, except for full dentures in which case the insurance company pays only 60 per cent. Annual premiums are determined on the basis of age, sex, marital status, and dental fees in the area. The rates were expected to range from $45 for an individual to $100 and $120 for the whole family.

Selecting a Family Doctor

In our highly mobile society many families move from one community to another, and the move usually necessitates a change in the family doctor, since most physicians practice within a limited area. There are a number of ways to select a family doctor and be assured that he is well trained. One of the easiest is to ask the local community hospital for a list of physicians associated

10 *Newark Evening News,* June 15, 1961, p. 13.

THE FAMILY AS CONSUMERS

with it who practice general medicine. An accredited hospital selects its physicians with care. They must be well trained and competent.

Another method is to ask either the hospital or the American Medical Association for a list of internists in the area. Recently the trend has been for doctors who care for the general problems of the family to be specialists in internal medicine. A physician so trained is well qualified as a family doctor.

A family could obtain the names of several very good physicians by either method. They then need to decide which doctor will be the best choice for them. Many families make inquiries of their neighbors about the doctor's policies: whether he makes home visits, what hospitals he generally uses, and what he charges. If this is not convenient, or you are in a large city, it is perfectly proper to telephone the doctor's office, explain that you are new in the town, that the doctor has been recommended by someone, and that you wish to inquire about a few things before a family emergency occurs. Still other families prefer to visit a doctor for a routine check-up. If they are happy with the doctor's procedure and manner, they will continue to use him; if not, they might try someone else on their recommended list.

Cutting the Cost of Drugs

The consumer has very little choice as to whether or not to buy drugs. If he chooses not to purchase, he does so at the most serious jeopardy to his health. For the same reason, he has little choice as to when to purchase a drug. He cannot put off his purchase until market conditions bring prices more to his liking and ability to pay. His pneumonia will not wait for the price of penicillin to drop.

Secondly, the consumer cannot make shopping comparisons and rationally decide which is his best buy. He and his family simply do not have the necessary knowledge. They are ignorant of the type of drug which is needed at the particular time. They do not know whether drug X, Y or Z is the most effective against the particular illness or condition. But even if they did, they are ignorant as to which brand within the type provides optimum value.[11]

At the present time most drugs are purchased and prescribed by brand names. Often the same drug is available for considerably less cost in a competing brand. For example, aspirin may be purchased under a certain brand name for seventy-three cents per hundred tablets; it may also be purchased as acetylsalicylic acid (which is the active ingredient) in boxes of 100 for as little as nine cents. In Table 15 a comparison of cost is made for some steroid drugs.

Drugs purchased under generic names must comply with the requirements of the Food and Drug Administration. It is to be hoped that the law will insure that drugs are sold under generic names so that the purchasers can compare prices for the same product. Until that time, however, patients can only

[11] Statement presented by Mrs. Sarah Newman, member of the Board of Directors of the National Consumers League before the subcommittee on Antitrust and Monopoly, Committee on the Judiciary, United States Senate, December 20, 1961, p. 2.

TABLE 15
Comparison of Drug Prices*

Generic Name	Brand Name	Tablets mgm.	Comparable Strength per Tab. mgm.	Retail Cost per 100 Tablets (Approximately)
1. Cortisone Acetate		25	25	25 mgm. $10.00
	(a) Cortone	25		21.00
2. Hydrocortisone Acetate		20	20	20 mgm. 10.00
	(a) Cortef	20		25.00
	(b) Hydrocortone	20		23.00
3. Predinsone		5	5	5 mgm. 5.00
	(a) Meticorten	5		30.00
	(b) Paracort	5		27.00
4. Predinisolone		5		5 mgm. 5.00
	(a) Delta Cortef	5	5	27.00
	(b) Meticortelone	5		30.00
	(c) Paracortol	5		27.00
5. Dexamethasone				
	(a) Decadron	75	75	0.75 mgm. 25.00
	(b) Gammacorten	75		24.00

* Prepared by the staff of the Ophthalmology Department, Montefiore Hospital, 1962.

urge their physicians to prescribe drugs by generic names. Under the present law a druggist must fill a prescription with the exact item prescribed. If a brand name is prescribed, the druggist must give the patient that brand name. The difference between drugs containing the same important ingredients may be only the flavoring, coloring, or some other unimportant ingredient.

Miracle Cosmetics, Drugs in Beauty Preparations

Those creams and lotions with estrogenic hormones in them—do they really "recapture youthful, radiant skin beauty?" Does the presence of the placental hormone, progesterone, in a skin cream really mean that it is "life-giving?" The skin treatments containing vitamins—can they provide nutrients when used externally and thus somehow *"feed complexions?"*[12]

[12] "'Miracle Cosmetics': How Safe, How Good?", *The Kiplinger Magazine* (April 1962), p. 22.

Dr. Rothman, a leading dermatologist, in an article in the *Journal of the American Medical Association*,[13] gave some reasons for opposing drugs in cosmetics: some drugs can be harmful if the cosmetics are used in large quantities; some drugs that are added to cosmetics are useless or in too low concentration for anything except advertising purposes; and medicated cosmetics encourage people with various sorts of skin problems to attempt to diagnose and treat themselves.

Some other reasons that have been advanced against drugs in cosmetics are: (a) Hormone additives may have some effect on individuals that we do not presently know about; (b) Vitamins added to cosmetics may be absorbed through the skin and result in an overdose, particularly of A and D; and (c) If antibiotics that are useful in serious illnesses and diseases are added in small quantities to cosmetics, people may develop an immunity or sensitivity that will prevent their effective use in serious illnesses.

The Government's Role in Good Health

Laws passed and enforced by federal, state, and local governments ensure a high level of community hygiene. The variety of services performed in the interests of public health by federal, state, and local agencies is immense. The food we eat must be pure; the water we drink must be safe; waste products must be disposed of in a sanitary manner. Swimming water is tested; swampy areas are sprayed to eradicate mosquitoes; garbage dumps are exterminated; vegetables and meats shipped from one area to another are inspected; and local food and drug retailers are licensed.

Government agencies also provide direct patient care, contribute funds for medical research, provide for the testing of food products, examine and control fishing waters, develop new varieties of plants, preserve vital watershed areas, and perform an almost infinite variety of other activities. The cost of these is enormous. In 1961 the federal government gave 157 million dollars in aid to state and local governments for hospital construction, 239 million for school lunches and the special milk program, and 88 million for health services and research. And these are only a few of the public health activities.[14]

Only a rich nation could afford such expenditures. Today improved national health can be purchased if sufficient public money is spent for the control of community health and individuals can afford or are supplied with adequate personal medical care.

While the various levels of government now perform a great many important and effective services for the general health of the nation, still more services are needed. "The complexity of modern industrial society and the growing

---

[13] Stephen Rothman, M. D., "Drugs in Cosmetics," *Journal of the American Medical Association* (1961), pp. 38-42.

[14] *Statistical Abstract of the United States, 1962* (Washington, D.C.: Government Printing Office, 1962).

Persons Whose Activity is Limited by Chronic Conditions*

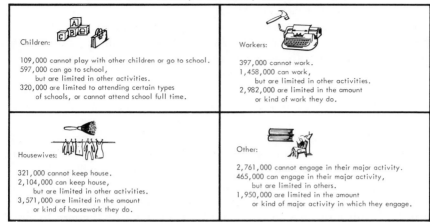

Children:
109,000 cannot play with other children or go to school.
597,000 can go to school,
    but are limited in other activities.
320,000 are limited to attending certain types
    of schools, or cannot attend school full time.

Workers:
397,000 cannot work.
1,458,000 can work,
    but are limited in other activities.
2,982,000 are limited in the amount
    or kind of work they do.

Housewives:
321,000 cannot keep house.
2,104,000 can keep house,
    but are limited in other activities.
3,571,000 are limited in the amount
    or kind of housework they do.

Other:
2,761,000 cannot engage in their major activity.
465,000 can engage in their major activity,
    but are limited in others.
1,950,000 are limited in the amount
    or kind of major activity in which they engage.

*Based on 17,000,000 persons.

FIGURE 62. *(Reproduced from* Patterns of Disease, *a publication of Parke, Davis & Company.)*

dependence of individuals upon each other have made it increasingly necessary for government to assume more responsibility in providing protection against the common health hazards."[15]

Automobile accidents have become a major health problem. One of the most significant causes of automobile accidents is the physical and mental condition of the driver, and that in most fatal accidents the drivers were either under the influence of alcohol or were speeding. More effective educational programs and stiffer penalties for driving while under the influence of alcohol and speeding would probably help.

Periodic medical examinations would prevent people who should not be driving from doing so. At the present time one can obtain a driver's license at age sixteen to eighteen and continue to drive as long as he wishes, with no further examination. People develop impaired vision, night blindness, and other serious physical limitations that impair their ability to drive safely. Nevertheless, until they are involved in a serious accident they can continue to drive, thereby endangering everyone else on the road.

The rapid increase in the number of automobiles on the road, plus the concentration of industrial plants in metropolitan areas, has resulted in air pollution or smog. Pittsburgh, once one of the areas with the worst smog problem, has demonstrated that a planned, vigorous program involving industry, car owners, householders, and government can change the atmosphere from smog to wholesome, clear air.

Occupational hazards in some industries need to be reduced. Management

[15] Harold Aaron, M.D., "How Can the Consumer Protect Himself in the Field of Medical Care?" *Selected Proceedings of the Fouth Annual Conference of the Council on Consumer Information* (Greeley, Colorado: Council on Consumer Information, 1958).

and unions have worked hard to improve the physical working conditions in many occupations, but there are still gaps.

Occupational injuries are frequent, as is evident from the size of the Workmen's Compensation payments. Studies have shown that many of these accidents are preventable with proper precautions and safeguards.

Shatterproof lenses should be required in all occupations where flying particles may be present. Workers in paint, chemical and dry cleaning industries need protection from harmful chemicals and fumes. Operators of many machine tools need better shielding to protect their hands.

Fluoridation of drinking water has been shown to be effective in reducing tooth decay.[16] Although at present considerable public controversy exists on the subject, it is possible that before long many communities will accept fluoridation of water as part of their responsibility in maintaining optimum health.

The United States is one of the few Western nations that does not have a national health insurance system. Some of the nations of Western Europe, such as Great Britain, have programs whereby the state bears the cost of medical care. In others, the employers and employees contribute to it.

Only the wealth and high living standards of the United States have enabled us thus far to manage without direct government health programs for large numbers of our population. However, the government has been involved in medical care and health to a considerable extent. In addition to the community programs of preventive health mentioned earlier, there are many federal programs of medical care. Veterans are able to get free care at many hospitals and centers maintained by the Veterans Administration. The number of patients cared for daily in 1961 in the Veterans Administration hospitals was between 114,000 and 115,000.[17]

Also, servicemen and their families may get free care at government hospitals. While these services are free to the eligible participants, they are financed by tax dollars levied on a large part of the total population.

With the mounting costs of medical care, and increased longevity, our low income families and citizens aged over 65 have been hard pressed to secure adequate care. The group over age 65 had the highest percentage of people requiring hospitilization, and also the largest number requiring medical care at home. As the richest nation in the world, we have a responsibility to provide all people with good medical care.

SELECTED REFERENCES

FAULKNER, EDWIN J. *Health Insurance.* New York: McGraw-Hill, 1960.
FOLLMANN, J. R., JR. *Medical Care and Health Insurance.* Homewood, Ill.: Richard D. Irwin, 1963.

[16] American Dental Association, *Journal of the American Dental Association* (June 1955), p. 657.

[17] Figures furnished by the Veterans Administration, East Orange, N.J.

HARMELIN, W. and R. W. OSLER. *Health and Medical Care in New York City.* Cambridge, Mass.: Harvard U. P., 1957.

SPEIGELMAN, MORTIMER. *Ensuring Medical Care for the Aged.* Homewood, Ill.: Richard D. Irwin, 1960.

WEEKS, HERBERT ASHLEY. *Family Spending Patterns and Health Care.* Cambridge, Mass.: Harvard U. P., 1961.

15

THE TEEN-AGE CONSUMER

Educating its young is probably a society's second most fundamental task—second only to the problem of organizing itself to carry out action as a society. Once organized, if a society is to maintain itself, the young must be so shaped as to fit into the roles on which the society's survival depends.[1]

A GROWING factor in the American economy is the influence of the teen-age consumer, both as earner and spender. So important has the teen-age market become that many research organizations are devoting much time, money and effort in an attempt to aid manufacturers, merchants and service concerns in choosing suitable and profitable items for this rapidly expanding consumer group.

The increasing consumer role of adolescents affects not only businesses catering directly to the young people of the nation but also the adolescents themselves. Their consumer role is a new aspect of their behavior as social beings. Parents, teachers, youth workers, and the community at large all have a vital stake in the solution to the problems raised by this new adoles-affluence. For there are problems: decreased parental control, unwise purchases resulting in health problems, and increasing numbers of automobile accidents.

The Teen-Ager:
A Social Psychological Review

Teen-age behavior has been the subject of much interest and study since the publication by G. Stanley Hall of his important book on adolescent psychology in the early years of this century. Adolescent economic behavior is one manifestation of the general behavior of teen-agers.

---

[1] James S. Coleman, *The Adolescent Society* (New York: The Free Press, 1961), p. 1.

What Is a Teen-Ager?

Some definition of the terms, "teen-agers" or "adolescents," is advisable, since no consensus seems to have been reached about the meaning of either word. For example, the Bureau of the Census defines "teen age" as from ages 13 through 19; in popular jargon the term often refers to junior and senior high school students; the Girl Scouts consider the 14- to 17-year-old group as teen-agers; *Seventeen Magazine,* which attempts to reach teen-age girls, focuses on the 15- to 19-year olds; while department stores generally designate as "teen" departments those which cater to 13- to 16-year-olds.

On the other hand, "adolescence" is generally given a more "scientific" definition, one which at the same time sets, by its very nature, somewhat more elastic limits to this nebulous period; that is, adolescence is defined as the "period that begins with the pubescent growth spurt and ends . . . with full social maturity."[2] Since what constitutes the onset of puberty is still open to question,[3] and since individuals vary greatly in physical and physiological development (regardless of what criteria are used), the beginning of the period may be as early as 10 years of age for some and as late as 16 for others. Similarly, "full social maturity" is virtually incapable of objective measurement.

The Adolescent: A Product of Industrial Society

Adolescence as we know it is uniquely a product of modern industrial society. Only after a society has achieved a high level of productivity can it afford to leave a large proportion of its able-bodied population in a dependent state, hopefully in order to better prepare these fledgling citizens to participate in and contribute to society.

Thus, the American teen-ager finds himself in an ambiguous position, considered neither child nor adult. In this transitional state, he receives few of the protective benefits normal to childhood nor is he given many of the responsibilities of adulthood.

A second effect of the uncertain status of the teen-ager is the conflict it often engenders with his parents. The "natural" tendency of parents in this culture is to overprotect their children. This engenders conflict with the teen-ager who is growing more self-assertive. The teen-ager, on the other hand, feeling more "grown up" than perhaps he is, may rebel unduly against even the mildest and best-intentioned restrictions placed upon him.

The Changing Family Relationship

Family relationships in American society have been altered drastically. No longer do the family members work as a unit to provide the material neces-

[2] L. Joseph Stone and Joseph Church, *Childhood and Adolescence* (New York: Random House, 1957), p. 269

[3] John E. Horrocks, *The Psychology of Adolescence,* 2nd ed. (Boston: Houghton Mifflin, 1962), Chaps. 10-12, esp. pp. 358-364.

sities of life, since one or two wage-earners can support a family easily and better than ever before. Thus, the adolescent is no longer a member of the "bread-winning team."

Another factor contributing to the decrease in interdependence between the teen-ager and his family is that the family no longer is able to provide him with the necessary skills to become economically self-sufficient. Most jobs require special abilities which the family is not equipped to teach; furthermore, many parents' occupational training has been in fields made obsolete by scientific and technological advances. This situation, plus the ever-increasing need for skilled workers, has led to the necessary lengthening of the educational process. Most states now require school attendance until age 16.

The sense of security derived from membership in a stable family setting is diminishing. There has been an increase in the number of broken homes. Even when the family remains together several trends have reduced family cohesiveness and added strain to the teen-agers' lives. One of these factors is the increased mobility of the typical American family: one out of every five people move each year, which means that teen-agers have fewer ties to a community, its values, and its people. Secondly, activities in which the family as a whole participates are on the decline. Family members tend to look outside the home for both work and play.

Changing Conditions: A Further Source of Insecurity

Any discussion of teen-age problems in the American culture would be incomplete without some mention of at least two factors, neither of them exclusively American, which seem to aggravate the sense of ambiguity and uncertainty which characterizes the typical adolescent. One is the feeling that society in general is no longer one of established values and clearly recognized roles; for example, the roles of men and women may overlap, as men diaper babies and women compete in fields heretofore the exclusive domain of men.

A second problem is the tense world situation, which makes difficult the looking ahead to any but an uncertain future and tends to emphasize the present. Teen-age boys must anticipate that whatever plans they make will be interrupted at some time or other by the obligation of military service; the girls, especially those contemplating marriage in the near future, are not unaffected by this consideration.

The Influence of the Peer Group

The importance of a teen-ager's friends and associates as an influence on his behavior has been noted by many observers. Yet its relationship to the totality of the adolescent personality has sometimes been so grossly distorted as to confuse the picture regarding its actual nature and scope.

Unlike the family, the peer group is a voluntary association. One may join it or not, may leave it at any time, and accept its structure and codes because they seem desirable and fitting, and not because one must. Riesman's "other-directedness" is perhaps the best-known description of this attempt to seek out and conform to prevailing modes in thought, dress, manners, and the like. Remmers and Radler's findings indicate that:

> . . . the typical teenager is responsive to the feelings and opinions of his peers on such questions as what to wear to a party, what clubs to join, how to act when out with the gang, and personal grooming (hair style, choice of clothes, etc.).[4]

The peer group (or subgroup) is unquestionably a molder of mores, and entrance therein is eagerly sought after.

The emphasis placed by teen-agers on peer-group acceptance and participation is, if not peculiar to American society, at least largely determined by it. What then are the factors in our culture which give rise to this situation?

One such condition has already been mentioned in another context, the lack of a clearly defined role for the adolescent to play in the American system as it exists today. This lack, and the resulting insecurity and confusion of self-identity—the teen-ager is told on the one hand to stop behaving like a child and on the other that he is too young and irresponsible to drive the family car—must somehow be counteracted. One way of doing this is to band together with others in similar predicaments as a means of self-protection.[5] Here at least the adolescent is among equals and can establish a place for himself on the basis of more clear-cut, if somewhat transitory, ideals.

The Teen-Ager as a Wage Earner

The teen-age population forms an increasingly important source of manpower for the American labor pool. Because of an increase in their leisure time and because they like (and in many cases, need) the extra money and the opportunity to spend it without supervision, many teen-agers are working part-time after school and during vacations. Others drop out of school to assume full-time jobs. Estimates of the number in this latter group run as high as one-third of the total teen-age population. The nature of much teen-age employment makes any figures cited open to question. However, the following statistics give at least a rough indication of the significance of teen-age participation in the American economy.

According to the 1960 census, a total of 4,181,093 persons between the ages of 14 and 19 were employed on some sort of regular basis; since the entire employed population numbered some 64 million, teen-agers comprised almost 7 per cent of the labor force. Also, since the number of those between

---

[4] Remmers and Radler, *The American Teenager* (Indianapolis: Bobbs-Merrill, 1957), p. 222.
[5] Philip R. Cateora, *An Analysis of the Teen-Age Market* (Austin: Bureau of Business Research, Univ. of Texas, 1963), pp. 27-28.

15 and 19 was slightly over 13 million, this means that somewhat between one-fourth and one-third of the teen-age population was regularly employed.[6] These figures do not reflect the number of those teen-agers working at odd jobs and in seasonal employment, both of which tend to go unreported. A study conducted in 1956 by Eugene Gilbert may have come closer to the actual picture; he found that over half the teen-agers interviewed held part-time and/or summer jobs.[7] Obviously, whatever the precise figure, it is large enough to indicate that a significant proportion of adolescents engage in some form of employment.

The question of adolescent earnings raises similar difficulties of measurement. The Small Business Administration reported that the average income of teen-agers in 1962 was between $10 and $15 per week, as compared to the 1940 average of $2.40.[8] Gilbert found (1956) that only one-third of those employed earned more than $10 per week. However, Gilbert also points out that 70 per cent of the teen-agers still attending school received allowances, which averaged $3.47 per week. He also estimated total teen-age income in 1956 to be $9 billion.[9]

The Teen-Age Market

The importance of the teen-age market in this country's economy has been growing steadily, especially since the end of World War II. Teen-agers make purchases not only for themselves but also for other members of the family; furthermore, their needs and desires influence the pattern of family spending. To quote two well-known writers on American education: "The young slowly are capturing an ever-growing share of the nation's market, both through their own purchasing power, and, more important, through effective dictation to parents."[10]

The Size of the Market

As was the case with the number of working teen-agers, wide variances appear among the several estimates of the size of the total teen-age market, changing with each survey and age group under consideration. Add to this the fact, which was mentioned before, that the influence of adolescents

[6] U.S. Department of Commerce, Bureau of the Census, *Statistical Abstract of the United States, 1961* (Washington, D.C.: Government Printing Office, 1961), Tables 2 and 5.

[7] Eugene Gilbert, *Advertising and Marketing to Young People* (New York: Printers Ink, 1957), p. 21.

[8] U.S. Dept. of Commerce, Small Business Administration, "Building Sales to Younger Customers," Small Marketers Aids, No. 80 (June 1962), p. 1.

[9] Eugene Gilbert, *Advertising and Marketing to Young People* (New York: Printers Ink, 1957), p. 21.

[10] Grace and Fred M. Hechinger, "Teen-Age Tyranny Extends Its Empire," *The New York Times Magazine* (March 19,1961), p. 21.

FIGURE 63. A teen-ager compares values. *(From* Farm Research, *Cornell Univ. Agr. Experiment Station.)*

on purchases made by the family is incapable of accurate measurement, and some idea can be gathered of the difficulties encountered in attempting to precisely estimate this ever-growing economic power. For example, the National Consumer Finance Association stated that the "youth market is rapidly attracting attention today as 16 million junior and senior high school boys and girls control $6 billion annual spendable income of their own."[11] Comparable figures cited by the Small Business Administration are 15 million and $10 billion, respectively.[12]

Amounts Spent by Teen-Agers

Various studies have attempted to determine the amounts spent by individual teen-agers. The survey of junior high school girls by Oppenheim found that girls spent an average of $3.94 per week, or $204.88 per year, on themselves. However, about half these girls also spent an average of $2.20 per week, or $114.40 per year, in purchases for the family, making a total average of some $319 per year.[13] This figure, of course, does not include those purchases made because of teen-age influence.

In another study, the National Education Association found that spending of teen-age girls varied widely within each grade level, ranging from $.30 to

[11] National Consumer Finance Association, "Finance Facts" (June 1960), p. 1.

[12] U.S. Dept. of Commerce, Small Business Administration, *loc. cit.*

[13] Irene G. Oppenheim, "A Study of the Consumer Role of a Sample of Young Adolescent Girls in Grades Seven, Eight and Nine in Irvington, New Jersey." (Ph.D. dissertation, New York University, 1961), pp. 313–314.

$8.50 weekly for girls in the seventh grade and from $1.65 to $19.50 for those in the twelfth.[14]

The automobile has become almost a necessary accoutrement for adolescent social functions. Teen-agers owned 1.5 million cars in 1960, while almost six million teen-agers were licensed to drive. Teen-age driving activities accounted for about 2.5 billion gallons of gasoline.[15]

Kinds of Items Purchased

Not surprisingly, a considerable amount of research has been done on the subject of the kinds of purchases made by teen-agers. A study of 5,000 adolescents, ages 13 to 19, produced the following breakdowns. Boys spent their own money to the indicated extents for these items: Sporting goods, 57 per cent; shirts, 40 per cent; slacks, 38 per cent; shaving cream, 36 per cent; razors, 27 per cent; to give some of the more important purchases. In the same way, girls the same age reported that 73 per cent spent their own money for lipstick, 43 per cent for hand lotion, 33 per cent for blouses, sweaters and skirts, 31 per cent for lingerie, and 27 per cent for dresses.[16] In addition, the following percentages of the 5,000 teen-agers interviewed indicated that, although the parents paid for the items, the choice was made by them: shoes, 94 per nent; fountain pens, 80; sports equipment, 70; radios, 55; watches, 44; and vacations, 38.

Adolescent Spending Habits

Adolescent spending like the rest of adolescent behavior is basically responsive to and conditioned by the adult society. Today's teen-agers, raised in a milieu which places great emphasis on thé attainment of material goods, learn very early that possessing the "right" things can lead to the achievement of status and success. "Keeping up with Tom or Mary" is just as important for the average teen-ager as "keeping up with the Joneses" is for his parents. The popularity and prevalence of new fads is a striking example of this tendency to conformity; clothing styles, hair-dos, and amusements come into fashion and decline with astonishing rapidity. Teen-age acceptance of certain recreational activities have helped fill bowling alleys, roller-skating rinks and ice-cream stands.

The general rise in family income has resulted in the fact that the money which teen-agers have at their disposal, whether allowances or earnings, is theirs to spend as they please. Most teen-agers do not have to contribute directly to the general family funds. A great proportion of working teen-agers hold jobs solely to provide themselves with consumer goods which otherwise

[14] Department of Home Economics, National Education Association, *Teen-Agers and Their Money* (Washington, D.C.: The Association, 1961), p. 3.

[15] Jessie Bernard (ed.), *Annals of the American Academy of Political and Social Science* (Nov. 1961), p. viii; quoted.

[16] Eugene Gilbert, "Seven Golden Years," *Sales Management* (June 4, 1957), p. 37.

they might have to forego. Among boys of driving age there is a strong desire for a car. As the Small Business Administration puts it, teen-agers are free to spend their wages "because these boys and girls pay no taxes, insurance, rent or grocery bills. Their parents provide such necessities.[17]

Teen-agers' consumption habits are more strongly influenced by their peers than by their family's socio-economic background. Cateora in the study previously cited found this to be the case. The study by Oppenheim confirms this view, while providing factual evidence of unavoidable differences in fulfilling consumer goals due to economic status. (The group under consideration was composed of junior high school girls in an urban community.) The results showed that while 13-year-olds spent more than 12-year-olds and 14-year-olds spent more than 13-year-olds, apparently each age sets up its own standards of expenditure and consumption, which increase with age. Similarly, while girls from poor homes were concerned primarily with getting enough to eat and putting together a decent minimal wardrobe, girls from somewhat better homes could afford to contemplate the purchase of attractive new clothes, and those from well-to-do homes placed great importance on high-fashion sweaters and skirts. Thus we can see that while differences exist among age groups and class groups as regards *attainment* of goals, the *goals* themselves are basically the same.

Conformity was not only evident in the purchases made by adolescents for themselves but also in those family expenditures over which they had any influence. For example, in Oppenheim's study the majority of the girls shared in family decisions to purchase food and soft goods. This was true regardless of socio-economic position.[18]

This conformity does not restrict itself to personal and family purchases. Cateora, in the study mentioned before,[19] found substantial agreement among them on a wide variety of economic questions, ranging from the desirability of specific articles and appliances to preferred methods of saving. Very few significant differences were found to exist among the various class levels represented in the sample.

The final point to be mentioned in this context is that the prevalence of conformity has tended to increase teen-age spending, since each new fad or fashion results in everyone buying the current "craze" item if possible.

The Social Effects of Teen-Age Spending

Teen-age spending also involves activities that are of concern to the community. A large number of teen-agers drive automobiles, and the accident

[17] U.S. Dept. of Commerce, Small Business Administration, "Building Sales to Younger Customers," Small Marketers Aids, No. 80 (June 1962), p. 1.

[18] Irene G. Oppenheim, "A Study of the Consumer Role of a Sample of Young Adolescent Girls in Grades Seven, Eight and Nine in Irvington, New Jersey" (doctoral dissertation; New York: New York University, 1961).

[19] Philip R. Cateora, *An Analysis of the Teen-Age Market* (Austin: Bureau of Business Research, Univ. of Texas, 1963), pp. 27–28.

rate among these youthful drivers is high. The Children's Bureau estimated that 306,000 youngsters classified as juveniles were involved in traffic accidents in 1960.[20] The Travelers Insurance Companies stated that "drivers under 25 were involved in 27.6 per cent of all fatal accidents in 1960."[21]

Teen-age drinking is another problem, one which is difficult to evaluate because the only available statistics are those for youngsters who have been involved in automobile accidents or court cases.

Many community groups are concerned about the apparent increase in teen-age smoking, seemingly reaching down even to the younger age groups. Although many states have laws forbidding the purchase of cigarettes by minors or the selling of them to minors by the stores, these laws are very frequently ignored. Reports from teachers and school principals indicate that a considerable number of youngsters even in the elementary grades have taken up smoking. Many current cigarette advertisements are aimed at young people, in spite of fairly conclusive medical evidence that a definite causal relationship exists between smoking and the incidence of lung cancer, as well as of heart disease.

Working with Teen-Agers

One of the important tasks for adolescents is to learn to use resources in a way which will help them to live satisfying lives. Many people feel that this education is no longer given in the home. Therefore, they have advocated that high school courses such as business education, economics, home economics and social studies devote more time to consumer education.

A more intensive approach was suggested for a coordinated program of school and community.[22] The aim would be to work with families through community agencies, adult education programs, or school-related programs, at the same time that teen-agers were studying consumer education in school. The feeling of the group which worked on this proposal was that it would be much more effective to involve families as well as teen-agers in the educational program.

The future of this nation may well depend more on the values and standards developed by our young people than on any other single factor. It behooves us, therefore, to give serious consideration to how we can help them develop a sense of responsibility for the ways in which they use their time and money.

[20] U.S. Dept. of Health, Education and Welfare, Children's Bureau, *Juvenile Court Statistics*, No. 65 (Washington, D.C.: Government Printing Office, 1961), p. 11.

[21] The Travelers Insurance Companies, *Deadly Reckoning, The Travelers 1961 Book of Street and Highway Accident Data* (Hartford, Conn.: The Companies, [n.d.]), p. 8.

[22] "Report of the Arden House Conference on Family Living," Arden House Campus, Columbia University, Harriman, New York, January 17–19, 1962.

SELECTED REFERENCES

BROWN, CHARLES H. "Self-Portrait: The Teen-Type Magazine," *The Annals of the American Academy of Political and Social Science* (November 1961), pp. 13-21.

COLEMAN, JAMES S. *The Adolescent Society*. Glencoe, Ill.: Free Press, 1961.

DUNSING, MARILYN. "Money Management Experiences of High School Students," *Journal of Home Economics*, Vol. 52, No. 9 (November 1960), pp. 756-762.

GILBERT, EUGENE. *Advertising and Marketing to Young People*. New York: Printers Ink, 1957.

HECHINGER, GRACE, and FRED M. HECHINGER. "Teen-Age Tyranny Extends Its Empire," *New York Times*, Magazine Section, March 19, 1961. pp. 27, 120-121.

KATONA, GEORGE. *The Powerful Consumer*. New York: McGraw-Hill, 1960.

LANTIS, MARGARET. "The Child Consumer," *Journal of Home Economics*, Vol. 54, No. 5 (May 1962), pp. 370-375.

SMITH, PAUL E. "Merchandising for the Teen-Age Market," *Journal of Retailing* (Summer 1961), pp. 9-14.

STONE, L. JOSEPH, and JOSEPH CHURCH. *Childhood and Adolescence*. New York: Random House, 1957.

U.S. Department of Commerce, Small Business Administration. "Building Sales to Younger Customers," *Small Marketers Aids*, No. 80 (June 1962).

16

THE SENIOR CITIZEN

It is well to remind ourselves from the start that old age is not an invention of our time but has existed as a respected and protected condition of man throughout recorded history. Our own contemporary preoccupation with aging reflects, first, the fact that many more of us are living to enjoy this ancient and honorable condition, and second, a growing awareness that neither our ideas nor our social arrangements are currently well adapted to making these added years the social and personal asset they should be.[1]

MODERN medicine has given longer life to many of our citizens, with the expectation of continued vigor and health. But the conditions of modern society have not kept pace to make the bonus of extra years a blessing.

National concern with the later years of life is evident in many ways. There is a new terminology to describe the study of aging, gerontology; and a new way of describing the older person, as a senior citizen. Individuals, public agencies, and private groups are trying to meet the personal and social needs of older people. Newspapers and magazines have had many articles on the problems or retirement and old age.

Although we are looking for ways to fit older individuals better into the social scene, we are still not completely happy and enthusiastic about the gift of longer life. Our society is youth-oriented. People tend to shy away from discussing the problems of aging or even recognizing that eventually most of us will join the ranks of the aged.

Our cultural values put great emphasis on youth. "Books by the dozen are published every year to teach us how to feel younger; clothes are advertised to accent that 'youthful appearance.' "[2]

---

[1] Elizabeth Wickenden, *The Needs of Older People*. (Chicago: American Public Welfare Association, 1953), p. 1.

[2] Mel J. Ravitz, "The Aged in American Society," *Journal of Home Economics*, Vol. 52, No. 6 (June 1960), p. 415.

The common practice of understating one's age is an indication of how most people dread older ages. The result has been that the aged are left to a separate, undefined category without status and role in our urban, industrialized society. Even those older people who can care for themselves physically and financially are usually considered apart from the mainstream.

The Evolving Situation of Senior Citizens

Changes have taken place in work and home life that are largely the cause of the undefined situation of senior citizens. Industrial jobs place a heavy premium on strength and endurance. Until labor unions developed power, older workers were pushed out.

As Americans moved from the farm to the city, independent activity declined. In an earlier social era, older people could remain on the family farm doing what little they could. Since they often owned the farm they were free to control it as they wished. Urban living has changed all this. There is little for older people to do that is productive in the home, and the skills that they used to earn a living are of little value in the household.

The Concept of Age

"Age is a relative concept."[3] With each passing year most people tend to revise their estimate of what is old. To a youngster of age 5 or 6, 25 is old; to a man of 35, 40 is still young. One man of 65 may be old and frail; another strong and vigorous.

Some people can't wait to retire; others would rather work as long as they can. Although we consider as the "aged" those who are 65 and over, we can generalize only to a limited extent about their requirements, health, or desires as they still are individuals with their own needs and ideas.

Why the Problems of the Aged
Are a National Concern

The concern about the aged on a large scale is quite new in the Western world, and there are few areas in which the needs of the aged are being adequately met. The unmet needs of the aged are part of the picture of the changing pattern of family life which leaves several groups inadequately cared for: the urban teen-ager, cultural minorities, and the aged.

The following is a brief overview of the situation of the senior citizens:

[3] Mel J. Ravitz, *ibid.*, p. 416.

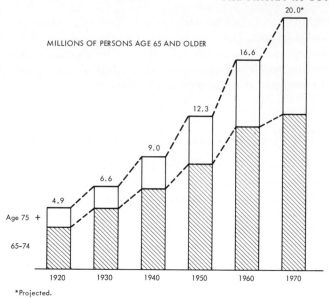

MILLIONS OF PERSONS AGE 65 AND OLDER

20.0*

16.6

12.3

9.0

6.6

4.9

Age 75 +

65-74

1920   1930   1940   1950   1960   1970

*Projected.

FIGURE 64. *(Courtesy of U.S. Department of Health, Education, and Welfare.)*

1. There were 17 million people age 65 or older in 1960, more than five times as many as in 1900.[4]

2. Life expectancy has increased more rapidly for women than for men, and this spread increases with age. In 1960 there were about 1.5 million more women over age 65 than men. There has been a great increase in the number of older widows, divorced, and single women.[5]

3. The number of people over 65 years of age increased 236 per cent between 1920 and 1960; the number over 75 increased 279 per cent; and those over 85 increased 920 per cent. Almost one million Americans were 85 years of age and older in 1960.[6]

4. In 1960 only one fifth of those over 65 were employed whereas in 1920 one third were employed.[7]

5. Projections indicate that the proportion of dependent older persons will increase in the coming years.[8]

[4] Federal Council on Aging, *1961 White House Conference on Aging Chart Book* (Washington, D.C.: Government Printing Office, 1961).

[5] U.S. Bureau of the Census, *United States Census of Population, General Population Characteristics, United States Summary,* Final Report PC(1) (Washington, D.C.: Government Printing Office, 1961).

[6] United States Senate, Special Committee on Aging, *New Population Fact on Older Americans, 1960,* (Washington, D.C.: Government Printing Office, 1961).

[7] United States Senate, Special Committee on Aging, *ibid.*

[8] Federal Council on Aging, *1961 White House Conference on Aging Chart Book* (Washington, D.C.: Government Printing Office, 1961).

AGED MEN BY SOURCE OF INCOME, 1960

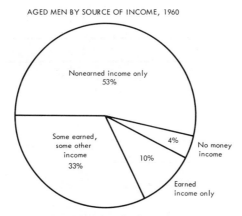

FIGURE 65. (*Courtesy of U.S. Department of Health, Education, and Welfare.*)

The Present Situation of the 65 Plus Population

Income

Many older people have outlived their own financial resources. Although some of the men and women who are now in their 70's and 80's thought they had made adequate provision for themselves, they have discovered that due to the falling purchasing power of the dollar, rising medical costs, and high living expenses they have insufficient money.

Social security benefits have done a great deal to provide large numbers of older people with some income. In 1963 nineteen million people received payments under the Old-Age, Survivors, and Disability Insurance Program. The average payment to a retired worker was $6.88 and to an aged widow $66.84.[9] (See Figure 65.) The benefits, however, were too small to enable most retired persons to live independently and adequately on this income alone in urban areas.

Some retired people received help from their families. The percentage who received cash contributions from one or more children was between 5 and 10 per cent. The median amount received by this group was $300 a year for couples and $240 for unmarried individuals.[10]

The average income of two-person families with the head 65 or over was $2,530 in 1960, and the income of persons living alone was $1,055. Even with public assistance many older people had too little money to live independently or adequately. (See Figure 66.)

[9] Statistical Abstract of the United States, 1964 (Washington, D.C.: Government Printing Office), pp. 285, 288.
[10] Alvin L. Schorr, *Filial Responsibility in the Modern American Family*, U.S. Dept. of Health, Education and Welfare, Social Security Administration (Washington, D.C.: Government Printing Office, 1960), p. 6.

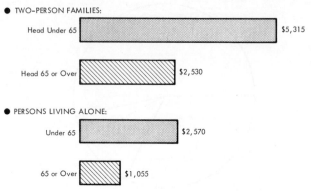

FIGURE 66. *(Courtesy of U.S. Department of Health, Education, and Welfare.)*

Health

Living longer inevitably subjects one to more of the diseases and disabilities of old age. Four of the five noninstitutionalized persons 65 years or older have been estimated to have at least one chronic condition. Thirty-one per cent have three or more chronic conditions.[11] Many are very limited in both energy and the ability to move about. (See Figure 67.) They visit doctors more frequently than do younger people, and require more frequent and longer hospitalization.

Legislation to provide health insurance protection for the aged has been the subject of much discussion. At the same time private health insurance programs for the aged have expanded greatly in the last few years. By 1962, 55 per cent of the noninstitutionalized aged population (over 9 million people) was covered by some form of health insurance.[12]

Insurance companies are permitting persons enrolled in health insurance plans to retain them upon retirement, usually with reduced benefits. Four out of five of the employees insured under group health insurance policies, issued by private insurance companies in 1962, have the right to retain these after retirement.

These private insurance programs are a big step forward in providing funds to enable senior citizens to obtain better health care. However, there is still inadequate coverage in amount for many insured persons, and large segments of the over 65 population are not covered at all.

[11] U.S. Dept. of Health, Education and Welfare, Public Health Service, *Health Statistics,* Series B-11, National Health Survey (Washington, D.C.: Government printing Office, 1959).

[12] J.F. Follmann, Jr., "Private Health Insurance Protection for the Aged," Director of Information and Research, Health Insurance Association of America. Talk given at the School of Public Health, University of California, April 30, 1963.

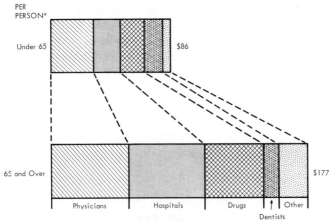

PER
PERSON*

Under 65 $86

65 and Over $177

Physicians | Hospitals | Drugs | ↑ | Other

Dentists

*In 1957–58; excludes private expenditure for nursing home care and
all care at public expense.

FIGURE 67. Average medical expenses in a year are at least twice as high in old age. *(Courtesy of U.S. Department of Health, Education, and Welfare.)*

Living Conditions

Satisfying living arrangements for the aged are often lacking. The smaller mobile family usually has little space for an aged parent. Moreover, most older people prefer to maintain their independence if their physical condition and income permit. However, with reduced financial circumstances many older people are forced "to live in dilapidated quarters under conditions that actually help to generate mental, physical and social ills."[13] What is critically needed is public and private provision for housing designed to meet the needs of the aging at a price they can afford. An interesting feature of a new housing development for retired couples in California is that health insurance is included in the rent. Medical insurance costs are included in the $93 to $103 monthly payments of a cooperative apartment being built at Seal Beach, California.[14]

Public housing programs have assumed considerable responsibility for elderly citizens. However, most projects have a minimum income requirement that many elderly people cannot meet. To help them it has been proposed to abolish the minimum rent requirement, build more utility or one-room apartments that cost less, and increase federal assistance to nonprofit or welfare groups to provide housing for particular groups of elderly citizens.[15]

[13] American Public Welfare Association, "Aging—Public Welfare's Role." A policy statement of the American Public Welfare Association, Chicago: American Public Welfare Association, 1960.

[14] *The Wall Street Journal*, January 4, 1962, p. 1.

[15] Hearings before the Subcommittee on Involuntary Relocation of the Elderly of the Special Committee on Aging, United States Senate, "Relocation of Elderly People" (Washington, D.C.: Government Printing Office, 1963).

Communities for retired people have been developed in Florida and other warm parts of the country. Most of these are housing developments of individual homes, although some are apartments. The housing is usually designed to meet the physical needs of the aging; no stairs, easy maintenance, and other conveniences are provided. Community activities and companionship with other retired people are available. However, since these "retirement communities" are concentrated in a few areas, retired people who wish to be part of such a community usually must move away from their old home and be willing to adapt to a new life. Moreover, to be able to do so, they need a considerably larger income than many retired people have.

The Need to Maintain Relationships with Family and Friends

Just as those of other age groups, older people have need of a satisfying role in their family, among friends and in the general community. Retirement is a period with many difficult adjustments. Family and friends are a continuing relationship that lend stability.

Relationships with friends and community activities are also important. Usually the elderly citizen has strong ties with his "old neighborhood." The church and civic groups may mean a great deal to him. Many public housing programs recognize the importance of these associations for older people and attempt to relocate within the same area the people they are forced to move. In the Senate hearings on relocation of the elderly, the need to provide more adequate housing while at the same time furnishing opportunity for maintaining ties with the neighborhood was stated many times.

In retirement it is necessary to find new ways to happily fill one's time. People past 65 have more hours per day and more days per year free of responsibility. Most men, in giving up work, are left without a satisfying means of filling their waking hours such as they had for the preceding forty or fifty years.

Many women find the transition easier because they busy themselves with housework which they have done for many years. However, it is as difficult for some women to adjust to a husband home all day as it is for the husband to adjust to being home.

About the time that parents retire, the relationship of the middle-aged child to his parents often undergoes a transition. The adult child begins to assume responsibility for the parent. Building or maintaining happy family relationships when parents and children have changed roles is difficult. The conflict which some middle-aged people find between their responsibilities to their parents and their own children complicates the difficulties.

Older people need to make new friends and develop new interests as old friends move away, become ill, or die. Interests and activities once enjoyed may not be possible because of limitations of energy, mobility, and income. Even if their children live nearby, they are often busy with their jobs and the demands of their own young children.

Golden age clubs and centers for senior citizens have tried to provide for these needs. This is a fairly new type of program and as yet reaches only a small segment of the senior population.

The Variety of Programs
Available to Serve Older Persons

At the present time most of the services and facilities for older people are located in urban areas. This is partly due to the heavier concentration of people in these areas, and partly to the difficulties of financing and providing facilities over widely scattered areas.

Some of the services available to older people are public, others are private, and some are jointly run by public and private groups. The following list will give some idea of the scope of services that presently exist.

1. Information and referral center.
2. Employment of a home economist on the agency staff.
3. "Friendly visitor" service.
4. "Meals on Wheels."
5. Housing services.
6. Special property consultants.
7. Special nursing home services.
8. Special medical services.
9. Senior citizen centers.
10. Homemaker services.
11. Special mental health services.
12. Rehabilitation services.
13. Foster home programs for the aged.
14. Provision for participation of older people in community programs.
15. Group recreational programs and clubs.
16. Protective services.
17. Commitment services.
18. Licensing services for institutions, nursing homes, foster, and boarding homes.
19. Special bureaus of aging.
20. Training programs for nonwelfare personnel working with older people.
21. Work relief on a voluntary basis.
22. Vocational counseling and training.
23. Intensive casework services.
24. Special employment services.
25. Health education programs.
26. Community organization leadership and planning regarding services for the aging.[16]

[16] American Public Welfare Association, "Administration of Services for the Aging Through Local Public Welfare Agencies," Report of the Institute held May 1961, p. 4. Reprinted by permission of American Public Welfare Association, 1313 East 60th Street, Chicago, Ill.

Many industrial concerns have programs to prepare workers and management for retirement. Coupled with retirement plans are counseling and health services, and in some cases special housing facilities for the retired worker.

Some unions have programs to help workers adjust to retirement. District 65 of the Retail, Wholesale, and Department Store Union conducts a class to prepare members for retirement.

A very promising development are the community programs, most of which have been developed since the White House Conference on Aging in 1961 which focused attention on the problem. Columbus, Indiana, organized its business, professional, and senior citizen groups into a Retirement Foundation. With the help of Purdue University a study was made of local retirement needs, and new programs for the retired developed. These include preretirement training, an employment service, a small industry, a health fair, home care service, bus tours, a senior day center, and a low-rent housing development.

A vigorous national association to serve the retired population has grown— The American Association of Retired Persons. Some of the activities and services they offer to members are:

1. European Travel Service—leisurely-paced group tours at the right price.
2. Non-Profit Mail Order Drug Service at savings of approximately 25% and more.
3. General Medical and Surgical Insurance Plans—broadest coverage for least cost.
4. Modern Maturity magazine and bimonthly News Bulletin . . .
5. Legislative Program—keeps members and legislators informed on retirement inequities—represents members' interest in vital areas of government.
6. Hearing Aids—over 30% savings on purchase price.
7. Housing Information—consultation and planning service in retirement housing.
8. Consultation and Referral Service with government agencies and private industry on employment, second careers, and preparation for retirement.
9. Local Chapters develop self-help in meeting community inadequacies.
10. Non-Profit Nursing Home—maximum care at minimum cost.
11. Hospitality House, St. Petersburg, Florida. . . .
12. Volunteer Service in Veterans hospitals and other facilities.
13. Citations for persons who have made outstanding contributions to enrichment of retirement living.
14. Co-sponsoring of projects to benefit retirees in cooperation with government agencies and industry.
15. Changing the image of aging to a positive philosophy of modern maturity.[17]

[17] From "Modern Maturity Is a Go-Ahead to Happy Retirement Living," p. 4. American Association of Retired Persons, Dupont Circle Building, 1346 Connecticut Ave., N.W., Washington, D.C.

FIGURE 68. Some modern apartments for the aged have been built with extra services, such as a community dining room. (*Courtesy of Medical Tribune and Crestview, Sylvania, Ohio.*)

The Senior Consumer

The consumption problems of the aged focus around two primary factors: most of the aged have inadequate incomes to enjoy the prosperous American life, and the variety of goods and services available are often not suited to the particular needs of the aged.

As the records of social service agencies amply document, a high proportion of the 10 per cent of the nation who are over 65 do not have sufficient income for more than minimal living. Efforts to improve the conditions of living for senior citizens have been channeled in two directions, to improve their "real" income and to improve services for the aged. Income for the aged has been increased through pensions, old-age and survivors insurance, and public assistance payments. Decreased taxation has increased income. People past 65 have a double personal exemption in computing federal income taxes. Most notable among improvements in the services for the aged have been the efforts to improve housing and medical care.

In a broad sense the consumer problems of the aged are public problems. Most of the people who are now aged are unable to provide adequately for themselves. Low-cost housing is not readily possible without massive governmental assistance. The high cost of urban land and construction makes it impossible for private industry to meet the needs of the aging at costs within their reach. Although medical insurance programs for senior citizens have been rapidly expanded and improved in the last few years, they are still beyond the income of many people.

The difficulties in achieving a satisfactory life past age 65 are compounded when one considers the plight of the culturally deprived groups in our midst. Most of these people worked at occupations that until recently were not covered by social security. Moreover, when they came under social security, their incomes were not insured at the maximum rate. If they are eligible for old-age and survivors insurance benefits they receive only minimal benefits, often as little as twenty or thirty dollars a month. Since public assistance programs are on a matching federal-state basis the benefits available to supplement old-age and survivors insurance benefits vary considerably from state to state. At best they are very minimal.

The question before the nation is, "What is our obligation to the aged and how can we meet it?" This discussion is based on the premise that the richest nation on earth has the duty to care for its old as well as its young, to make the last of life as rewarding as the younger and middle years.

Education and the Aged

Old age is something that we have to deal with right now as an emergency. It is a problem, partly because it is something that we have been afraid of, partly because

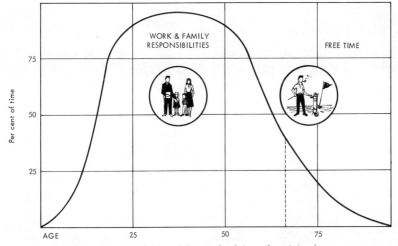

FIGURE 69. *(Adapted from Federal Council on Aging.)*

it is something our economy has not been prepared for. Therefore, there is the need to think temporarily of the whole aging population as a population that is special—a special category. But I would also like to talk about how we can rear a population from infancy on so that old age is not a problem and not a separate category, where it is a part of living . . . the way all human experiences and all crises are seen as a natural part of living.[18]

At present most people dread old age. A much more sensible approach would be to prepare for old age, to provide the conditions in which the aging population would have a place and a function, and to educate people so that their later leisure years are happy ones.

Facilities and good care are not enough. What is also needed is for people to approach the later leisure years with the attitudes and skills for a successful retirement. This is a job of education. Just as people now prepare for working years, they might also prepare for retirement ones.

Schools and community agencies could expand their function by helping people develop a constructive attitude towards older people and their own old age. They might also do more to help young people develop interests in activities they could carry on through their later years.

Community service projects also offer an opportunity to use the abilities of older people. Many could contribute more if the channels or communication were expanded so that older people would feel wanted and also learn where in the community they could function.

Modern science and medicine promise still longer life and healthier later years. Will this be a gift or a burden? The years after 65 can be useful and

[18] Dorothy Lee, "Attitudes and Values: Family, Community, and Individual," *Journal of Home Economics*, Vol. 54, No. 8 (October 1962), p. 691.

FIGURE 70. Older people also enjoy recreational activities. *(Leisure Village.)*

happy ones. Many people have an important part of their life after 65:
Eisenhower was President until after he was 70; Adenauer was the leader of
the West German Government until almost 90; Winston Churchill was
Prime Minister of England at an age when most people are in retirement.
Many public school teachers stay in the classroom until age 70. Some colleges
make a specialty of appointing retired professors over age 65 to enhance the
stature of the college.

SELECTED REFERENCES

AMERICAN PUBLIC WELFARE ASSOCIATION. "Planning Improved Serv-
    ices for the Aging Through Public Welfare Agencies." Report of the
    Institute on Aging. Chicago: American Public Welfare Association,
    1961.
BREEN, LEONARD Z. "Aging and Its Social Aspects," *Journal of Home
    Economics*, Vol. 54, No. 8 (October 1962), pp. 685-689.

FEDERAL COUNCIL ON AGING. *1961 White House Conference on Aging Chart Book*. Washington, D.C.: Government Printing Office, 1961.

GILES, RAY. *How to Retire*. New York: Fawcett World Library, 1959.

NICHOLSON, EDNA. "Physical and Psychological Adequacy," *Journal of Home Economics*, Vol. 54, No. 8 (October 1962), pp. 700-705.

SCHIFFERES, JUSTUS J. *The Older People in Your Life*. New York: Pocket Books, 1962.

SCHORR, ALVIN L. *Filial Responsibility in the Modern American Family*. U.S. Department of Health, Education and Welfare, Social Security Administration. Washington, D.C.: Government Printing Office, 1961.

STRYKER, PERRIN, AND THE EDITORS OF *Fortune*. "How to Retire Executives," Chap. 16; "When Should Workers Retire?", Chap. 17. *A Guide to Modern Management*. New York: McGraw-Hill, 1954.

The Nation and Its Older People. Report of the White House Conference on Aging, 1961. Washington, D.C.: Government Printing Office.

TIBBITTS, CLARK. "Economic and Social Adequacy of Older People," *Journal of Home Economics*, Vol. 54, No. 8 (October 1962), pp. 695-699.

U.S. DEPARTMENT OF HEALTH, EDUCATION AND WELFARE, Social Security Administration. *The Health Care of the Aged*. Washington, D.C.: Government Printing Office, 1962.

———. "Now That You Are Retiring." Washington, D.C.: Government Printing Office, 1962.

WICKENDEN, ELIZABETH. *The Needs of Older People*. Chicago: American Public Welfare Association, 1953.

17

SOURCES OF INFORMATION AND PROTECTION FOR FAMILIES

Goods and services provided free at public expense have in the main certain common characteristics. One . . . they represent values about which there is little or no dispute. . . . The second . . . is that the community as a whole has a stake in their widespread use.[1]

W E IN the United States enjoy one of the highest standards of health and sanitation of any nation in the world. Much of the credit for this lies in the effectiveness of our federal and state agencies. Most of the goods used by the average family in our highly industrialized society are produced in other parts of the country. Thus the major job of protecting families in the use of commodities is in the hands of federal agencies. Control over goods produced and sold within a single state are a function of the state governments.

Federal Agencies

As a nation of small independent farmers, there was little need for extensive federal regulation of commerce, food distribution, production, and transportation. Today, when the average urban family may have lettuce from California, meat from the Midwest, and fruit from Florida at one meal, there is need for regulations to insure the safety and cleanliness of food, to enable transportation to function in the national interest, and to develop means of communication that enable this commerce to take place.

United States Public Health Service

The accomplishments of the United States Public Health Service, the medical profession, and the various state services have been most impressive. Improvement in

---

[1] Hazel Kyrk, *The Family in the American Economy* (Chicago: The Univ. of Chicago Press, 1953), p. 151.

mortality has been remarkable; typhoid fever has been virtually eliminated; and diphtheria, measles, scarlet fever, whooping cough, infantile diarrhea, and small-pox are no longer the scourges they were in the past. Very large gains have also been made in the prevention and control of tuberculosis.[2]

The Public Health Service furnishes direct medical care through three divisions: the Division of Hospitals and Medical Care, the Division of Foreign Quarantine, and the Clinical Center of the National Institutes of Health. They also publish information on the frequency of illness and on industrial health and medical programs. In addition, they cooperate with state departments of health when needed. State and local governments are aided considerably by federal funds, advice, and supervision in carrying out public health activities.

The Public Health Service also promotes and conducts research. In 1952 a clinical research hospital costing $62.3 million was constructed at Bethesda, Maryland, "to integrate laboratory work with experimental application of that work to the patient."[3]

The Food and Drug Administration

At the turn of the century, food processing began to move from the home kitchen into large factories and commercial food processing plants. Home production of food was replaced with home consumption of processed food. This was the beginning of the commercial food production industry. Like many new industries the operating conditions were crude. Food preparation was unsanitary and unsupervised.

The first Pure Food and Drug Law was passed by Congress in 1907 to improve the sanitary level of commercial food preparation. Enforcement was placed in the hands of the Bureau of Chemistry of the Department of Agriculture. Dr. Harvey W. Wiley, who had led the nationwide campaign for the pure food law, was the first head. In 1927 the Food and Drug Administration was made a separate unit of the Department of Agriculture, and in 1940 the administration was transferred to the Federal Security Agency which was made the Department of Health, Education and Welfare in 1953.

WHAT IT DOES. The job of the Food and Drug Administration is to see that food, drugs, and cosmetics used by the American people are pure, wholesome, and sanitary. Food must be produced under healthful conditions; drugs and devices should be safe and effective; and cosmetics must be harmless and honestly described.

To protect the safety of foods, drugs, and cosmetics, as well as honesty in their labeling, the FDA carries out the following kinds of activities.

[2] Oscar N. Serbein, Jr., *Paying for Medical Care in the United States* (New York: Columbia U.P., 1953), p. 21.

[3] Oscar N. Serbein, Jr., *ibid.*, p. 252.

FIGURE 71. The Food and Drug Administration tests the safety of foods and inspects the manufacturing of drugs. (*FDA Photo.*)

Makes periodic inspections of food, drug, device, and cosmetic establishments and examines samples from interstate shipments of these products.

Enforces the law against illegal sales of prescription drugs.

Checks the manufacturers' evidence of the safety of all "new" drugs (about 40 each month) before they are put on sale to the public.

Checks the safety of all batches of coal-tar dyes for use in foods, drugs, or cosmetics.

Checks the labeling and range of usefulness of therapeutic devices, and takes action against dangerous or bogus devices.

Tests all batches of insulin and five of the most important antibiotic drugs for purity and potency before they are sold. The manufacturers pay for such tests.

Issues and enforces regulations specifying the kinds and quantities of new food additives that may be used in or on food products.

Establishes the amount of pesticidal residues that may remain on food crops without injury to consumers, and polices shipments to see that residues are within safe limits.

Sets up standards which guarantee the composition and real value of food products in line with the Congressional mandate to "promote honesty and fair dealing in the interest of consumers."

Checks imports of foods, drugs, devices, and cosmetics to make sure they comply with United States law.

Cooperates with State and local officials in the inspection of foods and drugs contaminated by disasters, such as floods, hurricanes, explosions, and fires, and in the removal of dangerous items from the market.

Assists industry in voluntary compliance with the law, and in setting up controls to prevent violations.[4]

HOW THE FDA OPERATES. In 1960 a major disaster occurred in the downtown section of Roseberg, Oregon. A truck with two tons of ammonium nitrate and dynamite exploded, wrecking two grain elevators, a soft-drink bottling plant, some drugstores, and an ice-cream stand. Glass and other foreign matter had contaminated food and drugs. The Food and Drug Administration stepped in to help sort and evaluate the condition of the remaining food and drugs. Contaminated products were destroyed, and the health of the community maintained.

An illegal but highly lucrative business is the diverting to commercial bakeries of unfertilized eggs that have previously been rejected by incubator operators. These rejected eggs are considered unfit for human consumption, but may be used for other purposes such as tanning of leather. However, bootleg operators sometimes purchase them, freeze them, and then sell them to large commercial bakeries. In the frozen state they appear to be good and eggs sold for human consumption command a much higher price than those sold for other things. When the FDA knows of such an operation, it can obtain a permanent injunction on the batches of rejected eggs so that they cannot be shipped from one state to another.[5]

The Food and Drug Administration has three ways of enforcing violations: (1) Contaminated products can be seized. The FDA asks a federal court to have the products seized and destroyed or changed to comply with the law. (2) An injunction against further interstate shipments can be obtained. (3) Criminal charges can be filed against the violators.

The FDA has been very effective in protecting our food and drugs. However, with the rapid changes in modern marketing methods and the wide and growing varieties of drugs and prepared foods, there is a constantly expanding need for vigilance. The budget of the Food and Drug Administration only permits inspection and spot checking of a very small fraction of the food and drugs purchased by the consuming public.

Meat Inspection Division, United States Department of Agriculture

The Meat Inspection Division supervises the safety of meat slaughtered for food and the preparation of meat food products. "Each working day, Federal meat inspectors keep some one million pounds of unfit meat from

---

[4] U. S. Dept. of Health, Education and Welfare, *Food and Drug Administration, What It Is and Does* (Washington: Government Printing Office [n. d.]), pp. 1-2.

[5] U. S. Dept. of Health, Education and Welfare, *The Annual Report of the United States Department of Health, Education and Welfare* (Washington, D. C.: Government Printing Office, 1960).

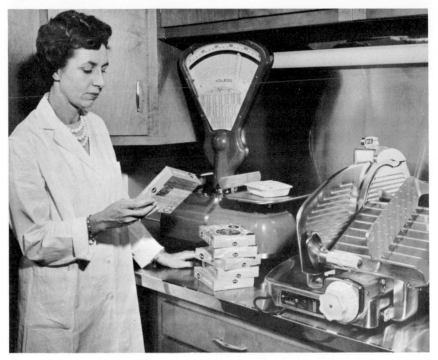

FIGURE 72. Packaged meat as well as fresh meat is checked and examined. *(USDA Photo.)*

U.S. dining tables."[6] (See Figure 72.) Meat inspection starts with the approval of plant construction to be sure that they provide sanitary and inspection facilities. Federal inspectors supervise and inspect sample batches of meat at every stage from the animal on the hoof through processing to the package and label.

Federal inspectors also inspect imported meat and meat products and approve United States meat before it is exported. The federal stamp on meat or packages tells families that the meat has been inspected and is safe and wholesome. It is not a grade.

The Federal Trade Commission

The Federal Trade Commission has the responsibility to maintain a free and fair competitive market. Their functions fall into two broad areas: to prohibit producers from restricting trade or forming monopolies in a particular industry and to see that advertising is truthful.

[6]U.S. Dept. of Agriculture, "Meat Inspection, The Protection It Provides" (Washington, D.C.: Government Printing Office, 1962.)

Much of the recent activities of the FTC have been devoted to the control of advertising. Their work in this area has been strengthened by several amendments to the original Clayton and Federal Trade Commission Acts. The Robinson-Patman Act of 1936 gave the Commission greater control of price discrimination, the Wheeler-Lea Act of 1938 gave greater authority in the control of advertising. The Wool Products Act of 1940 and the Fur Products Labeling Act of 1952 gave the Commission the job of surveilling labeling of these products. The Textile Labeling Act of 1960 expanded this function to fabrics. The Trade Mark Act of 1946 gave the Commission more careful duties regarding the use of trademarks. The McCarran Insurance Act of 1948 gave the Commission control of insurance, and in 1950 the Anti-Merger Act extended the Commission's authority to acquisitions of assets by corporations that adversely affect competition.

Action by the Federal Trade Commission is initiated by complaints from consumers, business competitors, or employees of companies. A complaint is investigated and if a violation of the law is uncovered, a formal complaint is issued by the agency. The case then goes to a hearing examiner of the FTC if the company involved does not voluntarily settle. At this point the FTC issues the initial decision, which is subject to review by the full Commission. If the decision is upheld by the full Commission, the challenged company can sign a consent order and agree to cease the practice on which it was challenged. If they do not desist, the FTC can issue a cease and desist order. The cease and desist order may be appealed in court by the company. However, once the order is upheld in court, violators are subject to fines. This is a lengthy and cumbersome enforcement process.

The Antitrust Division of the Department of Justice

The primary purpose of this agency is to reduce monopoly and to prevent price fixing. This agency enforces the nation's original antitrust law, the Sherman Act of 1890, and its subsequent amendments. The Act prohibits two types of conduct:

1. Concerted action by two or more people to restrict trade.
2. Monopolizing by one person or a group of persons.

Down through the years the courts have established that certain types of business conduct are traditional violations of the Sherman Anti-Trust Act.[7] The Sherman Act is both a civil and criminal statute. The criminal act permits prosecution for offenses, whereas the civil section permits the courts to order practices that will restore competition to an industry.

Unfortunately, the Antitrust Division operates on a very limited budget

[7] Monroe W. Karman, *Consumers Look at Federal Protective Services* (Greeley, Colorado: Council on Consumer Information, 1959), p. 23.

and has an enormous job in trying to restrict vertical integration and non-competitive practices. Many people feel they have done well with a few large monopolies, but not nearly enough with a wide range of areas.

The Postal Inspection Service

The purpose of the Postal Inspection Service is to prevent fraudulent activities involving the United States mail. The mails are frequently involved in such things as the sale of worthless stock and fake medical cures. To prevent fraudulent schemes of all kinds, the distribution of pornographic literature, and other undesirable practices the Postmaster General can prohibit solicitation of money or property through the mail. In such cases the Postal Department returns letters to the offender marked "Fraudulent" or "Unlawful." The Postal Department can also ask the United States attorneys to prosecute violators of postal laws.

The Institute of Home Economics of the Department of Agriculture

The major purpose of the Institute of Home Economics has been to help farm families manage their income more effectively. It is the oldest consumer education agency in the federal government and one of the smallest. The Institute was formed shortly after the Spanish-American War to promote higher living standards in the Philippine Islands. Its activities were increased to help southern families, and it later was joined with the Extension Service of the Department of Agriculture.

At one time the Institute tested large appliances, equipment, and textiles. However, at the present time most of their very limited budget is devoted to testing the efficiency of the use of time and space and to preparing materials for homemakers such as the booklet, "The Beltsville Kitchen-Workroom", that will increase their efficient use of time and space. Materials prepared by the Institute are used by the extension services of the states, home economists, and magazines.

The National Bureau of Standards

"Since we live in an exchange economy, the acts of weighing and measuring are repeated many times every day."[8] Over the centuries nations have had to determine standards for measurements and coins. The Constitution of the United States gave Congress the power "to coin money, regulate the value thereof, . . . and fix the standard of weights and measures."[9]

Since 1901 the National Bureau of Standards has been a center for testing the weights for federal agencies and states' measuring instruments. However, the Bureau is not a regulatory agency. Individual states vary considerably in their use of standard weights and in the adoption and enforcement of state laws covering weights and measures.

[8] Leland J. Gordon, *Economics for Consumers* (New York: American Book Co., 1961), p. 519.
[9] Constitution of the United States, Article I, Section 8.

Other Federal Agencies

Several other federal agencies have important responsibilities in protecting family interests. The Federal Communications Commission regulates interstate and foreign commerce in wire and radio communication. The type of service received by consumers and the rate charged are largely controlled by this agency.

The Interstate Commerce Commission oversees the transportation systems of the country. By their regulation of commercial transportation systems the interests of individuals are involved, particularly in the setting of rates and charges.

The Securities and Exchange Commission enforces the Securities Act of 1933, which requires full disclosure to investors of facts about securities publicly offered and sold through the mail or in interstate commerce.

The activities of the Federal Housing Administration and the Veterans Administration have contributed greatly to the trend to individual home ownership through their programs of insuring home mortgages. Both administrations make inspections of houses to be insured that furnish some degree of assurance of value to purchasers, although this has been subject to question.

The Agricultural Extension Service in each state provides considerable information for both urban and rural consumers. Each state has its own program. Many of these programs include the publication of informative leaflets, classes for homemakers, workshops, and the furnishing of information on a wide variety of subjects.

In February 1964 President Johnson appointed as his special assistant for consumer affairs, Mrs. Esther Peterson, Assistant Secretary of Labor. Mrs. Peterson's office is acting as a focal point for consumer interests at the federal level.

Evaluating the Federal Agencies

We should not be complacent about the effectiveness of our federal agencies. There are still many gaps in protection. More effective enforcement of existing statutes depends on stronger penalties for violations and more adequate funds and staffs for the watchdog agencies. Additional legislation is needed in many areas to provide greater protection for the individual consumer and also to ensure that national resources are used wisely.

State Agencies

Federal laws and enforcement agencies function only in situations where more than one state is involved or where commerce and products cross state lines. In many situations only state laws and agencies operate; for example, if food products are produced and sold within the state, if water supplies are available within the state, if trade agreements and marketing practices are used only within the state. Most states have counterparts to the federal regulatory agencies.

While in practice federal and state agencies often cooperate in the checking and enforcing of legislation, the quality of protection afforded families within a state—for those items and situations not covered by federal legislation—depends on the laws within the state and the enforcement of state agencies. As Leland J. Gordon, Director of the Weights and Measures Research Center, Denison University, pointed out in "Watch Your Weights and Measures",[10] state legislation and enforcement vary considerably. Many people believe that North Dakota has the best legislation, and California the most vigorous department for consumer education and information. The Consumer Counsel in California advises the Governor as to consumer legislation needs. This office was first established in New York State, with Dr. Persia Campbell as the Consumer Counsel, but was abolished with a change of administration.

Organizations that Test Products

Commercial Testing Services

The United States Testing Company, established in 1880, is the largest commercial testing company. For a fee the company will test a wide variety of goods for anyone. If a producer meets the required standard, he may display his Certified Merchandise Seal of Quality in advertising and labels. For the producer to continue to use this seal, the product must be tested periodically with samples both purchased in the regular market and taken from production lines.

The Better Fabrics Testing Bureau established by the National Retail Dry Goods Association tests textiles for a fee. The Bureau rates fabrics on a scale from poor to very good. If the textile is satisfactory for its use, the producer may use the Bureau's seal.

Consumer-Financed Testing Services

There are two consumer-financed testing services: Consumers Research in Washington, New Jersey, and Consumers Union in Mount Vernon, New York. The former publishes the *Consumers' Bulletin* and the *Annual Bulletin;* the latter publishes *Consumers Reports,* which includes an annual *Buying Guide Issue.*

[10] Leland J. Gordon, *Watch Your Weights and Measures* (Greeley, Colorado: Council on Consumer Information, 1957), pp. 30-31.

Both agencies test automobiles and primarily nationally branded merchandise. Consumers Research purchases test samples in the local area; Consumers Union has products purchased across the country sent to them for testing. The products selected for testing by Consumers Research are those that the staff and the readers' queries seem to think are most needed; at Consumers Union the testing program is based largely on subscribers' responses to their annual questionnaire. Neither of these testing companies accepts free samples from manufacturers, nor do they permit test results to be used in product advertising. Often manufacturers of products that are rated poorly consult these agencies to see how their own testing and checking can be improved. (See Figure 74.)

In general, the test results of both organizations on the same items are similar.[11] There is a small incidence of disagreement that may be due to the lack of standard test procedures for products. Consumers Union has a larger circulation, and thus a larger budget for operation. They test more products than Consumers Research. These two independent testing organizations furnish the only easily available comparison of standard products for prospective purchasers.

Private Testing Organizations

A number of private companies and magazines have product testing programs. For example, Sears Roebuck, J.C. Penney, and Abraham and Straus test many of the products they carry. Their services are very useful in helping them to decide which merchandise to stock and why merchandise is defective, but the results of their research are not generally available to the public.

Some magazines test products. *Good Housekeeping* gives a "Guaranty Seal," which reads, "Replacement or refund of money guaranteed by Good Housekeeping, if defective or not as advertised therein." The Consumer Service Bureau of *Parents Magazine* also guarantees refund or replacement by the magazine "if it is not as advertised therein," and also gives the use of a seal. Testing is done only on products submitted for advertising in the magazine. A product that is approved may be advertised with either the guarantee or the seal, and the manufacturer must agree to keep the product up to the standard at which it was tested.

Sometimes trade associations establish standards, test goods, and give approval seals. Two such seals are very widely used. The label "Underwriters Laboratories Inspected" on electrical equipment indicates that these products meet certain standards of safety under normal use. The round blue seal of the American Gas Association indicates that the equipment so labeled has been approved by the Association and meets American standards for safety, durable construction, and satisfactory performance.

[11] Eugene R. Beem, "Consumer-Financed Testing and Rating Agencies," *The Journal of Marketing* (January, 1952), pp. 272–285.

OCTOBER 1963/FACTS YOU NEED BEFORE YOU BUY/NO ADVERTISING/50 CENTS

CONSUMER REPORTS

76,000 Washing Machines and 32 Automobiles

A special report on rising repair costs—with brand comparisons

RAZOR BLADES

Vacuum Cleaners
RESULTS OF TESTS ON 14 LIGHTWEIGHT MODELS

Stereo Headphones
COMPARISONS OF 16 MODELS BASED ON TESTS

KNIFE SHARPENERS

UNABRIDGED DICTIONARIES
An expert evaluates the controversial Third Edition of Merriam's New International

For complete contents see third page

FIGURE 73. *(Above: Courtesy of* Consumer Reports. *Facing page: Reproduced by permission from* Consumer Bulletin, *published by Consumers' Research, Washington, New Jersey.)*

CONSUMER bulletin

THE ORIGINAL
CONSUMER
RESEARCH
MAGAZINE

ACME

OCTOBER 1964 — 50 CENTS

camera revolution

15 tested dryers

TO CHOOSE FROM

TRUE OR FALSE thermometers

trading stamps
COST YOU MONEY

BUY LIGHT —
NOT JUST
bulbs..........

THE IMPORTANT POINT IN
pencil sharpeners

45 STEPS TO
safer cars

HOW TO PREVENT
church fires

REPORTS ON PRODUCTS BY BRAND NAME
SINCE 1928 BY CONSUMERS' RESEARCH, INC.,
WASHINGTON, NEW JERSEY . . . COMPLETE CONTENTS ON PAGE 5

FIGURE 74. TOP: Testing a mattress for durability. LEFT CENTER: Repeated runs of standardized laundry loads test the automatic washing machines. RIGHT CENTER: Actual foods are prepared for a dishwasher test. BOTTOM: Freezers are tested in a controlled environment chamber for properly maintained temperatures. (Courtesy of Consumer Reports.)

Organizations That Furnish Information

Professional Associations

A number of professional organizations do a fine job of providing their members with consumer information. The American Home Economics Association, through their magazine *The Journal of Home Economics* and supplementary publications, provides information on research related to consumer problems, current legislation, and the needs of families. The Association also works with the American Standards Association in formulating standards for consumer goods, and is active in representing consumer interests at federal legislative and departmental hearings.

The Council on Consumer Information serves both professional people and members of communities who are interested in consumer problems. It is a nonpartisan, nonprofit organization that serves consumers through conferences and the publication of newsletters and pamphlets. The "Newsletter" gives a very concise summary of the progress of important federal and state legislation, as well as a summary of new programs, books, and materials of interest to people who work with consumer education and activities. The pamphlets explore in depth timely topics pertaining to consumer problems.[12] (See Figure 75.)

Other Sources of Information

The Better Business Bureaus of most large cities maintain an exchange of information on a wide variety of subjects. They also work with businesses to maintain ethical trade practices. The Better Business Bureaus carry considerable influence and can often exert adverse pressure against undesirable businesses. However, they are not enforcement agencies and can do little if local pressure is not effective. They usually keep lists of merchants and services which people have complained about. For instance, a family considering using a small moving company might check with the local Better Business Bureau to see if the moving agency is reliable. In some areas they publish pamphlets on consumer topics.

Changing Times, published by the Kiplinger Washington Editors, is a monthly magazine in very readable form that furnishes information on a variety of consumer topics.

Many newspapers and popular magazines have excellent articles on consumer topics. Most of the well-known magazines for women have a regular column or articles on family buying.

The Cooperative League of America and some individual cooperatives have educational programs and publish materials to help their members become more effective consumers. Some labor unions also have educational programs.

---

[12] Further information about the Council on Consumer Information can be obtained from the Executive Secretary, Dr. Ramon Heimerl, Executive Secretary, Council on Consumer Information, Colorado State College, Greeley, Colo.

FIGURE 75. Some publications of the Council on Consumer Information.

Other Sources of Help

No list of sources of help and assistance for consumers would be complete
without mention of the many activities of industries, trade associations,
and producer groups to improve products and services for consumers. New
methods of preparing, processing, preserving and packaging foods and supplies have been developed by producers and processors. Trade associations
of service industries work on developing better methods of servicing customers. For instance, methods of cleaning new types of fabrics have been developed by the National Institute of Dry Cleaning. The American Institute
of Laundering has tested fabrics for washing and finishing characteristics.
While there is no enforcement in its program, most laundry plants have
adopted its recommendations on washing and finishing of fabrics.

The Need for the Consumer to Be Heard

To a large extent the consumer's voice is heard in the marketplace. Products
and services are sold only if someone buys them. However, barter in the
marketplace is no longer a simple matter. Social pressures, the desire for the
"good life," advertising and promotion, and even the competition for shelf

space in the supermarket contribute factors that tend to complicate the buying job of Mr. and Mrs. John Q. Public. Often in the complexities of the modern marketplace, the voice of the small average consumer is not heard as clearly as that of the large producer, and legislation regulating trade practices is often not as up-to-date as new packages.

SELECTED REFERENCES

Annual Reports of the United States Departments of Agriculture; of Commerce; Federal Trade Commission; Postmaster General; and Department of Health, Education and Welfare. Washington, D.C.: Government Printing Office.

CAMPBELL, PERSIA. *Consumer Laws in Action.* Albany: State of New York, 1958.

COLES, JESSIE V. *Standards and Labels for Consumers Goods.* New York: Ronald Press, 1949.

Consumer Protection Activities of Federal Departments and Agencies. Eighth Report by the Committee on Government Operations, United States House of Representatives. Washington, D.C.: Government Printing Office, 1961.

Executive Office of the President. *First Report of the Consumer Advisory Council.* Washington, D.C.: Government Printing Office, 1963.

GORDON, LELAND J. *Watch Your Weights and Measures.* Greeley, Colo.: Council on Consumer Information, 1960.

HAMILTON, DAVID. *Consumer Protection in New Mexico.* Albuquerque, New Mex.: Pub. 54, Division of Government Research, University of New Mexico, 1958.

HAYHURST, DONALD. *Protection of Consumers in West Virginia.* Morgantown, W. Va.: Pub. 26, Bureau of Government Research, University of West Virginia, 1959.

KARMIN, MONROE W. *Consumers Look at Federal Protective Services.* Greeley, Colo.: Council on Consumer Information, 1961.

MAKRIS, JOHN. *The Silent Investigators.* New York: Dutton, 1959.

18

THE FAMILY AND
THE NATIONAL ECONOMY

> The basic demand on America will be less the
> effectiveness of our material investment than
> the effectiveness of our investment in men.[1]

THE GROWTH of industrialization has also resulted in more national influence on the economics of our daily lives. Thus as the federal government has expanded its influence on the daily lives of families has grown. To carry out its myriad functions, the federal government employed over two million people in 1961 and taxed most of the families in the nation.

Taxes

Laments over the size of the federal budget and the high rate of taxes abound. What is often overlooked, however, is the wide range of services provided by the government. In addition to expenditures for national defense and security, which consumes over half of our national budget, the government builds and maintains national parks, contributes heavily to the building of roads, gives assistance in building hospitals, supports medical research, services the national debt, makes payments to various segments of the population—the aged, veterans—develops experimental programs of farming, and provides thousands of other services.

The major source of revenue for the federal government is from personal and corporate income taxes. Deductions from salaries for federal taxes help to pay the cost of operating the federal government and its many services.

Definition of a Tax

A tax is a compulsory contribution of money to a government. Its usual purpose is to provide services for the common good.

[1] John Kenneth Galbraith, *The Affluent Society* (Houghton Mifflin, 1958), p. 355.

Payments made to a government for a service—such as the delivery of mail, which is paid for by postage stamps—are not a tax. No one is compelled to use the postal service.

A local community may have a tax on property to pay for the schools. Everyone who owns property must pay the tax whether they have children in school or not.

Direct and Indirect Taxes

The terms "direct" and "indirect" taxes are widely used, although this distinction is sometimes not wholly accurate. Generally, a direct tax is considered to be one levied on a particular segment of the population or on a type of commodity. Sales taxes and income taxes are usually considered direct taxes.

Indirect taxes are those levied on a particular item or service, but passed on to others indirectly. A tax on gasoline sold is imposed on the operator of the gas station but passed on to the motorist.

Some indirect taxes are called "hidden taxes" because many people do not realize they are paying the tax. Items like cigarettes and liquor have heavy taxes included in their retail selling price. Since the quoted selling price includes the tax, these are often considered hidden taxes. A similar situation exists with charges for household moving. Trucking firms pay heavy road use taxes that are passed on to the users of their services.

Distribution of the Tax Burden

The theory of the income tax, which increases in rate with larger income, is that those who can least afford it pay the least, and people with large incomes pay the most. A general sales tax on all merchandise assumes that people pay according to how much they buy.

Many people feel that the sales tax imposes an unfair burden on the poorer segments of the population. The people who can least afford it must pay a heavy tax on the necessities of living.

On the other hand, it is often argued that there must be an incentive in the form of reduced tax on high incomes to stimulate investment in productive enterprises that in turn help to create new jobs.

Types of Taxes

Local, state, and federal governments levy and collect taxes. The major types of taxes are income, personal and corporate; property; sales; inheritance; and gift.

Property taxes tend to be used by local communities, whereas income taxes are largely levied by the federal and state governments. Property taxes are levied on real estate or property that can be bought and sold. This type of tax is based on the old measure of land assets as a measure of a man's wealth and consequent ability to pay taxes. Although the most common type of property tax is on real estate, some communities place a tax on personal property in the home.

Real estate taxes are based on the assessed value of the property, which is in part related to the selling price of the property. Assessed value is determined by an appraiser selected by the community and based on certain criteria. The tendency is for older homes to have lower appraised values than new ones that sell at the same prices. The amount of tax is determined by multiplying the assessed value by the tax rate. (This is discussed more fully in Chapter 6, "Family Housing.")

One of the strongest arguments for property taxes is that since property is protected by government agencies, owners should pay for this protection through taxes. However, the people who are opposed to high property taxes claim that possession of land no longer is a fair basis for judging who can pay for the cost of government. Many people possess substantial assets, but do not own real estate.

Over half of the federal government's revenue comes from individual income taxes. Only about one third comes from corporate and excess profits taxes.

Every resident or citizen of the United States must file a federal income tax return if he or she earns $600 or over in a calendar year. Exemption is made for people over age 65; they do not need to file on less than $1,200. If you are in doubt about whether you need to file, consult your local Internal Revenue Office. However, if your income was under the limits mentioned above and you are entitled to a return of tax which was withheld, you must file an income tax return to obtain it.

WITHHOLDING OF THE FEDERAL INCOME TAX. Employers are required to withhold federal income taxes from the regular wages or salaries of their employees. (In some states they are also required to withhold an amount for state income taxes.) The amount that is withheld depends upon the income earned and the number of dependents an employee has.

At the end of the year, employers must furnish their employees, including part-time and temporary employees, with a statement of the amount that has been deducted on a form known as the W-2 form. This includes the wages paid and the deductions made for federal income taxes.

FILING A TAX RETURN. Two basic forms are available for use in preparing a tax return: 1040 and 1040A. Form 1040A is only a short card, and may be used if the total income is less than $10,000 and primarily from wages or salary. The longer form, 1040, must be used if you do not fall in the 1040A category or if you wish to itemize deductions. Many people are lured into using form 1040A because it is so simple and quick. However, if one has legitimate deductions, taxes are usually lower by filing the longer form.

Rules and regulations change. It is wise to read the latest edition of *Your Federal Income Tax,* which is revised annually and published by the Government Printing Office, Washington, D.C.

REPORTABLE INCOME. All income must be reported on the federal tax form, unless it is a kind of income exempt by law. (An example of an exempt income would be the interest on tax-exempt municipal bonds.) For most people, the tax year is January 1 to January 1. However, in special cases other dates can be used. All income during a tax year must be reported.

Interest on a savings account in the bank is considered income. Under the new system of automated reporting by banks, they report interest on savings accounts to the internal revenue service just as employers report earned income.

Dividends on stocks are reportable income. If the dividend is partly a return of principal, only the portion that is earned income is taxable. However, the first $50 of income on taxable dividends is excluded from taxes. If a couple files a joint return, the first $100 is excluded. This dividend credit may not exceed 4 per cent of the taxable income or the total income tax, whichever is smaller.

Rents and royalties are considered income. However, in both cases expenses may be deducted. For instance, the cost of typing a manuscript for an article that is sold or of repairing a house that is rented is a deductible expense. (For a fuller list, check with the Internal Revenue Service or an accountant.)

OTHER DEDUCTIBLE EXPENSES. Equipment and tools necessary to one's occupation can be depreciated—that is, their cost can be spread over a period of years and a certain portion written off as a deductible expense each year. For example, a doctor can depreciate his office equipment, a writer can depreciate his typewriter, a carpenter can depreciate his tools. Salesmen can depreciate their cars.

If a portion of one's home is used to conduct a business on which one earns an income, then the expense to maintain the portion of the home devoted to this activity may be deducted under certain conditions. For example, a doctor may use part of his house for his office, a writer may devote one room to a workroom. A professional photographer might have a darkroom for his work.

Capital gains, as was mentioned earlier, occur when one sells at a profit assets that have been held for more than six months. These are taxable at no more than half of the usual tax, and in any case no more than 25 per cent. Capital losses are those which occur when assets are sold for less than the price they were purchased. Up to $1,000 a year of capital losses may be deducted from federal income taxes. In the case of capital losses, there is differentiation between assets held for less than six months and those held for more than six months.

There are many complicated rules about handling gains and losses from securities. If you have any substantial amount of stock, it is wise to get the help of an accountant.

Social Security and veteran's pensions of persons over age 65 are not taxed.

However, income from other types of pensions is taxable if it is not return of principal. Annuities and some pension plans return a portion of the principal (the amount originally paid in to the fund) as well as interest. The portion that is principal is not taxed. (If this is the case, a statement is usually attached to the check indicating how much is interest and how much is return of the principal.)

Medical and dental expenses are important deductions for many families. Unfortunately, many of the people who have been hit hard by major medical expenses fail to realize how to deduct as much as they can. Although dependents who earn more than $600 cannot be claimed as an exemption on the return (this is discussed more fully, below, in the section "Exemptions"), if you contribute more than half of their support which includes medical expenses, the medical costs can be deducted from your return. Large medical expenditures can often be spread over two years so that one does not exceed the allowable limit in any one year for medical deductions.

There is a wide latitude allowed in medical deductions. They can include dentures, crutches, eyeglasses, hearing aids, wheel chairs, ambulance use, nurses' board, a gum course if prescribed, and premiums for health and accident insurance. Traveling costs to secure medical help are also deductible.

Casualty losses are deductible. This includes storm damage to your house, the cost of replacing shrubbery eaten up by insects, or the replacement of a car if these are not covered by insurance. The following are some deductible casualty losses: fire losses; losses due to natural causes—hurricane, rain, floods; automobile casualty—damage to a car when it is not due to wilful negligence; damage to home or property from explosion of a boiler or freezing of pipes; theft of cash, jewelry, or clothing.

Interest on debts is a deductible expense. For most people the largest item of interest is the amount charged on their mortgage. However, interest charges on installment loans, time payments, or personal loans are all deductible as interest.

Contributions to religious, charitable, scientific, and educational nonprofit organizations are tax deductible. These deductions may not exceed 20 per cent of your adjusted gross income in most cases. (Adjusted gross income is roughly the amount remaining after you have deducted from your total income business expenses, losses on the sale of property, sick pay, and half of any capital gains. This figure, adjusted gross income, is very important in determining one's tax liability.) Dues to organizations from which you receive benefits, other than those which are necessary to your business, are not deductible. For example a gift to the local YWCA would be deductible, but membership dues would not be. Gifts to friends and relatives are not deductible unless you can claim them as a dependent. (See the section "Exemptions" below.) In addition to cash contributions you can also include the value of clothing and furniture given to a charitable organization if you have receipts.

Taxes other than federal taxes are usually deductible. State and local income and sales taxes are deductible. So are personal property taxes and real estate taxes. Assessments for improvement of your property, however, are not deductible. Federal excise taxes, such as those on jewelry, handbags, and luggage, are not deductible.

A deduction is allowed for expenses of a working woman or widower for the care of children, or a physically or mentally incapacitated adult. However, this may not exceed $600 and can be taken only if the total income is below a certain level. A married woman may take this deduction only when she files a joint income tax return with her husband. She may take the full $600 if their combined income is below $4,500 per year. The amount which she may deduct is reduced if they earn over this.

Alimony or separate-maintenance payments are deductible expenses for the husband, but the separated or divorced wife must consider them as income. However, lump sum settlements and payments for the support of children are not deductible expenses. The law provides that any payments the husband deducts as expenses must be considered as income by the wife.

Automobile expenses can be deducted if a car is used for business, but not if it is used for pleasure only. If a car is used for both business and pleasure, then the expenses must be apportioned according to how much is used for business; for example, if a car is used two days a week for business, then one can deduct two sevenths of the expenses if these have not been reimbursed by the business.

There is a special provision for homeowners who sell their house at a profit and buy another. If a person sells their principal residence at a profit and buys within the year another which costs as much or more, which he uses as his principal residence, there is no tax on the profit. To take advantage of this ruling one must actually occupy the new dwelling within a year from the date of sale of the old one.

Uniforms and special clothes for work are deductible expenses. A nurse may deduct the cost of her uniform, a dentist the cost of lab coats, a waitress the cost of her uniforms if she is required to buy them, and so on.

Union dues and employment agency fees are deductible. Expenses incurred for business that have not been reimbursed are also deductible. For example, if you are allowed travel expenses for tourist air travel only, but must go first class because the tourist flights are cancelled, you may deduct the difference between what is reimbursed and what you spent.

JOINT RETURNS. The joint return procedure permits a husband and wife to file a combined tax return. This generally results in a lower rate of tax for the family. What happens is that the tax is computed on two halves of the family income, rather than on the whole. Since most wives earn no income or less than their husbands, it reduces the amount of tax paid on the husband's income. As income increases, the savings made possible by the joint return procedure become greater. Only a husband and wife can file a joint return. Even if they were only married for part of the year, they can file a joint return.

UNMARRIED HEAD OF HOUSEHOLD. An unmarried person or one who is separated or divorced may file as the head of household if (a) he occupied a home as a principal residence with related persons whom he could claim as dependents, and (b) he furnished over half the cost of maintaining the household. It is possible for a person to file as head of household if he is maintaining his dependent parents in a different home, but not if a parent is being maintained in a nursing home. In computing the cost of maintaining a household, rent, property insurance, property taxes, mortgage interest, repairs, utilities, and the cost of food may be included.

EXEMPTIONS. After subtracting *deductions* from total income, the next step is to subtract the amount allowed for *exemptions*. Each exemption entitles you to subtract $600 from your income for tax purposes. A taxpayer is allowed to count himself (or herself) as an exemption. Taxpayers age 65 or older can claim an extra exemption for themselves. A blind taxpayer is entitled to an additional exemption.

The wife of a taxpayer may be claimed as one exemption if the couple file a joint return. If they file separate returns, she may be claimed as an exemption if she did not have any income for the year and received over half her support from the husband. If she qualifies as an exemption, a double exemption may be taken if she is over age 65; an additional exemption may be taken if she is blind.

One exemption may be taken for each child, including stepchildren and legally adopted children: (a) If the child received less than $600 gross income. However, if the child is under age 19 or a student, this limitation does not hold. A student is one who during at least five calendar months of the year is a full-time student at an educational institution. (b) If the child received over half of his support from you, or from the wife if a joint return is filed. The term "support" means food, clothing, shelter, medical care, education, and other reasonable expenses incurred in the care of an individual. (c) If the taxpayer has not filed a joint return with his spouse. (d) If the child was a United States citizen or resident, or a resident of Canada, Mexico, Panama, or the Canal Zone.

You may also claim as exemptions other dependents for whom you furnished more than half the support if they (a) received less than $600 other income, (b) did not file a joint return with their spouse, (c) lived in your household for the year or were closely related to you (includes parents, grandparents, children, brother and sister-in-law, nieces, nephews, aunts and uncles), and (d) if they met the citizenship or residence requirements outlined above for exemptions.

ESTIMATING INCOME. Individuals who earn over $5,000, married couples or heads of households with income over $10,000, and self-employed individuals should file a declaration of estimated income for next year when they file their income tax return for the preceding year. (In certain situations estimates may be filed at a different date.) Quarterly payments are made on income from which federal taxes have not been deducted. If you have underestimated, the balance must be paid when you file your tax return; if you have overestimated, your tax return indicates that you are entitled to a rebate.

SAVING MONEY BY KEEPING RECORDS. It is important to keep careful records and receipts for expenditures that are tax deductible. When the Internal Revenue Service questions a tax return, they will examine your records of deductible expenses. If you can prove that your expenses were actually made and justifiable they will be allowed.

If your work involves travel, keep a day-by-day record of expenses and proof of hotel and transportation bills. Daily spending can include money spent for:

1. Train, plane, or taxi fare.
2. Meals and hotel expenses.
3. Tips, telegraph, and telephone costs.
4. Baggage charges, including insurance.
5. Charges for clerical help.
6. Costs of attending business conventions (within certain limits).
7. Automobile expenses for business away from home: gas, oil, maintenance, repair, garage rents, tolls, towing, and others.

Keep a careful record of all purchases involving interest, such as installment purchases, payments on a car, or mortgage payments. In the case of a house it is also wise to keep track of expenditures for improvements as well. When you sell the house, the cost of improvements can be deducted from the profits, if any, in computing the tax due.

Records of the costs of stock transactions and the dates of purchase and sale are also needed. All expenditures to produce income, in this case the brokers' fees and charges by any consultants, are deductible.

The cost of legal or tax advice is deductible as is the rent of a safe deposit box to hold securities or bonds. Keep receipts and cancelled checks to prove your payments. Even the cost of having someone prepare your tax return is deductible.

Contributions made in small amounts can add up. Since these are deductible, it is important to keep careful records of what is given and to whom.

Keep your records and cancelled checks for at least four years after the return is filed. If you are questioned, it is most likely that it will be done within four years. Remember that these records are your proof that you have paid these bills.

Sources of Help

There are many good sources of help with taxes. The local internal revenue office is glad to help you with questions that may arise in preparing your return. Except in the month before April 15th, when income tax returns are due, it is usually possible to talk with people in the Internal Revenue Service without a long wait. There is no charge for this help. Also, the members of the Internal Revenue Service are glad to help you get as many deductions as you are legally entitled to have. The law provides that you may figure your tax in more than one way and take the alternative that is least costly to you.

There are some good booklets available which can be of considerable help. The federal government annually publishes a booklet to help you figure your tax. It is available from the Government Printing Office, Washington, D.C. J. K. Lasser's *Your Income Tax* gives a step-by-step approach to filling out your income tax. This is revised yearly to keep it up-to-date.

An accountant is a good person to call upon if you have a complicated return, an unusual type of income situation or a large income. Sometimes, one can save the cost of the accountant's fee, or most of it, through savings on your income tax to which you are entitled but which you would not have known about.

People who advertise that they will fill out your income tax for very small sums, $5 or $10, are often not good sources of assistance. Frequently, they are not accountants well versed in the technicalities of federal income taxes. If your situation warrants getting outside help, by all means look for a qualified accountant.

The Responsibilities of Citizens in a Democracy

Today in the United States Americans have a way of life envied by most of the world. Social mobility and economic opportunities have enabled many families to achieve high standards of living. The rapid rise of a largely middle-class population where once most families were in the working-class group attests to this.

But high standards of living have not eliminated problems of family and community life. Although many groups have attempted to alleviate these problems, they have met with only limited success. We have public and private welfare programs, philanthropic groups, and a wide variety of organized community services.

There is a question, however, as to whether we have fully explored the possibility of educating families and their members for their roles as consumers of public and private goods and services. Education provided the basis for our present level of living. Much of our technical achievement and industrial development is closely related to the widespread opportunities for many people to develop their abilities through free universal education.

American education also laid the foundations for American democracy. It was in the public schools that the children of immigrants from many lands met, mixed together, and learned to read, to write, and to speak English. People of diverse backgrounds communicated with each other, worked to-

FIGURE 76. The old and the new. (TOP: *FAO Photo*. BOTTOM: *International Harvester Company.*)

gether, and played together. Through the schools, people of many lands learned to become Americans.

Education has also helped people to recognize the opportunities available to them. Generations of children have grown to adulthood believing that the "inalienable rights of man," coupled with the vast economic opportunities in the United States, make it possible for men to rise above the station to which they were born.

We are now at an important threshold. It seems very possible that the

United States can produce more food, commodities, and services than we will need. Harnessing the economic system in such a way as to make these things available to all families seems more difficult. So, too, does the job of educating families in wise consumption. It seems more difficult to ensure that the fruits of our modern industrial system be used in constructive ways than it is to increase our productive capacity.

The future of family life in this nation may well, depend not so much on the level of technology we are able to achieve, but more on the uses to which this technology and affluence are put, on the ways in which people channel their needs and desires in a society replete with many consumer choices. Education can and should help families to recognize the promises and possibilities of affluence for families as well as the individual's responsibilities to the community as a whole.

Individuals and families need to help all people achieve that level of living that should be accepted as the right of every human being. This "level of living" embodies certain essentials. Every child should have the opportunity to look forward to a life of good physical health, unfettered by preventable diseases and not hindered in his physical growth and development by the lack of an adequate diet. Economic conditions should not compel the mother of young children to work on the farm, in the field, or in the factory. Every child should have a right to an adequate education, one that not only enables him to read and write, but which helps him to develop the ability to think critically, to read widely, and to achieve awareness of his roles and responsibilities in society, and trains him to the best use of his abilities.

Effective thinking aimed at social improvement involves being willing to consider ideas that are not in the conventional or traditional pattern. Many ideas once labeled revolutionary or impossible look less so to succeeding generations. The idea of founding our nation from the poor, the immigrants, and the persecuted of many lands was revolutionary in 1789.

SELECTED REFERENCES

Federal Taxes (published annually). Englewood Cliffs, N. J.: Prentice-Hall.

How to Prepare Your Personal Income Tax Return (published annually). Englewood Cliffs, N. J. : Prentice-Hall.

Investor's Tax Guide (published annually). New York: Merrill Lynch, Pierce, Fenner & Smith.

LASSER, J. K. *Your Income Tax* (published annually). New York: Simon & Schuster.

U.S. Department of the Treasury, Internal Revenue Service. *Your Federal Income Tax* (published annually). Washington, D. C.: Government Printing Office.

GLOSSARY

BANK, TRUST, MORTGAGE, AND
REAL ESTATE TERMS[1]

Administrator. An individual or a trust institution appointed by a court to settle an estate (1) when the decedent has left no valid will, (2) when no executor has been named in the will if the decedent has left one, or (3) when the executor has died or is unwilling or unable to serve. If the individual appointed is a woman, she is known as an administratrix.

Amortization. The . . . [liquidation] of debt by periodic payments on principal.

Appraisal. An estimate of value; also, the process of preparing such an estimate.

Assessed value. The valuation placed on property by public authority for purposes of taxation.

Average daily balance. The average amount of money that a bank customer keeps on deposit, determined by adding the daily balances of his account for a given length of time and dividing the total by the number of days covered.

Bank directors. Persons selected by the stockholders of a bank from among their own number. The directors are responsible to the stockholders for profitable management and to government supervisory authority for operation of the bank according to law and sound banking principles.

Cashier's check. A check drawn by the cashier or other authorized officer.

Certified check. A depositor's check across the face of which an officer of the bank or some other authorized person has stamped the word "certified" and the bank's name and then signed his own name. By its certification the bank guarantees that sufficient funds have been set aside from the depositor's account to pay the check when payment is demanded.

Codicil. An amendment or a supplement to a will, executed with the same formalities as the will itself. A codicil is a definite part of the will and is probated with it.

Collateral. Specific property which a borrower pledges as security for the repayment of a loan, agreeing that the lender shall have the right to sell the collateral for the purpose of liquidating the debt if the borrower fails to repay the loan at maturity.

Collection items. Items (drafts, notes, acceptances, etc.) which are received by a bank subject to collection before payment will be credited to depositors' accounts.

Discount. A note on which the interest is paid in advance. A discount is distinguished from a loan by the fact that interest on a loan is collected at the time the note is paid.

Easement. An acquired right of use or enjoyment, falling short of ownership, which an owner or possessor of land may have in the land of another, such as a right of way.

Eminent domain. The inherent right

[1] Public Relations Council, American Bankers Association, 12 East 36th Street, New York 16, N.Y.

of sovereign power to appropriate all or any part of the private property within its borders for a necessary public use, with or without the consent of the owner or owners, by making reasonable compensation.

Encroachment. Occupancy of the land of another by the extension of a building or other improvement beyond the lot line.

Encumbrance. A lien or claim against title to property.

Executor. An individual or a trust named in a will and appointed by a court to settle the estate of the decedent. If a woman is named and appointed, she is known as an executrix.

Federal Reserve Banks (twelve in number plus branches). Federal banking corporations that deal principally with their member banks and with the government. They deal with the general public only to a limited extent.

Fee, fee simple, fee simple absolute. The highest possible degree of ownership of real property.

First mortgage. A legal instrument which creates or conveys a lien or claim against an owner's rights in property antecedent or prior to a lien created by any other mortgage.

Insurance trust. A trust composed partly or wholly of life insurance policy contracts.

Insured bank. A bank that subscribes to [an insurance plan, usually] the deposit insurance plan of the Federal Deposit Insurance Corporation. . . .

Intestate. Not having made and left a will; opposed to testate.

Joint tenancy. The holding of property by two or more persons in such a way that, upon death of one joint owner, the survivor or survivors will take the entire property.

Junior mortgage. A claim against or a lien on title to a property which is subordinate to that created by a prior mortgage.

Level-payment mortgage. A mortgage that provides for payment of a uniform sum at periodic intervals during its term, interest to be taken from this sum as earned and the balance to be credited to principal.

Life tenant. One who owns an estate in real property for his own life or for another person's life or for an indefinite period bounded by a lifetime.

Living trust. A trust that becomes operative during the lifetime of the settlor; to be distinguished from a trust under will (see Trust under will).

Mortgage. A legal instrument which pledges title to property as security for a debt; also, the lien created by such an instrument.

Mortgagee. One who lends money on the security of a mortgage.

Mortgage portfolio. The aggregate of mortgage loans or obligations held . . . as assets.

Mortgagor. An owner of property who executes a mortgage pledging that property as security for a debt.

Postdated check. A check dated ahead. It is not an effective order on the bank until the future date is reached. Thus, if a check dated July 15 is issued on July 1, it cannot be collected from the bank until July 15.

Purchase money mortgage. A mortgage executed by the purchaser to secure payment to the seller of all or a part of the purchase price of property.

Remainderman. A person who is entitled to the remainder of an estate after the life interest in the estate has terminated.

Service charge. A charge made by a bank for the cost of handling a depositor's account.

Tenancy by the entirety. Ownership of property by a husband and wife in such a manner that neither can dispose of his or her interest during the lifetime of the other except by joint action. Upon the death of either, the survivor takes the entire property.

Tenancy in common. The holding of property by two or more persons in such a manner that each has an undivided interest which, upon his death, passes to his estate and not to the survivor or survivors.

Testate. Having made and left a valid will; opposed to intestate.

Traveler's letter of credit. A letter addressed by a bank to its correspondent banks either in the same country or in foreign countries, authorizing the person named in the letter to draw drafts on the correspondent banks to the extent of the credit specified. The person in whose favor the letter of credit is issued deposits with the issuing bank a sum of money equal to the total amount of the credit plus the bank's charges for this service.

Trust institution. A trust company, state bank, national bank, or other corporation engaged in the trust business under authority of law. It is a trust institution if any department is engaged in trust business, although other departments may be otherwise engaged.

Trust under will. A trust created under the terms of a valid will, to become operative on the death of the testator; opposed to a living trust (see Living trust).

BUSINESS AND INVESTMENT TERMS[2]

Assets. Everything a corporation owns or due to it: cash, investments, money due it, materials and inventories, which are called current assets; buildings and machinery, which are known as fixed assets; and patents and good will, called intangible assets. (See Liabilities.)

Balance sheet. A condensed statement showing the nature and amount of a company's assets, liabilities, and capital on a given date. In dollar amounts the balance sheet shows what the company owned, what it owed, and the ownership interest in the company of its stockholders. (See Assets; Earnings report.)

Bid and asked. Often referred to as a quotation, or quote. The bid is the highest price anyone has declared that he wants to pay for a security at a given time; the asked is the lowest price anyone will take at the same time.

Bond. Basically an IOU or promissory note of a corporation, usually issued in multiples of $1,000, although $100 and $500 denominations are not uncommon. A bond is evidence of a debt on which the issuing company usually promises to pay the bondholders a specified amount of interest for a specified length of time, and to repay the loan on the expiration date. In every case a bond represents debt—its holder is a creditor of the corporation and not a part owner as is the shareholder.

Broker. An agent, often a member of a stock exchange firm or an exchange member himself, who handles

[2] From *The Language of Investing*, 1960, New York Stock Exchange, 11 Wall Street, New York 5, N.Y.

the public's orders to buy and sell securities or commodities. For this service a commission is charged.

Capital gain or capital loss. Profit or loss from the sale of a capital asset. A capital gain may be either short-term (6 months or less) or long-term (more than 6 months). A short-term capital gain is taxed at the reporting individual's full income tax rate. A long-term capital gain is taxed at a maximum of 25 per cent, depending on the reporting individual's tax bracket. Up to $1,000 of net capital loss—that is, when you sell securities at a lower price than you paid for them—is deductible from the individual's taxable income during the year reported. If the capital loss is more than $1,000, as much as $1,000 annually is deductible in each of the next five years. The amount of capital loss which may be deducted is reduced by the amount of any capital gain.

Capitalization. Total amount of the various securities issued by a corporation. Capitalization may include bonds, debentures, preferred and common stock. Bonds and debentures are usually carried on the books of the issuing company in terms of their par or face value. Preferred and common shares may be carried in terms of par or stated value. Stated value may be an arbitrary figure decided upon by the directors or may represent the amount received by the company from the sale of securities at the time of issuance.

Commission. The broker's fee for purchasing or selling securities or property for a client. On the N.Y. Stock Exchange, commissions average about 1 per cent of the market value of the stocks involved in the transaction and approximately one-quarter of 1 per cent on bonds.

Dealer. An individual or firm in the securities business acting as a princi-pal rather than as an agent. Typically, a dealer buys for his own account and sells to a customer from his own inventory. The dealer's profit or loss is the difference between the price he pays and the price he receives for the same security.

Dividend. The payment designated by the Board of Directors to be distributed pro rata among the shares outstanding. On preferred shares, it is generally a fixed amount. On common shares, the dividend varies with the fortunes of the company and the amount of cash on hand, and may be omitted if business is poor or the directors determine to withhold earnings to invest in plant and equipment. Sometimes a company will pay a dividend out of past earnings, even if it is not currently operating at a profit.

Earnings report. A statement—also called an income statement—issued by a company showing its earnings or losses over a given period. The earnings report lists the income earned, expenses, and the net result.

Fixed charge. A company's expenses, such as bond interest, which it has agreed to pay whether or not earned, and which are deducted from income before earnings on equity capital are computed.

Investment banker. Also known as an underwriter. He is the middleman between the corporation issuing new securities and the public. The usual practice is for one or more investment bankers to buy outright from a corporation a new issue of stocks or bonds. The group forms a syndicate to sell the securities to individuals and institutions. Investment bankers also distribute very large blocks of stocks or bonds—perhaps held by an estate. Thereafter, the market in the security may be over-the-counter, on a regional stock exchange, the American Exchange, or the N.Y. Stock Exchange.

Investment trust. A company which uses its capital to invest in other companies. There are two principal types: the closed-end and the open-end, or mutual fund. Shares in closed-end investment trusts, some of which are listed on the N.Y. Stock Exchange, are readily transferable in the open market and are bought and sold like other shares. Capitalization of these companies is fixed. Open-end funds sell their own new shares to investors, stand ready to back their old shares, and are not listed. Open-end funds are so-called because their capitalization is not fixed; they issue more shares as people want them.

Liabilities. All the claims against a corporation. Liabilities include accounts and wages and salaries payable, dividends declared payable, accrued taxes payable, fixed or long-term liabilities such as mortgage bonds, debentures, and bank loans.

Margin. The amount paid by the customer when he uses credit to buy a security, the balance being advanced by the broker. Under Federal Reserve regulations, the initial margin required in the past 20 years has ranged from 40 per cent of the purchase price all the way to 100 per cent.

Monthly Investment Plan (MIP). A pay-as-you-go method of buying N.Y. Stock Exchange listed shares on a regular payment plan for as little as $40 a month, or $40 every three months. Under MIP, the investor buys stock by the dollars' worth—if the price advances, he gets fewer shares and if it declines, he gets more shares. He may discontinue purchases at any time without penalty. The only charge for purchases and sales is the usual commission for buying

and selling, plus the regular odd-lot dealer differential. The commission ranges from 6 per cent on small transactions to slightly below 1½ per cent on larger transactions.

Mutual Fund. (See Investment trust.)

Over-the-counter. A market for securities made up of securities dealers who may or may not be members of a securities exchange. Over-the-counter is mainly a market made over the telephone. Thousands of companies have insufficient shares outstanding, stockholders, or earnings to warrant application for listing on a stock exchange. Others may prefer not to make public all the information which listing requires. Securities of these companies are traded in the over-the-counter market between dealers who act either as principals or as brokers for customers. The over-the-counter market is the principal market for U.S. government bonds, municipals, bank, and insurance stocks.

Paper profits. An unrealized profit on a security still held. Paper profits become realized profits only when the security is sold.

Proxy statement. Information required by SEC to be given stockholders as a prerequisite to solicitation of proxies for a listed security.

Short sale. [A short sale is made when someone sells a security he does not actually own. It is ordinarily made when a person believes the stock will decline in value.]

Split. The division of the outstanding shares of a corporation into a larger number of shares. A 3-for-1 split by a company with 1 million shares outstanding would result in 3 million shares outstanding. Each holder of 100 shares before the 3-for-1 split would have 300 shares, although his proportionate equity in the company would remain the same, since

100 parts of 1 million are the equivalent of 300 parts of 3 million. Ordinarily, splits must be voted by directors and approved by shareholders.

Ticker. The instrument which prints prices and volume of security transactions in cities and towns throughout the U.S. within minutes after each trade on the floor.

Unlisted. A security not listed on a stock exchange. (See Over-the-counter.)

Yield. Also known as return. The dividends or interest paid by a company expressed as a percentage of the current price—or, if you own the security, of the price you originally paid. The return on a stock is figured by dividing the total of dividends paid in the preceding 12 months by the current market price—or, if you are the owner, the price you originally paid. A stock with a current market value of $40 a share which has paid $2 in dividends in the preceding 12 months is said to return 5 per cent ($2.00 ÷ $40.00). If you paid $20 for the stock five years earlier, the stock would be returning you 10 per cent on your original investment. The current return on a bond is figured the same way. A 3 per cent $1,000 bond selling at $600 offers a return of 5 per cent ($30 ÷ $600). Figuring the yield of a bond to maturity calls for a bond yield table.

LIFE INSURANCE AND ANNUITY TERMS[3]

Annuity. A contract which provides a regular income for a definite number of years or for life.

Automatic premium loan. A provision that any premium the policyholder does not pay by the end of the grace period (31 days beyond date premium was due) will be paid automatically by a policy loan, if there is enough cash value in the policy to cover it.

Beneficiary. The person named in the policy to receive the insurance money, called benefits, upon the death of the policyholder.

Cash value. A gradually increasing sum of money, available in all permanent insurance policies. The policyholder can borrow this sum or can "cash in" the policy and take the money in a lump sum or as income. (If you "cash in" a policy, you give up its insurance protection. See Nonforfeiture values.)

Disability income. A provision for payment of monthly income in case of permanent and total disability.

Disability waiver of premium. A provision that a policy will be kept in full force by a life insurance company without payment of premiums should a policyholder become totally and permanently disabled.

Dividend. (See Policy dividend.)

Double indemnity. A provision that the company will pay the beneficiary double the face amount of the policy if the person whose life is insured dies by accidental means.

Endowment. A policy which pays the policyholder a certain sum of money on a certain date if he is then living. Should he die before that date, the face amount is paid to his beneficiary.

[3] Institute of Life Insurance, 488 Madison Avenue, New York 22, N.Y.

Extended term insurance. (See Nonforfeiture values.)

Face amount or face value. The sum of money the company agrees to pay at death or at the endowment date. (You will find this sum stated on the first page of your policy.)

Family income policy. A policy which combines permanent insurance (usually straight life) and term insurance to provide extra protection while children are growing up.

Family plan policy. A policy which combines permanent insurance for the breadwinner with term insurance for the breadwinner with term insurance for other members of the family. Children born after the policy is issued are included when they are 15 days old.

Grace period. Extra time given a policyholder after a premium is due (usually 31 days) during which he may pay the premium.

Group annuities. A plan under which retirement annuity benefits are provided for all members of a group under a master contract, usually issued to an employer for the benefit of the employees. The cost may be shared by employer and employees or paid entirely by the employer.

Group life insurance. A plan under which life insurance is provided for all members of a group under a master contract, usually issued to an employer for the benefit of the employees. The cost may be shared by employer and employees or paid entirely by the employer. No physical examination is required.

Industrial life insurance. Life insurance in small amounts, generally less than $1,000. Premiums are collected weekly or monthly by an agent who calls at the home of the policyholder.

Insured, the. The person on whose life an insurance policy is issued.

Level premium system. Distributing the cost of insurance so that the premium remains the same from year to year. This means paying more than the cost of the protection during the early years. The excess payments in the early years help pay the greater cost later on.

Limited payment life insurance. A policy which, while providing protection to the beneficiaries as long as the policyholder lives, telescopes premiums into a certain number of years. (After this, you pay no further premiums.)

Maturity date. In an endowment, the date when the face amount becomes available to the policyholder if he is then living.

Mortality table. A statistical table showing for a given number of people of a particular age how many will probably die during each year.

Nonforfeiture values. These are values guaranteed in permanent insurance policies if the policyholder stops paying premiums. These values may be taken:

• As "cash value" (lump sum or income), or

• As "extended term insurance" which continues the full protection of the policy for a limited time, or

• As "reduced paid-up insurance" which continues the protection of the policy for the lifetime of the policyholder, but for a smaller amount.

Nonparticipating insurance. Insurance on which the premium is calculated to cover as closely as possible the expected cost of the insurance protection and on which no dividends are payable.

Ordinary life insurance. Life insurance issued to individuals, usually in amounts of $1,000 or more. Premiums are paid annually, semiannually, quarterly, or monthly. This general classification includes term insurance, straight life, limited payment, endowment, retirement income, and combinations of these.

Ordinary life policy. (See Straight life insurance policy.)

Paid-up insurance. Insurance on which no more premiums are required.

Participating insurance. Insurance on which dividends are payable. The premium is deliberately calculated to provide some margin over the expected cost of the insurance protection with the intention of returning to the policyholder any portion of the premium that is not needed, as a dividend.

Permanent life insurance. Insurance from which someone at a future date will surely receive benefits—the beneficiary when the policyholder dies, or the policyholder himself. Permanent life insurance builds cash values. It includes straight life insurance, limited payment policies, and endowments.

Policy. The written agreement, or contract, between the policyholder and the insurance company.

Policy dividend. A refund of part of the premium paid for a participating life insurance policy. Such a dividend reflects the difference between the premium charge and actual cost as shown by experience.

Policyholder. The owner of a life insurance policy.

Premium. The amount of money a policyholder is required to pay periodically to a company for his policy.

Settlement options. The several ways in which the policyholder of the beneficiary may choose to receive the money from a policy, other than as an immediate payment in a lump sum.

Straight life insurance policy. A policy which provides protection throughout the life of the policyholder for his beneficiary, and on which premiums are payable as long as the policyholder lives. (Synonymous with Ordinary life policy.)

Term insurance. A policy which pays the face amount to the beneficiary only if the policyholder dies during the period it covers. Term insurance policies may be convertible or renewable. They seldom build cash values.

HEALTH INSURANCE TERMS[4]

Accident. An event or occurence which is unforeseen and unintended.

Accidental bodily injury. Injury to the body of the insured as the result of an accident.

Accidental death benefit. A lump sum payment upon the loss of life of an insured person due to the direct cause of an accident.

Association group. Group insurance provided to a trade or business association by which all members are protected under one master health insurance contract.

Blanket medical expense. A provision in loss-of-income policies providing payment for hospital and medical expenses up to a maximum amount.

Blanket policy. A health insurance contract which protects all members of a certain group against a specific hazard.

Blue Cross. An independent, nonprofit membership corporation providing protection against the costs of hos-

[4] Health Insurance Institute, 488 Madison Avenue, New York 22, N.Y.

pital care in a limited geographical area.

Blue Shield. An independent, nonprofit membership corporation providing protection against the costs of surgery and other items of medical care in a limited geographical area.

Coinsurance. A policy provision, frequently found in major medical insurance, by which both the insured person and insurance company in a specific ratio share the hospital and medical expenses resulting from an illness or injury.

Comprehensive Major Medical Insurance. A policy designed to give the protection offered by both a basic and major medical health insurance policy. It is characterized by a low "deductible" amount, coinsurance feature, and high maximum benefits —usually $5,000 to $10,000.

Deductible. Found in major medical insurance, is that portion of covered hospital and medical charges which an insured person must pay before his policy's benefits begin.

Disability. A physical condition which makes an insured person incapable of doing one or more duties of his occupation.

Elective benefits. Lump sum payments for certain injuries which a policyholder can choose instead of receiving weekly benefits.

Evidence of insurability. Any statement or proof of a person's physical condition, occupation, etc., affecting his acceptance for insurance.

Exclusions. Specified hazard for which a policy will not provide benefit payments.

Family expense policy. A policy which insures both the policyholder and his immediate dependents (usually spouse and children).

Grace period. A specified time, after a policy's premium payment is due, in which the protection of the policy continues subject to actual receipt of premium within that time.

Guaranteed renewable policy. A policy which the insured has the right to continue in force by the timely payment of premiums to a specified age (usually age 50), during which period the insurer has no right to make unilaterally any change in any provision of the policy while the policy is in force, but may make changes in premium rates by policyholder class.

Health insurance. Protection against the costs of hospital and medical care or lost income arising from an illness or injury. Sometimes called Accident and Sickness Health Insurance, or Disability Insurance.

Hospital benefits. Benefits provided under a policy for hospital charges incurred by an insured person because of an illness or injury.

Hospital expense insurance. Health insurance protection against the costs of hospital care resulting from the illness or injury of an insured person.

Individual insurance. Policies which provide protection to the policyholder and/or his family (as distinct from group and blanket insurance). Sometimes called "personal" insurance.

Lapse. Termination of a policy upon the policyholder's failure to pay the premium within the time required.

Limited policies. Contracts which cover only certain specified diseases or accidents.

Loss-of-income benefits. Payments made to the insured person to help replace income lost through disability.

Major Medical Expense Insurance. Policies especially designed to help offset the heavy medical expenses re-

sulting from catastrophic or prolonged illness or injury. They provide benefit payments for 75-80 per
cent of all types of medical treatment
by a physician above a certain amount
first paid by the insured person and up
to the maximum amount provided
by the policy—usually $5,000 or
$10,000.

**Noncancellable or noncancellable
and guaranteed renewable policy.** A policy which the insured
has the right to continue in force
by the timely payment of premiums
set forth in the policy to a specified
age (usually age 50), during which
period the insurer has no right to
make unilaterally any change in any
provision of the policy while the
policy is in force.

Partial disability. An illness or injury
which prevents an insured person
from performing one or more of
his occupational duties.

Pre-existing condition. A physical
condition of an insured person which
existed prior to the issuance of his
policy.

Proration. The modification of policy
benefits because of a change in the insured person's occupation or the existence of other insurance.

Total disability. An illness or injury
which prevents an insured person from
performing any duty of his occupation
or any other profitable work.

Waiting period. The duration of time
between the beginning of an insured
person's disability and the start of the
policy's benefits.

Waiver. An agreement attached to a
policy which exempts from coverage
certain disabilities normally covered
by the policy.

Waiver of premium. A provision
included in some policies which exempts the insured person from paying premiums while he is collecting
disability benefits.

INDEX